STUDIES IN STUART WALES

STUDIES
IN
STUART WALES

BY

A. H. DODD

CARDIFF
UNIVERSITY OF WALES PRESS
1952

TO
HAULWEN

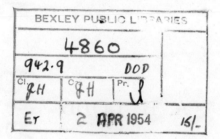

PREFACE

THE significance of the seventeenth century in Welsh history is apt to be overshadowed by the more obvious appeal of its predecessor and its successor. With the exception of a few heroic episodes like the defence of Denbigh and of Raglan, and a few romantic figures like the Earl of Glamorgan and John Jones the regicide, the age of the Civil War and Commonwealth in Wales lacks the picturesqueness of that of the Tudor settlement or the Methodist Revival—with the result that it has come to be thought of as a sort of King Arthur's cave, in which the spirit of the nation slumbers on after the sedatives administered by the Tudors, until it is roused to action by the trumpet blasts of Howel Harris and Daniel Rowland. Even in so admirably judicious and well-balanced a work as Professor David Williams's *Modern Wales* the age of the Stuarts wears something of the air of a footnote to English history, and tends to take its colour from the inglorious age that separates the Glorious Revolution from the Methodist Revival. It is part of the aim of this book to suggest a different perspective and to claim for the century its rightful place in the evolution of the Welsh people. The need for a comprehensive history of the period has long been apparent. The present writer has had on his conscience for some years a promise to contribute a volume on the subject to *Cyfres y Brifysgol a'r Werin,* and a preliminary sketch (from the political angle) was attempted in the Hartwell Jones Lecture for 1947;[1] but the writing of the promised volume had not advanced very far before it became clear that nothing like a concise and balanced survey could be hoped for until some of the more neglected topics had been dealt with at large. That, in brief, is the apologia for the present volume.

None of the studies included here have been published before, though the first two have been drawn upon for public lectures.

[1] Cymmrodorion Society's *Transactions,* 1948.

Each is self-contained within its own limits; but written as they have been at different times they occasionally overlap, and they may reflect differences in emphasis, as they certainly do in some mechanical details of presentation. It is hoped that in spite of this there will be found an underlying unity of theme and interpretation, as well as the more obvious bond of cross-references. Not that any claim is made that between them they constitute anything like a complete picture of Welsh society in this age of transition. On many important topics little is said, because much is (or soon will be) available in print. Not much space is devoted, for example, to religion. He would be a bold man who set out to add anything of substance to the massive researches of Dr. Richards into Welsh Puritanism; our knowledge of the Welsh recusants has latterly been clarified by the publication of Mr. Emyr Gwynne Jones's lectures on *Cymru a'r Hen Ffydd*; and for the Church in Wales the brief but compendious accounts of the period in Archbishop Edwards's *Landmarks* and Chancellor James's *Church History* can be supplemented from several excellent diocesan histories. Again, the Civil War is thinly represented, although an up-to-date version of Roland Phillips's work (now nearly three-quarters of a century old) has long been a crying need; but the story is gradually being built up county by county. Mr. A. L. Leach set a fine example in his account of the Pembrokeshire campaigns, and Sir Frederick Rees's invaluable *Studies* have now enabled us to put into proper perspective the whole of the first Civil War in the south and the second in both north and south. I hope to continue the work for some of the North Wales counties, starting in the forthcoming volume of the Anglesey Antiquarian Society's *Transactions*. Finally, although one of the studies that follow deals with elections, none of them covers the work of the Welsh M.P.'s at Westminster; the exploration of this field, begun in the Cymmrodorion *Transactions* for 1942 and 1945–47, is now being followed up by research students in the History and Welsh History departments at Bangor.

My indebtedness to the magnificent collections of family papers in the National Library will be obvious in almost every page, and I must here express my deep sense of gratitude to

the Trustees of the late Lord Leverhulme for the Research
Fellowship that made possible an uninterrupted spell of brows-
ing in these rich pastures during the session 1949–50. I have
drawn more sparingly on the Library's poetical collections
because here I could take advantage of the judicious excerpts
from seventeenth-century verse in the Brogyntyn Welsh collections published (with a wealth of illuminating comment) by
Mr. E. D. Jones in the Library's *Journal* during 1948–50.
What will not be so obvious to the casual reader is my indebtedness to the expert knowledge and consistent helpfulness of the
library staff, to which I should like here to pay the warmest
tribute. Among many others who have freely " lent their
minds out " to my great benefit I cannot forbear to mention
two old friends and colleagues: Dr. R. T. Jenkins, who (as
so often before) has saved me from pitfalls and cast new light
in many a dim corner after reading some sections in draft;
and Professor Thomas Parry, whose patience in guiding a
tyro through the intricacies of Welsh versification appears to
be inexhaustible. It would be an ill return to allow them to
be saddled with responsibility for any statements that may lay
themselves open to factual or interpretative criticism. What
this or any other publication of mine owes to the co-operation
and forbearance of my wife is more than can ever be told in a
preface or expressed in a dedication.

A. H. DODD

Bangor
June, 1952

CONTENTS

I THE SOCIAL ORDER . . . 1

II A LOST CAPITAL 49

III WALES AND IRELAND . . . 76

IV " NERTH Y COMMITTEE " . . . 110

V THE DAWN OF PARTY POLITICS . . 177

VI THE GLORIOUS REVOLUTION . . 216

ix

ABBREVIATIONS

A. & O.	Firth and Rait, *Acts and Ordinances of the Interregnum.*
A.C.	*Archæologia Cambrensis.*
A.P.C.	*Acts of the Privy Council.*
B.M.	British Museum.
B.B.C.S.	*Bulletin of the Board of Celtic Studies.*
C.C.A.M.	*Calendar of the Committee for Advance of Money.*
C.C.C.	*Calendar of the Committee for Compounding.*
C.C.P.	N.L.W., *Calendar of Clenennau Letters and Papers.*
C.J.	*Journals of the House of Commons.*
C.S.P.D.	*Calendars of State Papers, Domestic.*
C.S.P.I.	*Calendars of State Papers, Ireland.*
C.W.P.	N.L.W., *Calendar of Wynn (of Gwydir) Papers.*
E.H.R.	*English Historical Review.*
H.M.C.	Historical Manuscripts Commission (*Reports* quoted as " 1st *R.*", " *Cecil* ", etc.).
H.L.	Henry J. Huntington Library, San Marino, Calif.
L.J.	*Journals of the House of Lords.*
M.C.	Powys-land Club, *Montgomeryshire Collections.*
N.L.W.	National Library of Wales.
N.L.W.J.	*National Library of Wales Journal.*
P.R.O.	Public Record Office.
Phillips, *C.W.*	J. R. Phillips, *Memoirs of the Civil War in Wales and the Marches.* 1878.
Richards, *P.M.*	T. Richards, *The Puritan Movement in Wales.* 1920.
Richards, *R.D.*	Id., *Religious Developments in Wales.* 1923.
S.C.P.	I. ab O. Edwards, *Star Chamber Proceedings relating to Wales.* 1929.
T.A.A.S.	*Transactions of Anglesey Antiquarian Society and Field Club.*
T.C.S.	*Transactions of the Honourable Society of Cymmrodorion.*
T.C.H.S.	*Transactions of the Caernarvonshire Historical Society.*
T.H.S.L.C.	*Transactions of the Historic Society of Lancashire and Cheshire.*
Thurloe	*Thurloe State Papers*, ed. T. Birch, 1742.
T.R.H.S.	*Transactions of the Royal Historical Society.*
T.S.A.S.	*Transactions of the Shropshire Antiquarian Society.*
Williams, *P.H.*	W. R. Williams. *Parliamentary History of the Principality of Wales.* 1895.
W.W.H.R.	Historical Society of West Wales, *West Wales Historical Records.*
Y C.	*Y Cymmrodor.*

I

THE SOCIAL ORDER[1]

THE history of Wales in the seventeenth century is necessarily, in the main, the history of a class. Of those below
the rank of " gentry " we can know little at first hand.
They had neither the leisure nor the education to leave
their own account of themselves, and we have to glean what we
can from official records or estate papers, from popular ballads
or the correspondence of their betters. But this limitation need
not disturb us unduly, for the *gwerin*, if we confine the term to
those " with no estate above what they get by daily labour ",
was still a relatively small class, while the term " gentry " as
understood in Wales was a highly elastic and comprehensive
one, embracing all who could put up any sort of colourable
claim to descent from the old princes and *uchelwyr* and even
some who had lifted themselves out of the servile status of their
ancestors by judicious purchase, lease or marriage during the
long years when tribalism was in decay and the land market
kept fluid by the frequency of civil commotion. If an English
dramatist or pamphleteer wanted to raise a good-humoured
laugh, he had only to conjure up a Welsh " shentleman ", poor
as a church mouse but ready to rattle off his pedigree to the
ninth generation or even back to Brutus and Adam; and in
soberer mood Humphrey Llwyd himself, the learned Tudor
physician and antiquary, attributed the demand for his
countrymen in the service of English noble households to the
fact that " even in direst poverty they never forget their gentle
origins ".[2]

The keynote of the society with which we shall be dealing,

[1] Portions of this study were given as a lecture at the Annual Meeting
of the Historical Association, held at Cardiff on 3 Jan., 1951.

[2] " in summa paupertate nobilitatem generis agnoscentes " (*Commentarioli
Descriptionis Britannicæ Fragmentum*, 1572, fo. 49v).

I

in contrast to the Welsh society of to-day, is the pride it took in its patrician character, a pride shared to the full by those outside the pale. Yet it was far from being a narrow or even a homogeneous society; it embraced many gradations of rank, all of them strictly and piously observed (not least by the bards), from that of magnates like the earls of Worcester, living with the pomp of princelings in their castle of Raglan, down to small tenant farmers with a good pedigree or a scrap of freehold land to give them some claim to gentility. James Berry, whom Cromwell put in charge of Wales during the episode of the Major Generals, alleged that it was easier there to find fifty gentlemen of £50 a year than five of £100; yet in England even the landowner of £500 (the equivalent of about £5,000 in our money, if we allow for command over services as well as over goods) was generally reckoned among the smaller gentry.[1] Welsh " esquires " (in the strict sense of the *armigeri*, or men entitled to arms) were commonest in the south-east and south-west, where the counties of Pembroke, Glamorgan and Monmouth claimed more than thirty apiece; Montgomeryshire stood highest of the North Wales counties, with Denbighshire, Merioneth and even Radnorshire (despite its proverbial barrenness in men of substance) not far behind, and the rear was brought up by the remaining West Wales and Snowdonian counties, most of them with less than twenty. Very much the same pattern emerges from a study of assessments to the land tax when it was first imposed towards the end of the century.[2]

There was nothing of the fixity of a caste system, however, about these class distinctions. To rise out of one's class was not, as in the later days of Samuel Smiles, an ambition generally encouraged, but it happened from time to time, and with general acceptance, provided it was not done with indecent speed or too obtrusive a jingling of money bags; though it has been cogently observed that in Wales most of the " new rich " of whom we hear so much in this age were actually members of our oldest families who had retrieved in business or at court, at the bar or on the battlefield, the sunken

[1] Thurloe, iv. 316: cf. *Econ. Hist. Rev.*, x. 3.
[2] B.M., Harl. MSS. 4164 (fos. 29b–33), 6804.

fortunes of their fathers.[1] For the Welsh idea of gentility
was still one in which birth and breeding counted more
than cash:

> Gwell nac aur, gwell nac arian,
> ei air a'i glod i ŵr glan,

as a contemporary bard put it.[2] Even the style in which a
gentleman lived was less a matter of fortune than of rank. The
mortgages that lay so heavy on many Welsh estates, plunging
their owners ever deeper into debt, in the north to such men as
Sir Thomas Myddelton, the Denbighshire-born Lord Mayor
of London, or the Earl of Worcester in the south,[3] were often
incurred in the effort to keep up a style of living beyond the
yield of their estates; while those of humbler rank might easily
be better off in actual cash, and even in a position to lend to
their own landlords,[4] for the same reason that the non-
commissioned officer in the modern army may find himself
richer in practice than his company commander—because less
is expected of him.[5] In the earlier part of the century these
genteel poor were as a rule able to keep up with their mortgage
interest and to avoid a crash by lucrative matches, by working
minerals on their estates, or by the spoils of office, though sometimes a creditor would pounce, neighbours fail to come to the
rescue (especially if the family had made itself unpopular), and
another ancient household disappear from society; but it was
later in the century and on into the succeeding age that this
process of elimination reached its height, leaving behind it a
trail of farmsteads bearing the tarnished mark of their former
dignity as *tai cyfrifol*, and by their very closeness to each other
reminding us how numerous were the " gentry " of a vanished
Wales. Yet even then fresh mortgages were being taken out,
and those who had spare capital, if they wished to keep

---

[1] *T.C.S.*, 1948, p. 391.

[2] " Better than gold, better than silver, is his name and his fame to a
gentleman " (Richard Kynwal, *N.L.W.J.*, vi. 33).

[3] On Myddelton's loans and mortgages see U.C.N.W., Nannau-Hengwrt
MSS. 189, 207, 229, 240, 273, 287, 339–40, 357; N.L.W., Plymouth deeds
822, 913–4, 916; *N.L.W.J.*, i. 85–6; *C.W.P.*, 1017 (iii); *C.C.P.*, pp. 84, 129;
M.C., xxvii. 357. On those of the house of Raglan see *C.C.A.M.*, i. 210–217.

[4] E.g. Vaughan of Pantglas, 1640 (*T.C.H.S.*, x. 18).

[5] H.L., MS. EL., 7218.

their money at home, often found this the readiest form of investment.[1]

To this same urge to keep up a position beyond their normal means may be partly attributed the scramble for land and for office which was so pronounced among the Welsh squires of the age. This too did not appear in its more sordid form till after the Restoration, but already it had much to do with that passion for what a Denbighshire man picturesquely called "lawying",[2] which had long given them a reputation as

> yn gecrus—gwmbrus eu gwaith
> yn gyfrwys yn y gyfraith,[3]

and which made another critic of the age deplore that instead of cattle the country was now breeding two-legged asses good for nothing but braying in the courts.[4] As a career, however, the law had obvious attractions for a father intent on providing for his younger sons, and successful Welsh lawyers practising in London were apt to be besieged with offers of likely lads from home to be apprenticed as clerks.[5]

Though litigation made further inroads into their revenues, it was hard to avoid at a time when the complex task of fitting the classes of Welsh tribal society into the procrustean bed of English law was still under way, and when the Welsh squires (to say nothing of their younger brothers seeking a career at the bar, where so many of them won distinction in this age) were flocking to the Inns of Court for a sufficient smattering of the law to equip them as landowners and magistrates—in some years to the extent of a fifth of the total admissions, from a land containing perhaps a fourteenth of the total population.[6] Many of them had been first to a university, and an examination of the registers of four Cambridge colleges shows that they were fed by eleven different Welsh grammar schools; others no doubt were in closer touch with Oxford, where university

[1] E.g., N.L.W. MS. 12406 C (2 Apr., 1680).
[2] N.L.W., Llewenny MS. 3. 53.
[3] "cantankerous, crabbed, cunning in the law" (Edward ap Raff, *N.L.W.J.*, vi. 242).
[4] W. Vaughan, *The Golden Fleece*, 1626, pt. II, ch. vi.
[5] E.g., N.L.W. MS. 12 405 E (14 Jan., 1682) 12406 E (28 Jan., 1681, 4 Feb., 1682).
[6] *T.C.S.*, 1948, p. 22.

registers for the early seventeenth century contain a surprisingly high number of Welsh entries in proportion to the population. In addition to the endowed grammar schools there were obscurer private academies of which we get only passing glimpses, giving at least a grounding in the classics, and a host of unremembered " country schools " which were in effect preparatory schools.[1]

The result was that education, or at least literacy, extended well down in the social scale. It had been Humphrey Llwyd's boast that even the poorer Welsh gentry gave their sons a good schooling, and over eighty years later John Lewis of Glasgrug could indignantly exclaim, in repudiation of the charge of ignorance so often levelled by his fellow-Puritans against his fellow-countrymen, " Praise be to God we have . . . as able and knowing Gentry as ever ";[2] was he not himself a shining example of the claim—a small Cardiganshire squire with no university education, whose unforced quotations from the classics and the early fathers reveal the practised and reflective reader? Many a bard could write with almost equal ease in Welsh, English or Latin; many a squire could lovingly echo the words in Huw Machno's eulogy of Cynfal, the tiny manor house where Morgan Llwyd was born in remote Ardudwy, about

> llyfrau ar silffau sydd
> deg olwg gidai gilydd;[3]

and there is plenty of evidence that the books did not stay on their shelves. Lists of old or new publications to be bought at one of the London booksellers are among the most frequent commissions entrusted to friends on a visit to the capital; and concern for the education of their children breathes through the correspondence of the gentry even in the most troubled years.[4] Of the schooling of their womenfolk we know less, but such letters from them as have come down to us are those of cultivated ladies and emphatically of shrewd business women.

---

[1] *Id.*, p. 82: W. A. L. Vincent, *The State and Education, 1640–1660*, 1950, pp. 9–10, 52–3; A. Clark, *Reg. of the Univ. of Oxford*, II, iv. 26; N. L. W., Rowland Owen MS.

[2] *Evangeliographa*, 1656, p. 26.

[3] " Books together on their shelves—a comely sight " (Huw Machno, c. 1630, cited J. H. Davies, *Gweithiau Morgan Llwyd*, p. xviii).

[4] E.g., N.L.W., Edwinsford MSS. (unscheduled), 24 Aug., 1657.

A post-Restoration list of books collected by the sister of Sir Robert Owen of Porkington (Brogyntyn) and Clenennau comes not far short of two hundred volumes, most of them devotional books or household *vade mecums*, with a little contemporary drama, poetry and fiction—but not a single Welsh book save the *Gweddi Gyffredin*.[1] The existence of a humbler but quite extensive reading public is suggested by the output of Welsh printed books addressed (as Moris Kyffin put it) " i'r sawl ni wyddent ond y gymraeg arferedig ".[2] Even Sir Henry Salusbury's tailor could dun him for a long overdue bill of £20 13s. in a flowery letter opening with a string of complimentary quotations from the Scriptures almost in the manner of the minor *cywyddwyr*—save that this was all in English.[3] When we come down to the stratum of the sheer illiterates—if the gloomy pictures drawn by Vicar Prichard and others like him come anywhere near the truth—ignorance and superstition must have been indeed abysmal, though perhaps no worse than at the corresponding English level.

The fashion of letter-writing in English was becoming very general, except for an occasional young student's letter home or a farm bailiff's report on crops and stock. A man like John Jones of Maes y garnedd, trained (as younger son of a small squire) for business rather than polite society and using English for all his official and most of his personal correspondence, would turn to Welsh when writing religious exhortations to his relatives in Ardudwy, but with a diffidence he would never have felt in conversation.[4] English came readily enough to men inured to it in their student days—indeed it was indispensable to a man of any ambition at a time when (in the rueful words of a *bardd teulu*) " Seisneg arbennig yw'r byd ".[5] It had been the universal language of law and administration for over sixty years when James I came to the throne, and business—other

---

[1] N.L.W., Brogyntyn MSS. (unscheduled): " catalogue of my sister Ellen's books ", by Jane Owen.
[2] " to such as know only colloquial Welsh " (*Deffynniad Ffydd*, 1595: Annerch . . . at y Darllenydd).
[3] Llewenny, MS. 40. 42
[4] N.L.W. MS. 11440 D, fo. 117.
[5] " The world has gone all English " (Edward ap Raff, *c.* 1600, *N.L.W.J.*, vi. 41).

than the fundamental business of eating and drinking, buying and selling (with a vocabulary which William Salesbury dismissed as outside the literary pale)—was in the main an English import, carrying with it English ways of speech. Welsh written prose, on the other hand, was taught nowhere; and the Welsh of the bards was as unsuited to correspondence between gentlemen as was the spoken Welsh of kitchen or pot-house or market place, out of which a few pioneers like Gruffydd Robert, Moris Kyffin, Vaughan of Caer Gai and their successors (Anglican, Roman and Puritan) were trying to create a more flexible prose as a worthy medium for popular religious literature.

For all this, we must not exaggerate the decay of Welsh, especially in the north. Like so many other changes of the century, it went ahead most rapidly during its latter half. In James I's day a Merioneth gentleman like William Wynn of Glyn might adjure his son at Oxford to improve his English by eschewing Welsh in term time; his neighbour, Vaughan of Cors y gedol, might revel in the English poets and correspond with Ben Jonson; but both of them kept and cherished their own household bards and welcomed the itinerant bards on their *cwrs clera*, as did other northern households like Nannau, Plas y ward or Clenennau and a few like Pen y benglog in the south.[1] Others employed copyists to collect the literary treasures of the past, which they reverently preserved in their libraries. A few were qualified bards themselves, though there was a good deal of head-shaking over the growing laxity of admission to the bardic order and the intrusion into it of men of low birth and inferior skill who sang only for money. Many were skilled genealogists and antiquaries. Admittedly, for Wales this was not a creative age, for in literature as in politics it was *oes Lloegr*. To match the great developments across the border in drama and poetry, in memoir and essay, Wales could show only a few experiments in " popular " verse and prose. Rather was it an age of consolidation, distinguished by the grammatical works of Thomas Wiliems of Trefriw and John Davies of Mallwyd or the antiquarian researches of

[1] *T.C.S.*, 1948, pp. 81, 85, 197–8, 235–252, 365–410.

Vaughan of Hengwrt. That Welsh was the ordinary conversa-
tional medium of the rank and file goes without saying; this
was true even of Monmouthshire, at least till the middle of
the century, and in Radnorshire only a strip along the eastern
border had as yet succumbed to English influences. So when
the squire brought home (as he so often did) an English bride,
it paid her to pick up enough of the language to be able to
deal with tenants and menials; still less could her husband
afford (as a Glamorgan squire was reminded by the local
parson in the days of Charles I) to put himself at the mercy of
interpreters.[1]

The farmer and the labourer rarely left home unless to go
to market, and to the smaller squires a visit to " town " meant at
most a short stay at Ludlow and often only a trip to the shire
town; but legal and parliamentary business took the upper
gentry increasingly to London, especially after Ludlow's decline
as a provincial capital—to say nothing of those with jobs which
kept them hanging round the court for much of the year.

> Ledled oedd i Lwydlo deg
> ac i Lundain gu landeg.
> A hyn a fag, hen wyf i,
> adwy lydan o dlodi,

lamented a bard of James I's reign;[2] and Gruffydd Robert,
the Elizabethan grammarian, no doubt had grounds for his
complaint that " yn gytrym ag y gwelant afon Hafren neu
glochdai Amwythig, a chlywed Sais un dywedyd 'Good morrow',
a ddechreuant ollwng eu Cymraeg tros gof ".[3] This was why
some old-fashioned people resisted the pull of London. Sir
Roger Mostyn did not want his heir to stand for James I's
last parliament because it meant too prolonged a stay in the
capital; the objection did not apply to a younger son, since
he might in any case have to seek his fortune there. But the
Mostyns belonged to an age that was passing. Sir Roger's

---

[1] H.L., MS. EL 7466: *Red Dragon*, xi. 1887, p. 33. *T.C.S.*, 1948, p. 86.

[2] " Broad was the road to fair Ludlow and to dear, lovely London; and
this will make ('tis an old man who speaks) a wide gulf of penury to
yawn " (Edward ap Raff, *N.L.W.J.*, vi. 242).

[3] *Id.*, p. 250. " As soon as they come in sight of the Severn or the belfries
of Shrewsbury, and hear the Englishman say ' Good morrow ', they begin
to lose all recollection of Welsh " (*T.C.S.*, 1948, p. 250).

great-grandfather Richard ap Howel is said to have refused a place at the court of his kinsman Harry Tudor (whom he had followed to Bosworth) because he preferred to live among his own people; his great-grandson Sir Thomas was among the most assiduous collectors of Welsh literature even in the anglicising age of the later Stuarts.[1] Few others felt these scruples. It was soon after the Stuarts came in that Sir John Wynn of Gwydir resolved to spend most of the winter and spring in town;[2] wealthier folk like the earls of Worcester and an occasional bishop with private means went further and kept and staffed a town house. But of course these luxuries were beyond the means of most even of what we may call the parliamentary families. The Myddeltons of Chirk could afford the hire of one of the aristocratic palaces in the Strand, with a corresponding establishment, for their stay in London, but most of their fellow-members from Wales had to be content with humbler lodgings in one of the surrounding courts or side streets, with as brave a showing as could be provided by a temporary retinue of hired men like those who escorted Sir William Maurice of Clenennau as far as Shrewsbury on his way to the parliament of 1601, and whom he ruefully found he could not protect by his parliamentary privilege from arrest for brawling. They usually went loaded with commissions from stay-at-home neighbours—books or new Acts of Parliament to be procured, medicines or prescriptions to be wheedled from a city doctor, even a watch to be mended by a London jeweller; and at first they hurried home to their families as soon as the session or the legal term was over—sooner if they could get leave of absence from the Speaker or finish their legal business.[3]

Yet there were temptations in town, especially for those in whom education at the Inns of Court had bred a taste for the playhouse and the other gaieties of the London season; and the growing length of parliamentary sessions provided the necessary cover for a longer stay. This in turn caused difficulties

[1] Mostyn and Glenn, *The Mostyns of Mostyn*, pp. 74, 158; *C.W.P.*, 1186.
[2] N.L.W., Wynn of Gwydir MS. 348.
[3] *T.C.S.*, 1942, pp. 9, 15; Llewenny MS. 3. 107; Sweeney Hall MS. 7 (6 Jan., 1681); N.L.W. MS. 12406 C (28 Jan., 1681); Brogyntyn MSS. (unscheduled), R. Lawton to R. Mostyn, 11 Feb., 1685 (?); Chirk Castle MS. E.6088, and other family papers.

at home; a new gown from London might appease the
truant's womenfolk at first, but soon they would be clamouring
to see the sights themselves. Already in 1620 Sir James Perrot,
the unbending Pembrokeshire Puritan, was deploring the
extravagance into which the gentry were being led by these
feminine hankerings after the London season; two generations
later a letter from Richard Carne in London to Sir Edward
Mansell at Margam tells of his disgust at the concourse of
women flocking there from all over the country to see James II's
coronation, and his pious hope that Welshwomen would not
be tempted to follow the bad example.[1] This " urbanising "
process meant an increasing outlay not only on lodging but on
transport. When the master went to London with only a
servant or two he naturally rode on horseback; but when he
took his family they would soon be wanting their own coach.
The Salusburys of Llewenny had one as early as James I's
reign,[2] and the fashion spread after the Restoration.

For all the temptations of Vanity Fair, however, the real
centre of gravity for most of the Welsh gentry remained in
their own countryside and their own homes, at any rate till
well on in the century. The family in all its ramifications was
still by far the strongest social and political bond, and the
patriarchal sway of the *paterfamilias*, especially when exercised
by a forceful personality like Sir John Wynn of Gwydir or a
grandee like the Earl of Worcester, persisted long after the
children had grown up and married. Indeed the married
children often lived for years under the parental roof, while in
wealthy households this urge to *byw cyd* might be permanently
met by establishing the newly-married couple in a new wing
built on to, but separate from, the family home—an archi-
tectural practice especially characteristic of Gwynedd in the
sixteenth and seventeenth centuries.[3] If the son defied his
father's wishes he might be turned out (as happened to the son
of William Thomas of Aber during the Civil War) virtually
penniless save for what he or his wife might have in their own

---

[1] Nicholas, *Debates and Proceedings*, 1766, ii. 209–10; N.L.W., Penrice
and Margam MS. L. 182.
[2] N.L.W. MS. 1595 E., fo. 192.
[3] *A.C.*, xcvii. 98–112.

right.[1] Family quarrels of this sort, especially about property, were naturally common, and often came into the courts; but the affectionate tone of so many letters between husband and wife, father and son, aunt and niece, grandmother and grand-child, and even servant and employer, serves to remind us that it is not to the lawcourts we should look for a picture of normal domestic life.

Once at home, our squire had plenty to occupy him, both inside and outside his house. Apart from the claims of his estate and those of local government (which grew increasingly heavy under the early Stuarts, and led to many a peremptory summons back from town for those inclined unduly to prolong their stay), there were plenty of lighter diversions. This is how a contemporary bard describes the way the squires of Penllyn spent their leisure hours:

> At hyddod y tueddwn
> draw'n eu cylch i dreio'n cwn.
> Cawn fenswn, cawn fwy ansawdd
> a bîr a gwin heb awr gawdd,
> ac odlau a theg adlais
> bytheiaid, lawenblaid lais,
> a hela gwalch, hwylaw gamp,
> a hel pysg hwyl hapusgamp,
> a bowliaw gerllaw i'r llyn,
> llawen oll yn Llaniwllyn,
> ac englyn gan delyn dêg,
> gwych einioes, ac ychwaneg.[2]

Hunting was popular with all classes, from the wealthy squire with his organised stag hunt to the small farmer who begged the loan of a couple of greyhounds to avenge the damage the mountain deer had done to his oat field. Hawking was perhaps beyond the reach of the humbler folk, but the upper gentry still revelled in it as they had done four hundred years earlier,

[1] N.L.W., Llanfair and Brynodol MSS. (unscheduled), bundle 94 (20 Apr., 1644).
[2] " We will make a circuit of yonder stags to try the mettle of our dogs, feast on venison and fare more generously, with beer and wine and never an angry word; with songs and the grateful echo of the hounds—the voice of a merry pack; we'll hunt the hawk (a feat of skill), and fish, aglow with the joy of mastery; play bowls by the lakeside, light-hearted all in Llanuwchllyn; then an englyn sung to the lovely harp—a glorious life; and more besides." (John Vaughan of Caer Gai, *N.L.W.J.*, vi. 40.)

when Giraldus bragged of the prowess of a wild falcon of his beloved Pembrokeshire in despatching a Norwegian hawk of Henry II himself.[1] A letter to a friend by a Denbighshire squire not long before the Civil War shows the writer in a state of limp exhaustion after straining to keep up with a champion bird of his; and nothing could have been more welcome to the defeated Royalist colonel, Sir John Owen, in his days of political proscription after the war, than the gift of a goshawk sent from Ireland by his fellow-colonel, Marcus Trevor of Brynkynallt, with a request for the return gift of a couple of spaniels from Clenennau stables to " win their credit " over there. Similar gifts from Sir Roger Mostyn to a Flintshire neighbour during the same period confirm the impression that the Welsh Royalist gentry were not without means of amusing themselves while their enemies were in power.[2] Next to gifts of armour, hunting dogs were among the commonest objects of begging *cywyddau*, and when Thomas Davies of Gwysaney was away fighting on the continent his chief concern was that his dogs should be " made much of " in his absence. After the Restoration we begin to meet complaints among the west Denbighshire squires about neighbours who " spoile our sports by killinge the garowses on the mountains in the summer "; but in this part of the world poachers (or "fowlers ") had been disturbing the peace of mind of the gentry for the past thirty years.[3] Horse racing and cock fighting were the diversions of Sir Thomas Myddelton during his political exile under the Protectorate; as in England, both were found convenient cover for gatherings of political malcontents.[4]

Cock-fights were within the range even of the poor man, and he could also (in the mock pidgin-English of a contemporary broadsheet) " follow te pawling Togs over te hills, over te tales, over te titch, over te pales, to hunt te nimple

[1] *Itinerary*, I. xiii.

[2] Llewenny MSS. 3. 123, 130, 34; Brogyntyn MSS. (unscheduled), 5 July, 1657; N.L.W. MSS. 1595 E, fo. 293, 1593 E, fo. 158.

[3] E. D. Jones, " The Brogyntyn Welsh Manuscripts " (*N.L.W J.*, v–vii); N.L.W. MSS. 1593 E, fo. 203, 1595 E, fo. 300; Llewenny MS. 3. 55.

[4] W. M. Myddelton, *Chirk Castle Accts., 1605–66*, pp. 63, 65; H.M.C., *Kenyon*, p. 494; Thurloe, ii. 120–1, iii. 245, etc.

Hare, with te pugle by her side, and catch her if her can, and roast her for her supper ";[1] while in North Wales all classes seem to have joined, if only as spectators, in those Sunday hillside meetings where (according to an account written early in the century)

" theire harpers and crowthers singe them songs of the dooings of theire ancestors. . . . , and then they ripp upp theire petigres at lenght howe eche of them is discended from those theire ould princes. Here alsoe they spende theire time in hearinge some part of the lives of . . . the intended prophets and saincts of that cuntrie."[2]

These were the seventeenth-century counterpart of the modern eisteddfod—probably a closer counterpart than the original medieval eisteddfod which had had its last brief hour of glory under the Tudors. In the absence of a secular half-holiday, not only these assemblies, but the more boisterous diversions of the *gwerin*—their " twmpath chwareu, a'r bowliau, a'r tafarnau, a'r bel-droed, a'r denis "[3]—kept encroaching (to the grief of the more puritanical clergy) on Sundays and holy-days; and so did the practice of maypole-dancing to the tune of the pipes, which was spreading across the border from Cheshire and Shropshire.[4] Traditional games like *knappan* and *whippergundy* were more characteristic of south-west Wales; we know little of the latter, but the former appears in a contemporary description as a sort of primitive and more bloodthirsty Rugby, played with a wooden ball by whole villages (on horseback and afoot) on occasional Sundays and certain fixed holy-days, with a " field " that ranged over a broad countryside, thronged with caterers and with spectators yelling execrations and encouragements in Welsh. Other brands of football were popular further north, but players and spectators sometimes found themselves in the courts on charges of riot.[5]

A somewhat less boisterous type of village festival was provided by the *anterliwt*, handed down from generation to generation in village memory, and furbished up with a seasoning of

[1] *The Welchmans Protestation*, 1641.
[2] B.M., Lansdowne MS. 111, fo. 10.
[3] " Playgrounds and bowls and taverns and football and tennis " (Robert Lloyd, *Llwybr Hyffordd*, 1682: At y Darllenydd).
[4] *S.C.P.*, p. 67.
[5] Owen, *Description of Pembrokeshire* (Cym. Rec. Ser.), i. 270–2; *S.C.P.*, p. 58.

topical quips whenever occasion arose for a village merry-making. Only now and then would some master craftsman take a hand in it and leave a written version for posterity—as when Huw Morus (in the safety of the Restoration) made the Civil War his theme and Cromwell his villain.[1] The best Welsh acting talent no doubt went into the English companies, helping to satisfy the demand for the ever-popular stage Welshman. Wrexham had had its own band of strolling players as far back as Henry VIII's time, but as they included Shrewsbury in their tour their repertoire must have been such as an English audience could follow (unless they depended on the Welsh farmers and weavers who flocked in on market day); and this is obviously true of Welshmen who joined better-known companies, like Shakespeare's, which acted in London. None of the Welsh gentry who patronised their country's poetry—not even the princely third Earl of Worcester, whose company of actors was well known in many an English town—thought the native *anterliwt* worth taking under his wing, and neither playwright nor actor acquired anything like the status of the bard in Welsh society.[2]

The income level of the Welsh squires was no doubt substantially below the English average; it was observed that even in the parts of English shires bordering on Wales magistrates were often " men of mean estate, taken for want of others ", and the property qualification for jury service had to be fixed lower here—in spite of which the Sheriff of Anglesey sometimes had much ado to find a couple of dozen £4-a-year men to discharge the service.[3] But we need not treat Berry's chance remark as a sober statistical estimate; lists drawn up for the purpose of choosing sheriffs during Charles I's personal government show that even in a poor county like Anglesey there were then three landowners with over £1,000 a year, five between £500 and £1,000, and about twenty more over £100, while Glamorgan could show a dozen each in the first two categories and over a hundred between £40 and £200.[4] It was those at

---

[1] N.L.W., Cwrtmawr MS. 42.
[2] *T.C.S.*, 1948, pp. 170-83; H.M.C., *8th R.*, i. 428-31, *9th R.*, i. 249-51.
[3] *T.C.S.*, 1942, p. 57; *C.C.P.*, p. 60.
[4] H.L. MS. EL 7155; Symond's *Diary* (Camden Soc., 1859), pp. 216-17.

the middle level who were straining to keep up with the standards of their social equals (but financial superiors) in England in respect of seasons in town, enlarged and modernised houses and corresponding domestic staffs.

In great households the upper servants would not be divided by a very wide social gulf from their masters, for here as in England service with a family of standing, so far from being a bar to gentility, was a valued part of the education of both gentlemen and gentlewomen. Many of them could write a good letter; only the more menial servants would be *taeogaidd* and illiterate. These would include village girls brought in for a day's brewing to replenish the cellar or a day's spinning to replenish the linen-chest. To all of these, whether resident or not, the hall with its pastimes and festivities was the centre of social life. The village tailor himself was by way of being a retainer—in post-Restoration Anglesey at least, the Griffiths of Carreglwyd expected theirs to ask permission before he undertook a job for anyone else—but for the more modish items in their wardrobe even the middling families were now learning to look to London.[1]

The agent or steward was often himself a small landowner trained in the law, sometimes with deeper roots in the district than his own employer, and of sufficient standing there to be chosen as sheriff (as at Chirk and Powis castles); so he could advise as an equal on the management of the family estate and even of the family itself. He would often take up his quarters at the *plas* when the family was away, or permanently occupy a country house they had ceased to use, sending frequent and lengthy reports to his employer (an invaluable source of information to us to-day), and often at his wit's end to preserve the game and to keep peace among the servants over questions of precedence and allocation of duties. It was he who advised his employer which tenants could be trusted to let their rents run on and which should be pressed for prompt payment, or on purchases and sales and investments—generally with a strong bias against spending the revenues of the estate outside the country. It was he who managed elections by rounding up

[1] N.L.W., Carreglwyd MS. ii. 518, Llanfair and Brynodol MSS., bundle 91, letters of Grace Bold, 2 May, 1664, *et seq.*

the smaller freeholders while the candidate himself corresponded with his own friends; and he had to take charge of any
industrial undertakings on the estate. He was a very different
person from the agent as he appears in the pages of nineteenth-
century social critics—an alien (often a Scot), completely out
of sympathy with the tenants in language and religion, bent
chiefly on squeezing their rents out of them, evicting them if
they fell into arrears or voted in the wrong camp, and cutting
down expense on repairs and improvements. On the contrary,
the seventeenth-century agent's status made him just the right
intermediary between landlord and tenant and between buyer
and seller of land—even if, like his betters and his social
inferiors alike, he was not above making a little money on the
side on the deals he transacted for his employers, since (as a
prospective purchaser piously observed to one of them) " the
labourer is worthy of his hyre "[1]

Not that friction between landlords and tenants was as yet
at all common. Some of the latter, it is true, were miserably
poor, largely because of the backwardness of cultivation.
William Vaughan of Llangyndeyrn, a younger son of the house
of Golden Grove, who tried to relieve some of this poverty by
founding a Welsh colony of which more will be said later,
writes early in Charles I's reign, of lands " not halfe stockt "
and of " corne fields . . . so bare of Corne, that a stranger
would thinke that the earth produced such graine naturally
wild "; and a contemporary letter contrasts the good living of
the farmers of Arwystli with the squalor of some of the remoter
holdings in Anglesey where they lived " upon oate and barley
bread and butter milk and whaye, glassdwr and such like
trash ".[2] This was within a stone's throw of the house at
Penmynydd which, having given England its greatest line of
kings, now sheltered the obscure remnant of the parent stock,
permanently impoverished by their patriotic action in the
Glyn Dŵr movement two centuries earlier, and reduced to an
income of not much more than £200 a year.[3] But even

[1] Llewenny MSS. 3.43, 3.47, 3.55, 3.58, 3.84, 3.141-2, 3.158, et passim;
A. N. Palmer, Gresford, 1903-5, p. 107.
[2] Vaughan, Golden Fleece, 1626, II. vi. 29-36, II. xxiii; Llewenny MS.
3.141.
[3] H.L., MS. EL. 7155.

Anglesey's more substantial landlords were less interested in improving the yield of their estates than in rebuilding their houses after the fashion prevailing across the border:

> caer wen glaerwen eglurwaith,
> cerig a choed caer wych waith . . .
> a seler win ynghesel'r allt,
> neuadd deg, gwresog cegin,
> perl yw'r gwaith parlyrau gwin,
> uchel nen ai chloi'n unawr,
> a thair lloft rhwngthi ar llawr;[1]

and *Môn, mam Cymru* remained agriculturally backward for another century and more. For that matter, interest in agricultural improvement was rare everywhere till after the scientific movement which followed the Restoration, when it was an Anglesey parson, Henry Rowlands, who set his countrymen the example of using the discoveries of Boyle and the revelations of the microscope for the benefit of the soil and its produce.[2]

Poor as the living might be at some levels and in some regions, persistent mass pauperism was unknown, and the Elizabethan Poor Law, apart from its apprenticeship clauses and an occasional dole, sat lightly on most of the Welsh counties except Monmouthshire—probably the most populous, and certainly the most advanced part of Wales. Where vagrancy and mendicancy showed their heads it was because of some temporary and extraneous factor, such as the unauthorised landing of destitute Irishmen fleeing from famine to unwatched creeks on the Pembrokeshire coast early in Charles I's reign; it was probably for the same reason that Denbigh, which then lay on the main Irish road, had to find the money for a House of Correction. Money was collected for one in Brecknockshire too, but the county evidently found no need for it, since the sum was offered to the crown in lieu of a " benevolence " when the Addled Parliament dispersed in 1614 without voting

[1] " A fair citadel compact of the builder's noblest art, splendidly wrought of wood and stone, with a cellar of wine in the bosom of the hill; lovely hall and genial kitchen; a very pearl is the fashioning of the fine parlours; lofty vaulted roof, and three bedrooms 'twixt roof and ground-level." (Watkin Clywedog, N.L.W., Llanstephan MS. 122, fo. 511.)

[2] *Idea Agriculturæ*, written 1704, pub. 1764.

any taxes.[1] Local and personal charity, usually in the form of gifts of food, clothing or fuel from the *plas* at Christmas and Easter, could meet all normal calls; official action was necessary only in emergencies like death and pestilence, the return from the wars of a throng of disabled soldiers, the floods that overwhelmed the coasts of Glamorgan and Monmouth in 1606 (crippling the neighbourhood for a whole generation),[2] or the disastrous fire that burned down a quarter of the houses of Wrexham in 1643.[3] In extreme cases appeal would be made to the Privy Council to issue " briefs " authorising church collections outside the stricken area, even outside Wales. The Commons themselves made a collection for the flood victims of 1606, and the magistrates of Denbighshire, where the sea had also broken in near Abergele, wanted their plight considered too;[4] it was to a parliament much preoccupied with graver matters that an appeal went from Wrexham in 1648 for help in re-housing those still left homeless by the fire of five years earlier.

What agrarian disturbance there was arose mainly from the efforts of progressive landlords to consolidate their estates (a form of agricultural improvement they understood) by fencing off the waste for more profitable uses than the common rights of pasturage or wood-gathering which custom had given to tenants and cottagers, or by getting rid of those intervening patches of other men's lands still common in remoter areas untouched by enclosure. " A daily purchaser " is a common phrase in official correspondence about the qualifications of the local gentry for local office, and in their own unofficial correspondence no topic occurs more frequently than negotiations for the sale or exchange of pieces of land to round off their estates. Riots provoked by the enclosure of common (especially in North Wales) were frequent subjects of complaint in the Star Chamber or the Council at Ludlow; Elis Wyn of Lasynys was talking from experience when early in the next century he declaimed against " gŵr mawr a ddwg allan o'r

[1] *C.S.P.D.*, 1611–18, p. 261, 1628–9, p. 258; Llewenny MS. 3. 57.
[2] *Harleian Miscellany*, iii. 64–71; *C.J.*, i. 346; *C.S.P.D.*, 1635, p. 164; H.L. MS. EL, 7420.
[3] H.M.C., *7th R.*, p. 19; *L.J.*, x. 178.
[4] Llewenny MS. 3. 45.

mynydd ddarn o blwyf "[1] But the classic case in this area was that of Llewenny Green, near Denbigh, which cropped up again and again in the course of the century and was not finally settled till the next; and here the chief local landowners made common cause with the borough to resist the encroachments of an English intruder (apparently intent on some industrial development) who had the backing of the Privy Council.[2] In South Wales the most troublesome enclosure was that of Wentwood Chase in Charles II's reign. Here too many of the local gentry who were politically opposed to the Earl of Worcester (lord of the manor) helped to organise resistance when in the interests of his ironworks he tried to put a stop to the ancient common right of gathering firewood and timber there.[3] The Myddeltons had provoked resentment on similar grounds at Chirk a generation earlier, but there none of the smaller freeholders were wealthy enough to offer any effective opposition; nor, of course, was there any remedy against the " strangers " whose speculations in Flintshire land were popularly believed in Charles II's day to be " undoing the country " by " making land dear to the natives "—a complaint which could have been echoed from many other parts of Wales.[4]

Towards his more substantial tenants the landlord was generally considerate. Family pride dictated that those whose ancestors had been on the estate for generations should stay there, so eviction was rare, and however poor the farmer might be he at least had a reasonable measure of security.

> Dygwch drwy degwch draw
> ych deiliaid yn ych dwylaw
> a nad byth yr un di ball
> oth wyr att bennaeth arall :

such was a bard's advice to a young heir just succeeding to his

---

[1] " The great man who grabs a chunk of a parish from the mountain " (*Gweledigaetheu y Bardd Cwsc*, ed. Morris-Jones, 1898, p. 21).

[2] Llewenny MSS. 40.3, 3.6, 3.12, 3.20. 3.129; N.L.W. MSS. 1551 E (letter from T. Lloyd, 6 Oct., 1637), 12406 C (D. to J. Lloyd, 12 Dec., 1638); *C.S.P.D.*, 1636–7, p. 531; H.L. MS. EL. 7423; Williams, *Anc. and Mod. Denbigh*, pp. 196–7; Dodd, *Industrial Rev. in N. Wales*, p. 82.

[3] H.M.C., *9th R.*, iii. 116–17.

[4] N.L.W., Edward Owen deeds 31, 38; N.L.W. MS. 12406 C (T. Williams to E. Lloyd, 1 Aug., 1679).

estate in 1626; and the advice was better heeded than many of
the bardic moralisings.[1] When John Jones (the regicide) heard
from Ireland that his Merioneth tenants could not pay their
rents because a bad season had prevented them from selling
their starved and scraggy cattle, he suggested that in lieu of
rent they should send some of the beasts over to him to be
fattened in Irish pastures; and under the restored monarchy
tenants on the Powis Castle estate who were as much as three
years in arrear with their rents were let off in bad times with
corn, cheese, butter, " an ox or cow to kill for the work folks ",
or even a spell of work at the plough or harrow. " The best
tenants fayle ", writes a Flintshire agent during a summer of
incessant rain under the Merry Monarch, " and I can not
finde in my heart to urge yt much; knowing how it stands
with them."[2]

For on old-fashioned estates the relationship between landlord and tenant retained even now something of its tribal or
patriarchal character. The Vaughans of Trawscoed were still
levying payments under the name of *cymortha* a century after
the Act of Union had strictly forbidden them, and up to the
end of the century rents often took such forms as " 6½ teals of
tye or pilcorn at Christmas, a heriot of the second best beast,
six chickens at Whitsuntide, two geese at Michaelmas, a fat
hog at Christmas, a hen at Shrovetide, two men to reap, two
horses to carry corn, two horses to carry turf and two horses
to harrow ". Indeed on this estate food rents were occasionally
paid even in Napoleonic days, labour rents almost as late; and
the collection of *ebediw* or " heriot "—a sort of death duty
consisting of the payment to the landlord of the deceased
tenant's " best beast "—remained common in many parts of
the country till the end of the century.[3] The tenant took
a reciprocal pride in the family at the big house. His letters to

[1] " By even-handed dealings keep thy tenants at thy side, and come what
may let not one of thy men become another's liege." (Richard Kynwal,
Brogyntyn MS. 3, fo. 376.)

[2] *T.H.S.L.C.*, n.s.i. 1861, p. 232; N.L.W., Powis Castle MSS., letter 402
(cf. *N.L.W.J.*, iii. 140); N.L.W. MS. 12406 (T. Williams to E. Lloyd,
2 July, 1680).

[3] N.L.W., *Cal. Crosswood Deeds, passim*; N.L.W. MS. 12406 C (T. Williams
to E. Lloyd, 6 Feb., 1680, 6 and 17 May, 1681); Llewenny MS. 3.58.
On survival of " Cymorthas " cf. *T.C.S.*, 1916–17, pp. 128–9.

landlord or agent (often in English, with highly picturesque
and original spelling) bear the usual crop of complaints, but
never a hint of class hostility or envy. He hardly needed the
reminder which appeared in a Flintshire Elizabethan lease,
that he was " not to serve any other man by badge, livery, fee
or wage " nor to vote at election time for any but his landlord
or his landlord's friend;[1] for to follow him to the polls was as
natural in the early seventeenth century as to follow him to
more perilous fields had been (and was to be again) in less
peaceful times.

These conditions did not always apply to the relations
between the landlord and the small cottager who lacked the
protection of written agreement or the heritage of tribal
custom. It was this amorphous class, of uncertain and perhaps
fluctuating size and distribution, recruited from the floating
population bred in times of transition, that was apt to suffer
when a landlord of commercial views tried to make his estate
" pay " after the English fashion by rack-rents or prohibitive
fines, swelling at one and the same time the acres of his own
parkland and the ranks of the rural proletariat; for this was
really an indirect form of enclosure, accompanied by rural
eviction and helping to provoke the occasional agrarian riots
that came before the Star Chamber. It was commonest in
areas like Pembrokeshire which were advanced agriculturally
and susceptible to " progressive " influences from outside;
but even in a remote and outlying part of the estate of an
enterprising and anglicised landlord the villagers might be
startled out of the use and wont of centuries by the ominous
descent on them of an English surveyor to measure and value
their holdings—as happened to some Anglesey tenants of the
Llewenny estate when Charles I was king.[2] As for the poor
labourer, the patriarchal relationship that gave him protection
under a good master put him at the mercy of a bad one; for
dismissal left him with little hope of employment on a neighbour's estate, and if he tried to run away there was always the
chance he might be met, recognised and chased home (like

[1] *E.H.R.*, lxv. 221–2.
[2] E. Jeffreys Jones, " Rents and Fines in S. Wales ", *Harlech Studies*,
pp. 215–44; Llewenny MS. 3. 53.

the Flintshire servant who had thought to take advantage of the unsettled conditions that marked the last days of the Rump) by some friend of the family. But cases like that of the Denbighshire carter whose master fined him a whole week's pay (amounting to eighteenpence) for taking an unauthorised short-cut across the park, were apt to recoil on the oppressor's head in the ostracism of his neighbours.[1]

The houses of the tenantry varied widely from district to district. At the bottom of the scale comes the squalid earth-floored cottage of the *tyddynwr* in the more backward parts of Anglesey and elsewhere, often unpartitioned and innocent of glass, but sometimes with an extra room in the form of a *croglofft* perilously approached by ladder. A grade above this, and widely spread in the seventeenth century, was the " long-house " with its *pen uchaf* for the family and *pen isaf* for the livestock; at the top the characteristic stone farmhouse of Pembrokeshire which may have reflected the county's long intercourse with Bristol and south-western England, or the timber-framed dwelling with walls of stone, brick or wattle-and-daub, which was spreading from the English border to the adjacent parts of Denbigh, Montgomery and Radnor; these in turn faded imperceptibly into the smaller manor houses of the gentry. Roofing, save where slate or fissile stone was quarried, was generally of thatch, and there were still good thatchers everywhere, especially in the vale of Glamorgan. The style of the house itself, as well as of its furnishings, thus depended (in an age when the state of the roads precluded long hauls of material) on the natural resources of the district and its craft traditions, as well as on the social standing of the occupants. However hard material conditions might be, there was no lack of variety, picturesqueness or scope for craftsmanship in Welsh country life of the seventeenth century.[2]

With rents uncertain, capital locked up in stones and mortar, and income dribbling away in lawyers' fees, mortgage interest, and lavish housekeeping, the Welsh gentry were often far poorer than their outward showing would suggest. In

---

[1] N.L.W. MSS. 1593 E, fo. 156, 1600 E, fo. 256.
[2] I. C. Peate, *The Welsh House* (*Y Cymmrodor*, xlvii).

Anglesey it was alleged (probably with truth) that of the twenty or thirty gentlemen with fortunes adequate to put them in the running for the office of sheriff, not more than three could lay their hands on as much as £300 at short notice.[1] Failure to sell a load of oats at a critical moment reduced Vaughan of Caer Gai, the poet and translator, to borrowing four or five pounds from his son-in-law (with a hint that even less would be acceptable) when he was still sheriff of his county. What Archbishop Williams called " the Spanish fleet of Wales, which brings hither the little gold and silver we have " was her droves of cattle, squelching their way annually along the traditional tracks that converged from all parts of the country on the Smithfield market. The licensed drovers were the chief men of substance outside the ranks of the landed gentry, with fortunes far more fluid. They were the bankers of the age, ready to make advances in ready cash, to negotiate bills, or to act as agents for the transmission of large sums to London, whether for private or for public purposes. They could make upwards of £100 a year, and more than once a drover's name was put forward as sheriff, though the suggestion never bore fruit.[2] The works of Edward Morris of Perthi Llwydion, the Denbighshire drover poet, remind us too that he might be a man of good education. Until this " Spanish fleet " reached port there was a chronic shortage of cash everywhere, and much needless friction might have been avoided if English officials could have been persuaded to realise this. The stoppage of the cattle sales during the Civil War almost brought the economic life of the country to a standstill and, when it was over, John Glynne, the leading Welsh lawyer on the parliamentary side, induced his fellow-M.P.'s to vote a group of drovers the sum of £3,000 in compensation for their losses—a striking tribute to the magnitude of the traffic.[3] The chief

[1] Llewenny MS. 3. 53.
[2] Brogyntyn MSS. (unscheduled), R. Vaughan to W. Wynne (15 Mar., 1643); C.W.P., 1748; H.L., MS. EL. 7147.
[3] Williams, Anc. and Mod. Denbigh, pp. 220–1; A.C., I. i. 332–3, VII. ii. 249–50: T.R.H.S., IV. ix. 135 ff.; C.W.P., 1724, 1728, 1834, 1878A; Llanfair and Brynodol MSS., bundle 94, petition of 6 Apr., 1644; A Particular Charge or Impeachment . . . against . . . Master John Glynne, 16 June, 1647, p. 12.

competitors of the Welsh cattle were those from Ireland, and both under James I and again under Charles II the Welsh M.P.'s strongly supported legislation to restrict their importation. It was a bitter blow to Welsh expectations when the final passage of this measure was followed by the poorest cattle fairs in living memory.[1]

Next in importance to the sales of cattle came those of butter and woollens. Butter from south-eastern Wales to the estimated value of £12,000 a year crossed the Bristol Channel to feed south-western England; woollen cloth woven and spun by unorganised peasants of the north in the upland districts of Merioneth, Montgomery and Denbigh went overland to Shrewsbury to be sold by the municipal Drapers' Company. Both were the subject of monopolies which the London merchants, with their strong prejudice in favour of open markets, made the most strenuous efforts to break down by legislation in parliament. The speculators in butter had powerful friends at court, but the London merchants, and the parliamentary opposition in which they figured so prominently, were too strong for them, and in James I's last parliament the London market was thrown open to Welsh butter, subject to a proviso empowering the magistrates in each county to keep local supplies at home in times of scarcity; export was not allowed, despite pressure from some who saw the possibility of a Welsh butter mart at Hamburg. This Act, which remained on the statute book till the time of George III, cannot have been very effective, for fourteen years after it was passed there were still complaints in Glamorgan of poverty caused by the cornering of butter, and two years later a Welsh member was turned out of the Long Parliament as one of the guilty parties.[2]

The cloth monopolists were even stronger, for the Shrewsbury Drapers were an old and powerful corporation who could base their claim to the sole right of selling Welsh cloth on an

---

[1] *T.C.S.*, 1942, p. 57; *C.S.P.D.*, 1619–23, pp. 396, 498; Cunningham, *Eng. Ind. and Commerce*, 1919 ed., ii. 372; *C.J.*, ix. 589, 613, 621; *Old Parl. Hist.*, iv. 340, 345; Carte, *Ormonde*, 1736, ii. 234; Clarendon, *Life*, 1759, iii. 704–26; N.L.W. MS. 12406 C (T. Williams to E. Lloyd, 28 Jan., 22 Mar., 1681), Chirk Castle MS. E. 6370, Carreglwyd MS. ii. 118.

[2] *T.C.S.*, 1942, p. 50; *C.W.P.*, 1205; *C.S.P.D.*, 1611–18, p. 507, 1619–23, pp. 273–4.

Elizabethan charter; and in their numerous efforts during the first two Stuart reigns to stop the London merchants from buying cloth in Wales itself, and so saving the middleman's profit, they generally had the sympathy of the crown. But once again parliament asserted the principle of freedom of trade, and the same House that opened the London market to Welsh butter opened it also (on paper) to Welsh cloth, with the strong backing of the Welsh members. But since the Shrewsbury Drapers dug their heels in and refused to go to Wales for cloth, the Act was circumvented by the economic pressure they could exert on a countryside where there were no capitalists to give the industry an independent organisation; and the monopoly lingered on till the middle of the next century. It enabled Welsh cloth even in the seventeenth century to reach a market extending over most of Western Europe and as far as Archangel and the Guinea coasts; but the profits stuck with the Shrewsbury middlemen and the London exporters, and did little to enrich the Welsh countryside.[1]

Of industries not directly connected with farming, Wales had as yet but few. In this respect, as in many others, the most developed region was the coastal plain of South Wales, which for geographical reasons had been in the van ever since the Bronze Age.[2] In Elizabeth's reign the Gloucestershire Hanburys had begun their long connection with industrial Monmouthshire by opening the Pontypool ironworks; Sir Henry Sydney, the greatest of the Presidents of Wales, had developed the industry in Glamorgan; and the Tintern foundry and wireworks had been founded by one of the Elizabethan joint-stock companies for industrial development. Initially at least most of these enterprises were worked in the main by imported labour, but under the Stuarts they began to draw more extensively on local man-power. Early in the century the earls of Worcester were developing the iron industry on their Monmouthshire estates, while the Hanburys extended

[1] *T.C.S.*, 1942, pp. 48–9, 1946–7, p. 67; *A.C.*, VII. ii. 220 ff.; *Economica*, 1929, pp. 197 ff.; *C.S.P.D.*, 1619–23, *passim*; *A.C.P.*, 1619–23, *passim*, 1627, p. 254.
[2] V. E. Nash-Williams (ed.), *A Hundred Years of Welsh Archæology*, pp. 67–70.

their enterprises into Brecknockshire; by Charles II's time the Mansells of Margam and the Morgans of Tredegar were turning out small quantities of iron from the Machen and Tredegar forges. Charcoal was the agent for smelting, and we have seen how this extension of the industry led to a more jealous guardianship of timber stocks, to the detriment of those who had exercised common rights in the woods and forests of Gwent; but coal was used in the forge and foundry, with the result that exploitation of the coal measures of the south was greatly stimulated, and the use of coal as domestic fuel was spreading in regions where pits had been opened. In the broken country further inland exploitation had to wait another century, till the road-builder and the canal "navvy" had made transport possible.[1]

The Elizabethan pioneers had also opened up the lead mines of Cardiganshire with a view to extracting silver from them, but no great success was achieved until in James I's reign Sir Hugh Myddelton, the Lord Mayor's younger brother, took a lease from the Mines Royal Company, extended his activities as far as south Caernarvonshire, and made fabulous profits, which he used (with no great advantage to himself) to improve London's water supply in preference to sinking further capital in his native soil.[2] He was followed by another Gloucestershire prospector, Thomas Bushell, whose success was cut short by the Civil War. Cardiganshire silver played its part in promoting the national dignity as well as the material prosperity of Wales, for orders were given for Myddelton's silver to be separately minted and stamped with the Prince of Wales's insignia, and Bushell was even allowed to set up his own mint at Aberystwyth.[3] But little further development took place here till towards the end of the century. After the Restoration lead-mining spread inland into Montgomeryshire, where Lord Herbert of Cherbury tapped a promising vein near his home, as well as others on his Caernarvonshire property; the small ironworks on the

[1] D. J. Davies, *Econ. Hist. of S. Wales . . . to 1800*, sec. III.

[2] *Ibid.*; *D.N.B.*, xxxix. 436 ff.; *A.P.C.*, 1618–19, p. 100, 1621–3, p. 515, 1623–5, pp. 159–60, 169–70; *C.S.P.D.*, 1619–23, pp. 544, 593, 1623–5, pp. 289–90, 425; *C.W.P.*, 1008, 1366–7; H.M.C. *5th R.*, p. 355, *7th R.*, p. 254; cf. Howell, *Dodona's Grove*, 3rd ed., 1645, p. 32.

[3] J. W. Gough, *The Superlative Prodigall*, 1931; *C.S.P.D.*, 1623–5, p. 73, 1638–9, pp. 47, 289.

neighbouring Powis Castle estate (a refuge for persecuted Quakers under Charles Lloyd of Dolobran and his friend Abraham Darby, the great Quaker ironmaster) had begun to wreak indiscriminate havoc on Powis woodlands even before the Civil War.[1]

In mid-Wales industrial development was held back by lack both of coal and of transport; here the north-eastern counties were luckier. Before the middle of the century the Mostyns' coal mines, for which the Dee estuary provided a natural outlet, were already deep enough to suffer from fire-damp, and Flintshire's long-exploited wealth in lead gave a market nearer home; the fortune the family lost in the King's service was largely retrieved by their lead-smelting enterprises. Further south the Flintshire coal measures were near enough to Chester to supply the grates of its citizens, who felt the draught very literally when the Roundhead siege cut them off from their supplies; and coal, iron and lead works developed rapidly after the Restoration, when prospectors and surveyors were busy up and down the coalfield. The exploitation of the Denbighshire coal measures owed much to the Myddeltons of Chirk, heirs to most of the Lord Mayor's fortune; by mid-century they too were installing machinery in their pits, and an iron forge on the estate (with three others in close proximity) helped to absorb the output and to meet the local demand for malleable iron. Wrexham had been the resort of a wide variety of workers in iron since long before the day when Guto'r Glyn addressed to the abbot of Valle Crucis a *cywydd* thanking him for the gift of a sword and buckler, *prickswng y siop o Wrecsam*, and the industry went forward briskly in Charles II's time. There were also workers in lead, dependent on spasmodic revivals of the ancient workings at Minera. Even the thin and broken coal seams of Anglesey were worked to provide fuel for lime burning, with beneficial effects on agriculture; and the Wynns of Gwydir interested themselves in the lead and copper ores of the Conway valley, using the river as waterway.[2]

[1] *N.L.W.J.*, iii. 41, 148; Dodd, *Ind. Rev.*, p. 19; *T.C.S.*, 1948, p. 89 *n.*
[2] Dodd, *op. cit.*, pp. 18–19; Palmer, *Town of Wrexham*, pp. 10–11; Mahler, *Chirk Castle and Chirkland*, pp. 158–9; N.L.W., Bettisfield deeds 320, 323, 707, 812, 815, 1052, 1318–21, 1468, 1567, 1581, 1634, 1700, Rhual deed 304; N.L.W. MS. 12406 C (T. Williams to E. Lloyd, 3 July, 1679, 5 Mar. and 2 Apr., 1680, 9 Apr., 1681, 30 Jan. and 9 Feb., 1683).

In relation to the life of the country as a whole these industries were less important than the space they occupy here
might suggest. They created no new classes of capitalists or
labourers; for the capitalist was usually, as we have seen, the
owner of the soil (Hugh Myddelton, Thomas Bushell and the
Hanburys being the chief exceptions), and the labourer, apart
from a few imported skilled men and some forced labour,[1]
normally a peasant who gave only part of his time to industry.
We hear, of course, the usual complaints about the extravagant
demands of workmen and servants, whether industrial,
agrarian or domestic, especially of those who claimed in virtue
of specialised skill a higher rate than the shilling, sixpence or
even threepence a day that sufficed for the day labourer; and
just before the Civil War Sir Thomas Myddelton had to deal
with pleas for a rebate of rent on holdings subject to encroachment from " thous ill Condisioned Collyars "—a complaint
echoed both here and in Flintshire in Restoration days. By
then the industrial age had begun to cast its shadow before it:
in the lead district of Flintshire a couple of London merchants
had contracted with the owner of some local mines and
smelteries for the entire output over a term of years, at £10
a ton for pig lead and £4 15s. for ore—but with the significant
proviso that the landlord was still free to oblige his friends with
small quantities for their own needs; an east Denbighshire
squire made a similar deal with a neighbour who had opened
an iron forge, to supply him with wood fuel in exchange for
pig iron, and estates in Flintshire were being stripped of timber
to satisfy the same voracious maw.[2] But there was nothing in
all this to disturb the balance of society or to undermine its
traditional standards. The total stock-in-trade of the Machen
forge, with bars, pigs, scrap, coal, wood and plant, was valued
in 1683 at only £625, and a little earlier a sum of £420, received
by Lord Herbert of Cherbury for the largest sale of ore yet
made from his south Caernarvonshire mine, was more than
swallowed up in arrears of wages and outstanding debts for

[1] D. J. Davies, *op. cit.*, pp. 56–7.
[2] Chirk Castle MSS. E. 3297, 3299, 3301; Brogyntyn MS. 1018; Rhual
MSS., letter 167; Edward Owen deed 77; N.L.W. MS. 12,406 C (as
above); *L.J.*, xii. 401–26.

stores extending over eighteen months. Even the Myddeltons
at Chirk were less concerned with the market than with the
needs of their neighbours for iron to make or repair farm
implements; *noblesse oblige* was not yet swamped by the higgling
of the market.[1]

Indeed, the strains set up by these new developments were
psychological rather than economic; we can see them in
miniature in the obstructions met by the wealthy Myddeltons,
with their new-fangled London ways and ideas, at the hands
of old-fashioned Chirkland neighbours like the Edwardses of
Plas Newydd, with roots in the area going deep down in its
history and fostering a love for the ancient ways alike in
religion (for which they sacrificed much of their fortune) and
in culture (as Thomas Wiliems bore witness when he called
the Edwards of his day " gwir ymgeleddwr yr iaith Gymraec ").[2]
Men like this bitterly resented the power of a *parvenu* " usurer "
to buy an ancient dignity like the lordship of Chirk, which
they wished to see resumed by the crown; they accused the
newcomers of using their powers tyrannically, trampling on the
rights of the commoners, and denuding the forests for their
private gain, and they put every obstacle they could in the way
of enterprises that threatened the familiar way of life.[3] Naturally
the longer purses and the new ideas won the day when matters
came to an issue, but as England offered a far more profitable
field for investment of capital, there was as yet but a barely
perceptible ruffling of the surface of ancestral modes and
standards at home.

With the exception of the woollen ware sold at Shrewsbury,
the butter shipped to Bristol or London, and the cattle driven
to Smithfield, the market served by Welsh industry was in
general a narrowly local one. This was obviously true of the
products of the village smithy or corn mill or the handiwork
of the itinerant shoemaker or carpenter; and in the existing
state of the roads fragile commodities like slate or coal could

[1] Penrice and Margam MS. L.167; Powis Castle MSS., letter 402;
Chirk Castle MS. E.558.
[2] " A true lover of the Welsh people " (or " tongue ") (H.M.C., *Welsh
MSS.*, ii. 1056).
[3] Edward Owen deeds, 31, 38 *et passim*.

reach a wider market only when they were found near enough to a good harbour to be shipped overseas—which in turn demanded at least a rudimentary organisation. The slate quarries of North Wales, so important in the next century, had hardly yet reached this stage, but for two or three centuries past they had been used on a small scale to meet local housing needs, travelling at times by sea to Chester, and latterly even to Ireland.[1] There was also a small export trade in slates from Cardigan to Ireland by the end of our period, and a more considerable one in coal from Swansea and Pembroke to Ireland and occasionally to France; in the north it was only the Mostyn pits that could compete in the former market, and that was the farthest their shipping resources would allow. The product of the cottage loom, excepting in the three counties where the Shrewsbury Drapers had spread their tentacles, rarely travelled beyond the nearest market town, though there was some small export of leather from Cardiff, and the Denbigh glovers and corvisors, with their strong gilds, were able to sell their wares overland through most of North Wales and for some distance over the border.[2] The limited character of Welsh trade is illustrated by the relatively small number of marketing offences which came up before the court at Ludlow from the thirteen counties during the early years of the century—not much more than a tenth as many as those arising in the four border counties, and these all concentrated in three shires of South Wales.[3]

There was always a strong prejudice against the movement of farm produce, especially corn, out of the county where it was grown; we have seen how allowance had to be made for this in the Act for free trade in butter. But there was rarely any corn to export, except in a few rich areas like the vale of Glamorgan and the Pembrokeshire plain. A little was shipped overseas from Cardiff, and Pembrokeshire sent its surplus coastwise both to south-western England and to the more backward counties of North Wales; but even in this premier

[1] *Record Society for . . . Lancashire and Cheshire*, lix. 241; Brogyntyn MSS. (unscheduled), W. Hatfield to Sir J. Owen, (5 July, 1657).
[2] D. J. Davies, *op. cit.*, sec. III; Dodd, *op. cit.*, p. 8.
[3] *T.C.S.*, 1916–17, p. 136.

agricultural county, where sheep-rearing was giving place to arable farming as the once-flourishing cloth industry succumbed to competition from the south-west of England and from mid-Wales, the leading gentry (with those of Carmarthenshire) strove as hard under the early Stuarts to check the outward flow of both corn and wool from their counties as their fathers had done when Elizabeth's Commons voted down a Bill to stop wool exports from the whole area.[1] Within each county the chief distributive agencies, apart from the few shops (like Guto'r Glyn's *siop o Wrecsam*) that disposed of local handicrafts, were the weekly markets and (often catering for a wider area) the periodic fairs, of which there was one in process somewhere or other in Wales about four days out of every seven—not excluding Sundays, for Llanelly held its on Whitsun Day. The great fairs of Wrexham and Carmarthen, lasting several days, were the chief means of spreading once or twice a year, through the northern and southern counties respectively, produce that came from a greater distance; those of Pembrokeshire, at the beginning of the century attracted buyers and sellers not only all over West Wales but from as far north as Trawsfynydd in Merioneth or Cemmes in Montgomeryshire.[2]

It was the market towns—many, though by no means all of them, chartered boroughs with a measure of self-government —that sheltered what urban life there was in Wales. But there was no sharp division between town and country. Towns were small, few had gilds of any importance (since skilled crafts were spread through the countryside rather than concentrated in the towns), and so in municipal government and parliamentary representation alike they tended to lean on the support and protection of the neighbouring gentry for the maintenance of their privileges and the furtherance of their trade. Hugh Owen of Orielton took on the mayoralty of Pembroke in 1632 for " the raysinge of trade which is now decayed "; and when the Earl of Suffolk fell from power in 1618 he dragged down with him the Oswestry cloth market,

---

[1] D. J. Davies, *loc. cit.*; *A.P.C.*, 1621–3, pp. 72–3; *C.S.P.D.*, 1619–23, pp. 529, 546, 1629–31, pp. 384, 394, 445, 512; *T.C.S.*, 1942, pp. 10–11.
[2] *Llyfr Plygain*, 1612 (1931 reprint), pp. 35–46; *B.B.C.S.*, vii. 284–318.

which as lord of the manor he had defended against the
encroachments of Shrewsbury. The county borough of
Haverfordwest, with its body of merchants trading with
London and Bristol, provides perhaps the nearest approach to
urban conditions, but even here the surrounding squirearchy
had great influence.[1]

Few of the Welsh seaports could accommodate ships of any
considerable draught. Swansea, still theoretically a subordinate
" creek " of Llanelly along with Neath and the Pembrokeshire
ports, possessed a dock of sorts by the early years of the century,
and we have seen that each of this group had by now a fairly
brisk traffic in corn and coal. Cardiff and its creek of Newport
were outlets for the seaborne agricultural produce of the south-
eastern counties rather than coal ports; Chepstow exported
the ironware of Monmouthshire. Along the shores of Cardigan
Bay the staple commodity was the herring, shipped coastwise
from Cardigan and Aberystwyth, and as far afield as Ireland
and France from the Pembrokeshire ports. That the fisheries
flourished in the later seventeenth century appears in the
efforts of the impecunious father of Edward Lhuyd the antiquary
(a small squire of the Oswestry region) to retrieve his sinking
fortune by wholesale dealings.[2] Along the north coast maritime
trade, concentrated in the port of Beaumaris and its creeks of
Caernarvon, Conway and Pwllheli, was even more limited.
Indeed the whole volume of Welsh shipping did not amount to
much. There was only one vessel over 200 tons in the whole of
South Wales in 1635, even Pembrokeshire carrying its trade
to Bristol, Ireland and France in ships of twenty to thirty
tons' burden. At the very end of the century the joint shipping
of the more westerly ports of South Wales, from Swansea to
Milford Haven, was no more than 73 vessels averaging 35 tons,
while Chepstow and Cardiff had not much more than half
the number and less than half the tonnage. As for North
Wales, one would strongly suspect a deliberate underestimate
in the allegation made in 1626, when it was a matter of sup-
plying ships and men for the navy, that the six counties between
them could not find more than nine vessels, ranging from six

---

[1] H.L. MS. EL. 7135: *Economica*, 1929, p. 201; *infra*, p. 185.
[2] D. J. Davies, *loc. cit.*; Sweeney Hall MSS. 3 and 5.

to thirty tons, were it not that seventy-five years later Aberystwyth had but a single ship of fourteen tons.[1]

Reference has already been made to the reflections of William Vaughan of Llangyndeyrn on the poverty of the land; he attributed it to lack of enterprise, and (being a considerable traveller himself) was especially severe about the backwardness of his countrymen in maritime adventure. He even declared in 1626 (no doubt with some exaggeration) that the whole country did not possess more than ten ships as against 150 in Devonshire, with its inferior natural advantages. His remedy was colonisation, and in 1616 he obtained from the patentees for Newfoundland a grant of land for a Welsh colony on the extreme south-east tip of the island, to be called Cambriol. He transported the first batch of settlers there (at his own costs) in the following year—three years before the Pilgrim Fathers set sail. Their provenance is indicated by the names they gave to their settlement—Glamorgan, Pembroke, Cardigan, Breckonia—all names that have disappeared without trace from the map of Newfoundland. A further batch, under a governor appointed by Vaughan, followed in 1618, but most of the first pioneers were sent home as unsatisfactory—some, perhaps, to perpetuate the memory of their year's adventure by calling their farms " Newfoundland ", a name long current in the Carmarthenshire countryside. Vaughan himself, delayed by ill-health, did not join his colonists till 1622, and was back again in a few years to commend his project by tongue and pen to the King, the President of Wales, the Earl of Pembroke, Bishop Williams and other leading public figures, as well as to the reading public at large, while his patron Lord Falkland appealed to Buckingham as Lord High Admiral to deal with the urgent problem of piracy in Newfoundland waters by appointing as commissioners himself and Vaughan, with Vaughan's brother-in-law Salusbury of Llewenny and

---

[1] Davies, *loc. cit.*; P.R.O., S.P. 16/35, No. 12; cf. S.P. 14/109, No. 9 (3 May, 1619), where it appears that Beaumaris and Caernarvon had between them six vessels ranging from 10 to 17 tons, and thirteen " traders by sea ".

others of his clan. A second visit in 1628 was cut short by the urgent need to settle his personal finances, on which the colony was still dependent.

For Cambriol never became self-supporting, its planters being no more successful in withstanding the rigours of the climate, the depredations of French, Spanish and renegade British pirates, or those of the lawless fishermen in Newfoundland waters defending their livelihood against the interlopers, than Gilbert's or Raleigh's first Virginian settlers had been in establishing themselves on the mainland; but for a different reason—a dearth rather than an excess of the " gentleman-adventurer " type. Even the help of Lord Baltimore, the future founder of Maryland (who took over part of the colony, with no better luck) failed to set Cambriol on its feet; but in 1630 Vaughan was heartened by the prospect of colonists of substance from North Wales, including Sir Henry Salusbury, a restless spirit who had also had his eye on an Irish home. Two years later, however, Salusbury died without ever visiting Cambriol, and the colony itself did not survive much longer. Its founder, though a man of immense learning and energy, had in him more of the medieval schoolman than of the modern coloniser, and his dream of a Welsh colony never fully emerged from the wrappings of fantasy and allegory in which he loved to present it to the world (preferably in Latin) as part of an all-embracing scheme of morals and politics. Yet there is no hint of religious or political dissidence in all his speculations, and although many of his followers came from those regions where Puritanism gained some of its few Welsh footholds, they were no Pilgrim Fathers. Vaughan's own loyalty to the Anglican establishment was unaffected by his fervid Calvinism or by the passion for Protestant unity that made him in later years look with charity even on the " crabbed zeal " of the " holy separatists "; his belief that parliament (as the Tudors conceived it) was the very soul of the body politic was matched by an equally strong conviction that democracy " of all regiments is the very worst "; and a boyish admiration for Elizabeth's Earl of Essex and his Welsh steward Sir Gely Meyrick left unimpaired his lifelong devotion to the crown as the sheet anchor of

Protestantism and to the Act of Union as the palladium of Wales.[1]

The spirit of maritime adventure to which Vaughan of Llangyndeyrn appealed was either swallowed up in the general colonising movement of the age or else found its outlet on the high seas themselves. It was natural that South Wales, with the greater capacity of her harbours, the wider range of her shipping, and above all her contacts with Bristol, should take the lead in both these fields of adventure. Under Charles I North Wales, according to her own vice-admiral, had not more than forty men who earned their living on the sea, mainly in coastal fishing, while few could handle a boat as far as Land's End.[2] Those of the southern counties, on the other hand, were used to longer voyages, not only to Ireland (which accounted for about sixty per cent of Welsh overseas exports) but across the Channel to France; they were thus able to supply experienced and adventurous crews for Sir Thomas Button when he went in James I's time to explore the northwest passage or (under that other great Glamorgan sea-dog Sir Robert Mansell) to clean up the pirates of Algiers, or again to patrol the Irish Sea for Charles I. But the north also produced one of the leading seamen of an age of naval decadence in Sir Sackville Trevor, a Denbighshire man (with two brothers serving the navy ashore) who commanded his first ship as a mere stripling under Elizabeth and lived to win distinction in the few continental expeditions of Charles I.[3]

The navy was by now afloat continuously enough to afford something like a professional career; and although we had as yet no standing army, experience in the continental wars was creating also the rudiments of a class of professional army officers. This class was well represented here, for the pugnacity

[1] E. R. Williams, *Elizabethan Wales*, ch. xiv; Lansdowne MS. 53, fo. 182; W. Vaughan, *Poematum Libellus*, 1598, *Erotopaignion pium*, 1598, *Speculum humanæ condicionis*, 1598, *Golden-grove*, 1608, bk. III, *Spirit of Detraction*, 1611, pp. 315–23, *Cambrensium Coroleia*, 1625, *Golden Fleece*, 1626, pt. II, pp. 29–36, pt. III, chs. iii–vi, *Directions for Health*, 3rd ed., 1633, *Church Militant*, 1640; N.L.W. MS. 1595 E, fo. 165.

[2] S.P. 16/32, No. 12.

[3] *T.C.S.*, 1948, pp. 18–19, 34–5.

and valour of the Welsh was as proverbial as their poverty and their touchiness in point of honour—though it was no doubt they themselves who invented the current proverb, " Three Welshmen, two soldiers; three Englishmen, two thieves; three Frenchmen, two traitors ", and so on.[1] Sir Charles Morgan of Pencarn, nephew of the stout Elizabethan warrior Sir Thomas, fought abroad most of his life—accompanied on some of his campaigns by a band of Welsh followers glorying in a leader who " beheaves hymselfe bravely "—and he married and died there; but during an interlude at home under James I he served as magistrate for his native Monmouthshire, and he sent his foreign-born daughter home to be naturalised and to marry another Monmouthshire Morgan.[2] His younger neighbour Sir Thomas Morgan of Llangattock began his military career as a monoglot Welsh lad of sixteen by serving as a volunteer in the Thirty Years' War, and he came home at thirty-eight to fight for parliament in the Civil War; knighted by Richard Cromwell for service in Scotland, he fought abroad again under Charles II, and ended (though almost illiterate because of his early enlistment) as the very successful governor of Jersey. The Devereux influence promoted a strong military tradition in south Pembrokeshire: both Rowland Laugharne and Sir John Meyrick had followed the third earl to the continental wars before the latter became General of Ordinance to parliament and the former led its forces in his own county. In Montgomeryshire there was Sir Charles Lloyd, kinsman to his namesake who built the Mathrafal forge. Descended from the Princes of Powys through Sir Griffith Vychan, a hero of Agincourt, he was great-grandson to one of the leading spirits in the settlement of mid-Wales under the Act of Union; but his grandfather sold the ancient family estate (heavily mortgaged to Sir Thomas Myddelton the Lord Mayor), and his father Brochwel Lloyd made his living as a soldier of fortune, first abroad and then at home in the Bishops' Wars. Sir Charles himself learned the

---

[1] *A True Copy of the Welch Sermon Preached . . . by Shon up Owen*, 1646, p. 2.
[2] *T.C.S.*, 1945, p. 17; *A.P.C.*, 1625–6, p. 492, 1627, pp. 229–30, 340, 421; H.M.C., *5th R.*, p. 75, *Cecil*, vi. 165, 205, 361, xi. 291, xvi. 207, xvii. 235; N.L.W. MS. 1595 E, fo. 100.

new art of fortification while on service in the Netherlands, and came home to receive a life appointment as general-in-chief of engineers and quartermaster general of all fortifications in the British Isles, in which capacity he served Charles I in the Irish rebellion and the Civil War, and was succeeded on his death after the Restoration by his brother Godfrey, his companion in Holland.[1]

There were others who combined with a strong professional interest in soldiering the normal pursuits of a country gentleman. A good example is Sir John Owen of Clenennau in Caernarvonshire, eulogised by bards as *gŵr purffydd* and *gŵr a nerthai'r Goron*;[2] he had served his military apprenticeship before he succeeded to the estate, and was consequently placed in charge of the forces raised for Charles I in Snowdonia. After his defeat he was regretfully unable to accept an invitation from Prince Rupert to lead a Welsh force into the French king's service, and when the Restoration came he settled down to the humdrum duties of county magistrate; but the only addition he made to the library at Clenennau, founded by his great-grandfather Sir William Maurice with an assortment of well-thumbed legal and theological works, was a single book on the art of gunnery.[3] Robert Ellice of Croes Newydd in Denbighshire was another North Wales squire who had gained military experience abroad (under Gustavus Adolphus) before he placed it at the disposal of Charles I;[4] and in Radnorshire Charles Price of Pilleth, son of an Elizabethan warrior-squire, began his career as second in a duel and ended it as victim of another while he was in the royal army during the Civil War, having meanwhile fought in Ireland and abroad and represented his county or its borough with great vigour and independence in seven successive parliaments.[5] Many of these

---

[1] *D.N.B.*, xxxiii. 408, 420–1; Lloyd, *Sheriffs of Montgomeryshire*, pp. 3–17, 280–90; *M.C.*, xxvii. 354 ff.; *T.C.S.*, 1946–7, p. 84.

[2] " A man of unsullied faith . . . a bulwark of the crown " (Huw Machno, *N.L.W.J.*, vi. 35).

[3] *Id.*, v. 169; Brogyntyn MSS. (unscheduled), *passim*; *T.S.A.S.*, II. iii. 13–54.

[4] Palmer, *Old Parish of Wrexham*, pp. 82–90.

[5] *T.C.S.*, 1948, pp. 19, 23, 31, 41, 48–51, 53–4; Howell, *Familiar Letters*, 1892 ed., pp. 337, 454; Herbert of Cherbury, *Life*, 1886 ed., p. 101; *Lord George Digby's Cabinet*, 1647, p. 26.

distinguished soldiers took abroad with them a contingent of tenants and dependents, and news of how these were faring in the war took pride of place in their letters home.[1] There was thus a considerable body of Welshmen of all ranks who were familiar with continental military tactics—a factor of some importance when the Civil War broke out.

The colonels and even the sea captains, when they were not in the field or afloat, often subsided in this way into civilian country gentlemen; the best representatives of the professional classes proper are the parson, the lawyer and the doctor. Not that we can draw a sharp dividing line between them and the squires, for they were usually their younger sons, and they often had estates of their own. Enough has already been said about lawyers to indicate their importance in country society. A few of the greater families retained standing legal agents in London: for example, Sir William Dolben had served his kinsmen the Wynns of Gwydir in this capacity for nearly a quarter of a century before Charles II made him a judge. But the practice was naturally not liked by the country lawyers; Sir John Wynn's son believed they took it out of the old man by hampering him at every turn when he failed to consult them.[2]

The country doctors showed the same jealousy of their wealthier colleagues in London. But about this class we know very little; it must in any case have been very thinly represented in Wales, where those who could not afford a trip to London or one of the big cities were generally content with the traditional country remedies, the abundance of which is testified by the many surviving manuscript collections of recipes, prescriptions and charms in Latin, Welsh and English— naïve admixtures of ancient lore, genuine observation and sheer black magic. Siôn Dafydd Rhys, the Anglesey philologist who had taken his medical degree at Padua in Henry VIII's time, was apparently still practising in Brecknockshire after Elizabeth's death, and his younger contemporary and fellow-philologist Thomas Wiliems, who lived well on into the new century, is believed to have served Llanrwst in the dual capacity of doctor and parson. During his later years he had to compete

---

[1] N.L.W. MS. 1593 E, fos. 161, 201, cf. 12440D (24 May, 1673).
[2] *C.W.P.*, 1008.

for the custom of the neighbouring "big houses" with a Scots physician who settled at Holt early in the century, and their mutual denunciations suggest that medical etiquette was as yet as undeveloped as medical science! Yet not long after Wiliems's death an agent at Llewenny who needed medical attention could find no physician nearer than one at Chester, whom he suspected of scamping the job because his patient had previously consulted a London doctor (unless it was just incompetence); so he asked his employer to procure him some "playsters and directions" from the latter on his next visit to town.[1] After the Restoration a Denbighshire lady suffering from the King's Evil was able to consult three "able and proficient men in physicke" in or near the county, all of whom prescribed the royal touch as the only cure. About the same time there were but three licensed physicians in the whole diocese of St. David's.[2] In a remote Montgomeryshire village like Llanymawddwy it was the local parson who prescribed for the sick at the very end of this period, and we still possess a set of his prescriptions, with correspondence from his patients.[3]

Far more important than the village doctor, and equal, if not superior in importance to the village squire himself, was the village parson. He belonged, of course, to the same social class—often enough to the same family. For since the Reformation, patronage had fallen largely into the hands of the lay landowners, and they naturally chose such friends or kinsfolk as were in orders. This practice was no doubt responsbile for a certain intrusion of worldliness, but it did ensure that so long as no social and cultural gulf yawned between squire and *gwerin* Wales would not be faced with the problem of an alien clergy out of touch with the life and language of their parishioners. Occasionally in North Wales, and more frequently in the south, this essentially eighteenth-century problem was already casting its shadow before it, as for example when a monoglot English vicar of Llanrhaeadr ym Mochnant, at

[1] Morrice, *Wales in the Seventeenth Century*, pp. 307–10; Llewenny MS. x. 3. 107; *C.W.P.*, 523, 527, 580; *Y.C.*, xl. 188–206.
[2] N.L.W. MS. 12402 D, letter of J. Lloyd, 4 Apr., 1664; Richards, *Wales under the Penal Code*, pp. 168–9; see also Edwinsford MSS., letter of W. Nicholson, Carmarthen, (18 June, 1659).
[3] N.L.W. MS. 1595 E, fo. 125.

D

loggerheads with his churchwardens, begged Archbishop Laud
to transfer him to a Vale of Clwyd parish where " many English
families " were resident.[1] But the affection which the clergy
generally inspired in their flocks is reflected in the work not
only of the recognised bards, but also of the popular and by
no means mealy-mouthed ballad-mongers. The gentry, in
spite of frequent tiffs over tithes and glebe lands, testified their
devotion to the church by the gifts of plate which are so
prominent among the benefactions of the century—conscience
money, perhaps, for the depredations of their grandfathers in
the age of the Reformation.[2] And many of the clergy themselves were well fitted for spiritual and intellectual leadership
in a Welsh society, whether poets like Edmund Prys, arch-
deacon of Merioneth, whose metrical translations of the
Psalms are still loved and sung; or philologists like John Davies,
rector of Mallwyd, to whose fine scholarship his countrymen
largely owe a standardised (perhaps too rigidly standardised)
literary language, and its application to a purer version of the
Scriptures, as well as an enrichment by translation of their
stock of devotional literature; or humbler copyists like Humphrey Davies, rector of Darowen, credited with a knowledge of
five languages but occupied during most of his leisure moments
in copying the works of countless Welsh poets which, in the absence of facilities for printing them, might otherwise have been
lost to posterity.[3] It is true that in post-Restoration days (when
Welsh admissions to the universities were probably falling off)
Bishop Lloyd had to excuse his departure from the normal practice of restricting ordination to graduates on the plea that there
were more benefices than qualified candidates but he added cau-
stically that the graduate did not always make the best parson![4]

The frequent complaint that few of the clergy could preach
a Welsh sermon is credible enough (however heavily we may
discount Walter Cradock's estimate of an average of one per
shire)[5] when we remember how novel was the idea that the

[1] C.S.P.D., 1637–8, pp. 280–1.
[2] See, e.g., E. A. Jones, Church Plate of the Diocese of Bangor, 1906.
[3] Morrice, op. cit., pp. 123–9, 310–21; A. I. Pryce, Diocese of Bangor during Three Centuries, 1929, introduction; N.L.W.J., v. 234–6.
[4] D. R. Thomas, St. Asaph, 1908, i. 131.
[5] The Saints' Fulnesse of Joy, 1646, p. 34; Richards, P.M., pp. 9–10.

service was "barren" without a set sermon in which the preacher must "dod rannau a phynciau'r ffydd" (as a bard urged the Bishop of St. Asaph to do)[1] in the everyday language of his flock—after learning them in the formal English and Latin of the schools. Lack of skill in a task they had never been trained for did not necessarily argue either indifference or ignorance or lack of Welsh, especially in days before the vernacular Bible had come to the homes of the people to familiarise them with the appropriate vocabulary. The leaders of the Church were doing their best to fill the gap: the Welsh translation of the Book of Homilies, which came out in 1606, must have helped many a lame dog over the stile; bishops like William Morgan and John Owen at St. Asaph arranged that at least the members of the cathedral chapter should preach regularly in Welsh in the cathedral itself and in their own parishes;[2] the numerous editions of the *Llyfr Plygain*, from Elizabeth's later years onwards, placed in the hands of the laity a manual of devotions which also served the purpose of a secular almanac in Welsh; and, as we have seen, clerics and laymen alike were struggling with the task of translating standard religious and moral works in English into a new literary adaptation of the Welsh of the market place.

The prime obstacle everywhere was the abject poverty in which the Reformation had left the Welsh Church. Where the tithes had passed (as they so often had) first to a monastery and then to the layman who acquired it, it was common for the actual cure of souls to be paid at £10 or £20 a year or even less. It is not surprising that at one time the living of St. Peter's, Carmarthen went a-begging because no sufficient person could be found to fill it at £7 a year! If the vicar had no private means (and luckily many of them inherited or married into land), it was only by flagrant pluralism that he could keep up the style of living expected of him; and pluralism meant at worst complete neglect of one or another of the accumulated livings, at best scrambling through the service at

---

[1] "Expound the faith point by point" (Richard Kynwal, *N.L.W.J.*, vi. 41); cf. O. M. Edwards, *Gwaith Edward Morus*, p. 23.

[2] D. R. Thomas, *St. Asaph* (Diocesan Histories, 1888), pp. 77–8: Browne Willis, *St. Asaph*, 1801, i. 112–13.

one church to leave time for jogging on horseback to the next. The worldly and " dumb " parsons whom Puritan critics denounced often had some extenuation, if not a complete excuse, for their neglect.[1] And the parson's wife (another novel phenomenon in Welsh society) was far too busy selling butter and eggs to her neighbours to help her husband in parochial affairs as her successors are expected to do to-day.[2]

Even the upper clergy were by no means well off when they had no private fortunes. The bishoprics of Bangor and Llandaff were worth only some £130 each—less than half as much as Gloucester, the poorest English diocese—and St. Asaph only £185; the bishop of St. David's alone among his Welsh colleagues approached the £500 stipend of his brother of Exeter, and that was well down in the English scale, nor was the stipend generally regarded as adequate compensation for the desolate character of the countryside and what Bishop Field called the " Welshly tedious ways " that led there—with the consequence that St. David's was commonly used as a stepping-stone to English preferment for English-speaking clerics. In Llandaff too the only Welsh-speaking bishop appointed in the first half of the century owed his election to Archbishop Laud, whose theological views he shared, and who (as an ex-bishop of St. David's) had strong feelings about choosing bishops who could minister in Welsh. The northern sees, on the other hand, had a succession of bishops who not only spoke but promoted the language, and filled the livings in their patronage with men of good family and university education—in sharp contrast with the general level of incumbents in the southern dioceses where episcopal patronage was rarer. As for deaneries, that of Bangor (to take a single example) was worth £22 in the middle of the century; even later, when it had risen to £100, Dean John Jones (the great patron of the S.P.C.K.) assured Bishop Humphreys that the extra £50 he would get by exchanging for it his living of Beaumaris would not meet the additional expenses involved.[3] No wonder there was a

[1] Richards, *op. cit.*, pp. 1–6.
[2] Llewenny MS. 3.163.
[3] *The Charges Issuing forth of the Crown Revenues*, 1647, p. 53 (cf. Harl. MSS. 4133, fos. 5b–7b, 6381, fos. 41–2); *C.S.P.D.*, 1629–31, p. 84; N.L.W., Plasgwyn MS. 79.

scramble for livings *in commendam* to supplement these slender incomes—and to swell the volume of absenteeism.

By the time the Stuarts came, the Welsh Prayer Book had influenced a whole generation, and it was now generally accepted and widely loved, though there were still those who doubted whether prayers in the vulgar tongue could be as effective as the old Latin devotions.[1] Indeed the late Chancellor Fisher showed in his fascinating lecture on *The Private Devotions of the Welsh* how half-understood relics of the missal and the breviary survived in the home for generations after they had been banished from the church. The Welsh had long been known for their special cult of the Virgin, and the Reformation did not destroy it even in such staunch Anglicans as Edmund Prys or James Howell the historiographer; but this could and did find vent in carols, hymns and prayers outside the hours of public worship. Two patriotic *motifs* strengthened the hold of Protestantism on the Welsh people: on the one hand the argument that Rome was responsible, through St. Augustine's mission, for impairing the purity of primitive Celtic Christianity and the legendary learning enshrined in its monasteries; on the other, the identification of the papacy with the despised *Gwyddelod* and the dreaded *dynion duon* of Spain—both of them standing threats to the long and defenceless Welsh coast.[2] The regions where there was disaffection from the Church as standing too near to Rome and too far from Geneva were generally those which lay open either to the depredations of Spanish galleons or to the infiltration of Puritan ideas from English urban centres like London itself or the border towns of Bristol, Hereford, Shrewsbury and Chester. Nowhere was there any movement towards separation from the Church till the crisis of Charles I's reign. If for no other reason, the new sects had little attraction for a society where rank and kindred had counted so much, even in religion, that the very saints had flaunted their pedigrees; for as an English broadside shrewdly

[1] Richards, *P.M.*, p. 8.
[2] *T.C.S.*, 1948, pp. 24–6; but contrast W. Vaughan, *Church Militant*, pp. 118–19.

put it, no Welshman would desire to " be call'd brother when her was none of her Kinred ".[1]

The number of those alienated from the Church—at any rate to the extent of abstention from its services—for the opposite reason, was also small. An estimate made at the very beginning of our period shows only 800 recusants for the whole of Wales as against 200,000 regular churchgoers.[2] They too were concentrated chiefly on the borders, especially the south-east border—where they had the powerful protection of the earls of Worcester even during spells when the head of the house conformed to the Anglican order—and in Flintshire, with its flocks of pilgrims to St. Winefride's well; and there were smaller bodies of recusants clustering round the houses of a few other Catholic squires like the Pughs of Penrhyn Creuddyn or the Edwardses of Chirkland, who from time to time were able to smuggle in priests to minister to them. For missionary priests from the continental seminaries kept coming in sporadic-ally, often paying with their lives for their defiance of the penal laws, until the Jesuits organised regular missions to North and South Wales from headquarters at Holywell and Cwm respectively. Only after the last great martyrdoms of 1679 did this dynamic and heroic epoch in the history of Welsh Catholic-ism give place to one in which the popish population settled down to the accepted status of a harmless, stabilised and inactive minority. Meanwhile their numbers fluctuated in response, now to political events, now to the personality of a well-loved priest or the effectiveness of the printed propaganda by which both priests and their lay converts kept enriching the volume of Welsh devotional literature. Yet it is doubtful whether at any time after Gunpowder Plot the number of active recusants went much beyond a thousand. Rome had missed her opportunity in Elizabeth's reign, largely because the stiff Spanish influences then dominant at the Vatican were not such as to promote a sympathetic understanding of the

---

[1] *The Welchmans Protestation*, 1641; cf. Griffith (or William) Phylip's injunction to Sir John Owen to make the Brownists more amenable (*ystwyth*) by his victories in the field (*N.L.W.J.*, vi. 244, 260).

[2] Harl. MS. 280, fo. 157; cf. H.M.C., *Cecil*, xvii. 374, where the number for St. Asaph is given as 140 in 1600 and 400 in 1605, and see E. G. Jones, *Cymru a'r Hen Ffydd*, 1951, chs. i and ii.

problems of a land like Wales; and by the end of her reign the
old religion here was already succumbing to what Archbishop
Mathew calls "encirclement and slow starvation".[1]

No survey of Welsh society would be complete without some
reference to Welshmen of the Dispersion. In the early days
of James I the Elizabethan exiles on the continent were dying
out, or else drifting home to make their peace with the government, but Hugh Owen, the irreconcileable Caernarvonshire
Catholic, was still advising the court at Brussels on English
affairs, as he had done for thirty years past, with a hand in
every plot against the heretic state. Although the Welshman
in him was never quite sunk in the cosmopolitan, Elizabeth's
government had successfully cut his communications with
home, and before the first Stuart reign was over he died at
Rome at the age of eighty, having disinherited his heir at law,
John Owen, the Protestant epigrammatist.[2] On the other
hand, we have seen how Welsh soldiers of fortune came home
from the continent to play their part in the Civil War or to
settle their families on Welsh estates, and Welsh missionaries
from Rome or Douay to seek their country's conversion. But
on the whole, Welsh communications with Europe were less
brisk than they had been in the preceding age. Now that the
Renaissance had permeated the English universities there was
less occasion (except for the Catholics whom they banned) to
seek those of Europe, and political and religious exiles became
rarer after the storms of the Reformation began to subside;
yet a dozen or more Welshmen went to Padua (most popular
of the continental universities) in the course of the seventeenth
century, and certainly not all were Romanists.[3] In general,
however, apart from the knights errant and the few families
rich enough to indulge in the Grand Tour for their children,
Welshmen who travelled abroad now did so in one of two

[1] *The Celtic Peoples and Renaissance Europe*, p. 76, and pp. 29–92, *passim*;
Richards, *Penal Code*, pp. 54–5. On the effects of Gunpowder Plot on Welsh
opinion cf. Richard Hughes's *englyn* in *Cynfeirdd Lleyn*, p. 215.

[2] *T.C.H.S.*, i. 47–8.

[3] H. F. Brown, "Inglesi e Scozzesi all' Universita di Padova" (*Mono-
grafie storiche sullo studio di Padova*, Venice, 1922). I owe this reference to
the kindness of Mr. E. S. de Beer.

capacities: some went as merchants, like Lewes Roberts of Beaumaris, who in 1638 wrote *The Merchant's Map of Commerce*, the first systematic treatise on British trade (with sound economic advice to Welsh readers and complimentary verses from Anglesey friends and relations), or Maurice Wynn of Gwydir, who tried to develop the European market for Welsh cloth, lead and butter as factor to a merchant at Hamburg, and came home to be Receiver General for North Wales under the Commonwealth;[1] others as diplomats, like Sir Thomas Parry and Lord Herbert of Cherbury, James I's ambassadors to France, or Sir John Herbert, Sir John Trevor and Sir Leoline Jenkins, all of whom went on missions to the continent before they became Secretaries of State. Such men, however, belong to English more than to Welsh history.

Nearer home the flourishing Welsh community in Ireland brought considerable wealth into Wales, strengthened Protestant sentiment here, and was already on the way towards giving Dublin something of the character of a secondary capital for Welsh society. This must be the subject of a separate study, but we shall miss much of the significance of the Act of Union if our picture fails to bring into focus the London Welsh. For they played a vital part in the evolution of Wales; some by retiring here and giving their countrymen the benefit of their experience and wealth, or by settling their children on Welsh estates; some by using their fortunes to promote Welsh causes; yet others by holding a watching brief for Wales at court as public officials, or in parliament as members for English constituencies.

It would be hard to exaggerate the influence of Sir Thomas Myddelton, alike in the field of religion and in that of economics. His financial support for the Welsh press, and especially the *Beibl bach* of 1630 which at last put the Scriptures into the hands of the people as well as of their pastors, was perhaps the greatest single factor in preserving the language; his frequent loans on mortgage shored up many a North Wales estate, while his foreclosures drove the last of the Lloyds from Leighton in Montgomeryshire and of the Owens from Plas Du, the Caernarvonshire home of the exiled Hugh.[2]　Sir Hugh

---

[1] *C.W.P.* 836, 865, 964, 1023, 1078, 1083, 1154, 1205, 2032, etc., cf. 1160.
[2] *M.C.*, xxvii. 357; *C.C.P.*, pp. 84, 129.

Myddelton the goldsmith retained a lifelong and intimate connection with the borough of Denbigh (of which he was Recorder) and presented both it and Ruthin with gold cups— a benefaction matched by his fellow-tradesman John Williams, the King's goldsmith, with the gift of an exquisite chalice to the church of his native Beddgelert.[1] The younger Sir Thomas Myddelton, settled by his father as lord of Chirkland, became the focus of what opposition there was to Charles I in North Wales, the General of the parliament's forces there, and the ancestor of a long line of Whiggish squires to balance the prevailing Toryism of the next century. Even those Myddeltons who settled permanently in England did not at first lose touch with Wales; it was probably in the family of the Lord Mayor's younger son, whom he had set up as an Essex squire, that John Jones of Maes y garnedd learned the earnest Puritanism that made him a regicide, and the business experience he used in helping to govern Ireland for the Saints.[2] Alderman Rowland Heylyn, who also helped with the *Beibl bach*, was another London merchant sprung from old and distinguished Welsh stock; his nephew Peter, the biographer of Laud, would have bought back the family estate of Pentre Heylyn, near Oswestry, had he not ruined himself by backing the losing side in the Civil War.[3] And at the end of the century it was from London that the impetus came for the educational work of the Welsh Trust and the S.P.C.K. The Tudors have often been blamed for draining the best blood of Wales to the English capital; it may well be asked whether these enterprising Welshmen could have done as much for their country if they had stayed at home.

What Tudor statecraft accomplished in London, Stuart intolerance achieved across the Atlantic. It will be shown later how after the failure of Cambriol, land-hungry Welshmen turned their faces towards Ireland rather than New England.[4] Sometimes the younger son would seek his fortunes as a " head-

---

[1] A. I. Pryce, *op. cit.*, p. xxiv; *D.N.B.*, xxxix. 438.
[2] Chirk Castle MS. E.5602.
[3] Morrice, *op. cit.*, pp. 70–81, 108–9; G. Vernon, *Dr. Peter Heylyn*, 1682, pp. 3–4.
[4] Infra, III.

right " (financed by wealthier friends or relatives) in Virginia;[1] a few South Wales Puritans attached to the new separatist congregation of Llanfaches appear to have gone out, with others from the " mother church " at Bristol, to the Plymouth colony in the early days of the civil war, but they no doubt returned in the same company when things looked brighter at home;[2] an occasional Catholic recusant sought refuge in Maryland, but generally the influence of Raglan sheltered Welsh papists from the worst penalties of the law until the Popish Plot of Charles II's reign—by which time Maryland was little safer than Britain.[3] Even the flight of John Miles the Baptist to Massachusetts from the Clarendon Code was an isolated phenomenon, for only one member of his congregation is known to have fled with him.[4] It was the migration of Quakers and then Baptists from mid-Wales and west Wales to Pennsylvania from 1682 (a delayed fruit of what Dr. Richards has called the " great spiritual awakening " inaugurated by the Puritan preachers after Naseby and under the Commission for the Propagation of the Gospel) that created for the first time a real (though not, as they had first hoped, a self-contained) community of Welshmen across the Atlantic; and for well over a century—almost until the beginning of the mass migrations of the mid-nineteenth century—Pennsylvania remained the New Jerusalem for Welshmen oppressed in spirit or in body by conditions at home.[5]

[1] *Virginia Magazine of History*, xxvi. 208: cf. Theo. Jones, *Brecknockshire*, 1805, ii. 22, 177.

[2] *Publications of Col. Soc. of Mass.*, xxii. 70–71: cf. Hutchinson, *History of . . . Mass. Bay*, ed. Mayo, 1936, i. 177–8n., Richards, *R.D.*, p. 51.

[3] *Infra*, p. 89; Lloyd, *Powys Fadog*, iii. 16.

[4] Joshua Thomas, *Hanes y Bedyddwyr*, ed. Davies, 1885, p. 95.

[5] Richards, *P.M.*, p. 218; D. Williams, *Cymru ac America*, 1946, pp. 23–31; MS. minutes of Pennsylvania Welsh Society (1798 ff.) *penes* Pennsylvania Hist. Soc., Philadelphia.

II

A LOST CAPITAL

AMONG the many towns whose historical claims to be
the true Welsh capital have been canvassed in these
latter days, no one seems to have given a thought to Ludlow.
Yet no other town has ever had so long and continuous a
career as a social and administrative centre for the thirteen
counties. True, Ludlow is an English town, and its jurisdiction
extended beyond the Wales of the Acts of Union to that nebulous
marchland which a chief justice of Great Sessions once referred
to as " the shires between England and Wales "[1] But even
after the lawyers at Ludlow had abandoned their wider claims
(under heavy fire from the lawyers and borderers in the Long
Parliament), a proposal was officially advanced that this border
town should qualify as a metropolis for Wales itself by incorpora-
tion, along with Monmouthshire, as " a parte of the Princi-
palitye ". The author of the scheme was almost certainly
Richard Lloyd of Esclus (near Wrexham), a Welsh lawyer of
ancient family who had recently been appointed attorney
general for North Wales, and who now threw his legal skill
into the struggle for survival of the Welsh Council as he was
soon to fling his sword into the struggle for survival of the
monarchy itself.[2] He failed in both endeavours; what would
have happened to Wales had he succeeded is an enticing theme
for fancy to play upon, but it lies outside the sphere of sober
history. It may be of interest, however, to glance back at
Ludlow's hour of glory as a provincial capital, the seat of a
sort of viceregal court, and to pass in review the course of
events that brought about its downfall and left Wales without
a capital.

[1] H.M.C., *Cecil*, xi. 460.
[2] H.L. MS. EL, 7466, 7539; D.N.B., xxiii. 431; J. E. Griffith, *Pedigrees*,
pp. 328, 330.

The special position of Ludlow arose originally from the fact that it had been the administrative centre of the Mortimer inheritance, the earldom of March; and the late Dr. Caroline Skeel has shown[1] how the devolution on the crown of this inheritance made possible the gradual amalgamation of the Council of the Earls of March with that of the princes of Wales and the evolution of the body which came to be known comprehensively as " The Lord President and Council of the Dominion and Principality of Wales and the Marches of the same " (more briefly The Council in the Marches, or in its later days The Welsh Council, *tout court*). Statutory authority was conferred on it by the Acts of Union, but it never had a statutory seat, and in fact it did meet from time to time in a number of border towns; but by usage and convenience Ludlow became its normal meeting place, and the castle the official and sometimes also the private residence of the President.[2] When the Shrewsbury poetaster Thomas Churchyard described it, in the year before the Armada fight, it had already something of the air of a metropolis; in fact Churchyard obviously regards it as the capital of Wales:

> It stands for Wales, most apt, most fit and best,
> And neerest to, at hand of any place . .
> The rest of townes, that in Shropshiere you have,
> I neede not touch, . . . I know they cannot crave
> To be of Wales.

He goes on to describe the armorial bearings on the castle walls which gave it the air of a viceregal seat:

> . . . the armes, the blood and race
> Of sondrie kings, but chiefly noble men,
> That here in prose, I will set out with pen—

—and he thereupon abandons all pretence at verse and lists the arms of presidents and councillors that adorn the chapel, concluding with " the armes of Northwales and Southwales, two red lyons and two golden lyons, Prince Arthurs" in a new and adjoining chamber. In the town itself (he adds in his marginal notes) were houses built by various councillors for their stay at the court. Forty years later the youthful Richard

[1] *Council in the Marches*, intro. and ch. i.
[2] *Id.*, ch. vii.

Baxter, staying at Ludlow as pupil of the chaplain to the Council, was to learn from experience how the swarm of flunkeys, hangers-on and minor functionaries that came in its train could give the town some of the darker aspects of a metropolis in the temptations it offered to the raw and unwary.[1]

But if Ludlow was the capital of Wales it was no Welsh capital, for the atmosphere of the town was wholly English. It is a curious fact that when Daniel Powel, son of the pioneer historian of Wales, put on record *The Love of Wales to their soueraigne Prince, Expresed in a true Relation of the solemnity held at Ludlow . . . vpon . . . the day of the Creation of the high and mighty Charles, Prince of Wales* (in which he was " not altogether an idle Actor "), he had not a single scrap of Welsh pageantry to describe.[2] Whitehall did better, for although the investiture itself was robbed of half its pomp by the prickly aloofness of the delicate young Prince, he was regaled two winters later by an ante-masque of Ben Jonson's (*For the Honour of Wales*) in which the poet conjured up an atmosphere even more Welsh than that of his earlier effort for the first Prince (Charles's lamented elder brother), with the help of a backcloth on which a conventional Mount Atlas did duty for " Craig-Eriri ", and dialogue and dance liberally seasoned with what a spectator summed up as " goats and Welsh speeches ".[3]

When Churchyard wrote his uninspired verses the second Earl of Pembroke had just succeeded to the presidency at Ludlow, so successfully held for over a quarter of a century by his father-in-law Sir Henry Sidney; and his own tenure of office, not yet marred by the onset of chronic illness, showed promise of an equal brilliance. Sidney was an Englishman, but one who identified himself closely with both the economic development of his " province " and its cultural interests. He made Ludlow castle his home, except during the long spells when the Queen ordered him to similar but less congenial

[1] Churchyard, *The Worthines of Wales* (1776 ed.), pp. 76–96; Baxter, *Autobiography* (Everyman's Library), pp. 7–8, 14.

[2] Clive, *Ludlow*, pp. 61–80.

[3] McClure (ed.), *Letters of John Chamberlain*, ii. 31, 128; *C.S.P.D.*, 1611–18, pp. 403, 522; Ben Jonson, *Works* (ed. Cunningham), iii. 63–71, 127–33; Pennant, *Tours*, 1888 ed., ii. 301–2.

duties in Ireland and he had to rule Wales from across the Irish Sea through vice-presidents; and he arranged for his second son (who became his heir when the eldest, Sir Philip, perished at Zutphen) a South Wales marriage which gave the family a footing in Welsh society for several generations. But Pembroke, while a man of great wealth and influence at the English court, was a Welshman who took pride in his Welsh descent and his command of the language (his father, indeed, is said to have been tongue-tied in any other), and who was thoroughly at home in the labyrinth of Welsh genealogy. No one could have been better fitted for his post than the man whom Thomas Wiliems aptly called *llygad holl Cymru*.[1] The courts he held at Ludlow were brilliant social occasions when a broad section of Welsh society met to pay homage to the President, with a round of banquets, masques and other gaieties " where " (in the words of a spectator of one of his last Christmas courts) " a young man might have learned as much good behaviour and manners as should have stucke to him ever after whiles he lived "[2], and where county politics were brought into focus with the broader perspectives which the President could open to his countrymen.

The Christmas courts were the high lights of the President's term of office, but throughout the year his influence as lord lieutenant of the crown in all Wales and the Marches was wafted to every shire through the local gentry whom he either appointed directly or recommended to the crown as his deputies, the principal channels through which he conveyed, in terms appropriate to the local situation, the orders that kept pouring in to him from above. These in turn percolated from the deputy lieutenants to their fellow magistrates, and so to still broader reaches of county society. Another and more formal channel of communication was provided by the circuits of the eight justices of Great Sessions. The President's advice was often sought on their appointment too,[3] and some of them always sat on the Council, wielding, by reason of their permanence and

---

[1] " The eye of all Wales " (*Y Greal*, 1805, pp. 61–7); *T.C.S.*, 1948, pp. 10–11.

[2] Stradling, *Storie of the Lower Borowes* (ed. Randall and Rees), S. Wales and Mon. Record Soc., i. 74; cf. *C.W.P.*, *passim*.

[3] E.g., *C.W.P.*, 954.

their specialised skill and knowledge, an influence out of
proportion to their numbers and comparable to that of Privy
Councillors and royal officials in the House of Commons.
Frequently, but by no means invariably, the senior justice
acted as the President's deputy at Ludlow when he was away
or during an interregnum in the succession of Presidents. The
judges in turn carried to the grand juries in their respective
circuits such orders, directions and information as the Council
wished to have published abroad, and brought back reports
about the state of county feeling and grievances that had been
presented to them for redress.

In some ways, however, the professional judges were less
effective as intermediaries than the lay deputy lieutenants.
For one thing they had not necessarily any local roots, nor
even a knowledge of the language; a proposal had been made
by a distinguished Lancashire lawyer, who was Sidney's deputy
at Ludlow during one of his Irish absences, that at least one
of them should always be Welsh-speaking, but unfortunately
nothing came of it.[1] Their prestige was also affected by their
relatively low rate of salaries (as compared with those of
English judges), which forced them to eke out a living by
practice at the English bar.[2] On the whole, the tendency of
the judges was to be more concerned with the royal prerogative
than the interests of Wales; in 1621 they opposed the repeal of
a clause in the Act of 1542 empowering the King to issue supplementary laws for Wales by prerogative, although James I
himself had offered to forego the right seven years earlier.[3]
Among the non-judicial duties of the judges was that of drawing
up for the President each autumn, from their knowledge of
the local gentry, lists of those suitable for the office of sheriff;
from these comprehensive lists, often bristling with information
about the fortunes, family ties, capacities and loyalties of all
who counted in the shire, the President selected three from
each county for the final choice of the King in Council.
Sheriffs were often councillors as well;[4] in any case they were

---

[1] Skeel, *op. cit.*, p. 110.
[2] H.L. MS. EL, *loc. cit.*
[3] H.M.C., *13th R.*, iv. 260–1.
[4] Skeel, *op. cit.*, p. 279.

important links between capital and counties in respect of finance and elections, as the deputy lieutenants were in the all-important field of military organisation. The judges also co-operated with the Council in advising the Lord Chancellor on his choice of local magistrates, those " Tudor maids-of-all-work " on whom fell the chief burden of carrying out the day-to-day orders of the Council; and the councillors themselves were *ex officio* magistrates.[1]

Thus there existed in theory a well-integrated network of communications between Ludlow and the shires; yet in practice there was constant friction. Not only did the county gentry need frequent presidential reminders that " some must governe, some must obey " and that the minds of public officials cannot be " united in publique defence " while they are " devyded by privat quarrells ",[2] but there were parts of the country where the prevalence of the old religion undermined Pembroke's authority when he tried to enforce the aggressively Protestant policy forced on him after complaints of his father-in-law's leniency to recusants.[3] This was particularly true of South Wales, which the long arm of Ludlow could not always reach, in spite of Pembroke's lavish hospitality at Cardiff castle. In the south-east there was a rival centre of influence at Raglan, where the Somerset family—descended (with a bar sinister) from royalty, and rewarded for support of Harry Tudor with the earldom of Worcester—had for a time threatened to usurp the towering position of the Herbert clan by virtue of the first earl's marriage to the heiress of the Yorkist Herberts. The revival of the earldom of Pembroke in favour of a bastard but extremely vigorous offshoot of the old Herbert stock, and the judicious acceptance of the Reformation by the new line of earls while Raglan clung to the ancient faith, changed the complexion of things. A Romanist could not hope to become President of Wales, but he could still exercise a powerful patriarchal sway at home; and the Somersets had identified themselves fully with the people among whom their lot was

---

[1] 34 and 35 Hen, 8, c. 26, s. 55: H.M.C., *4th R.*, p. 336.
[2] *C.C.P.*, p. 31.
[3] *Efrydiau Catholig*, ii. 12; *A.P.C.*, 1580–1, p. 59; Collins (ed.), *Letters and Memorials of State*, 1746, i. 276.

cast. The third Earl of Worcester was acclaimed by a Gwentian bard as " Tew Wilim o Went ", a veritable Herbert among Welshmen; " ni rusia ddywedyd cymraec, a'i hymgeleddu, a'i mawrhâu yn anwylgu Vrytanaidd ", boasted Thomas Wiliems of his son.[1] The special position of the house of Raglan in south-eastern Wales had been recognised and guaranteed in one of the Acts of Union,[2] and any intrusion of Ludlow into its special sphere of influence was always resented (as we shall see again and again), until at last the Somersets deserted their ancestral faith and the presidency itself fell to a descendant of *tew Wilim*—in time for him to sing the swan-song of Ludlow.

The challenge to his authority in the south-east was by no means alone among the " causeless crosses " of which Pembroke found occasion to complain.[3] Not least among these was his own ill-health, which set in soon after his presidency began and became chronic from about 1595, confining him for long spells to his Wiltshire property (now his principal seat) with only spasmodic visits to his Welsh estates or to Ludlow or the English court.[4] This in turn opened a wide door to intrigue against him both at Ludlow and at Whitehall. In his own court there had long been jealousy between the official and the lay members—a reflection in miniature of the jealousy between magnates and royal officials in the King's own Council which had been the marrow of English constitutional history since the Middle Ages. The expert resented being made to sit cheek by jowl with men whose only qualification was that they were " well seene in Welsh Stories "[5]—a qualification which perhaps contributed more towards greasing the wheels of government than their more learned colleagues were prepared to recognise. The territorial magnates for their part resented having to jostle with "Bushops and meaner Men" for places they regarded

---

[1] " Yn un a Harbard trwy'n iaith " (Dafydd Benwyn, in Bradney, *Monmouthshire*, ii. 14); "He made no secret of speaking, cherishing and exalting Welsh, dearly-loved Briton that he was " (*Y Greal, loc. cit.*).

[2] 27 Hen. 8, c. 26, s. 33.

[3] H.M.C., *Cecil*, ix. 415.

[4] *Id.*, viii. 219–20, ix. 142, 351, 358, x. 408, xi. 3–4, 9, 13, xii. 14, *13th R.*, iv. 257; Collins, *op. cit.*, I. ii. 372, II. 120–4, 130, 152, 187, *et passim*.

[5] Skeel, *op, cit.*, p. 109.

E

as their birthright. Pembroke's absences gave the professional element its chance to flout his authority and to obtain from Whitehall fresh instructions (in which he had not even been consulted) severely limiting his powers, particularly in respect of control over the appointment of local officials.[1]

More serious still was the trouble that blew up from another quarter—this time the south-west. It was while Pembroke was incapacitated for much of the year by illness that the dashing and feather-brained young Earl of Essex was busy gathering round him that motley crew of devoted companions-in-arms, disgruntled Puritans, disgruntled Papists and mere place-seekers, by means of which he hoped (without any other clearly-defined policy) to displace the Queen's present advisers and to distribute offices among his *entourage*, with himself as a sort of Mayor of the Palace. His Welsh steward and factotum Sir Gely Meyrick might be called his party organiser in Wales, and he found plenty of material at hand in Essex's Welsh tenants and dependents in West Wales, his own family circle in Pembrokeshire and his wife's in Radnorshire, young Welsh blades who had followed the earl to the wars and come back with knighthoods and other honours, and smaller squires (many of them with leanings towards the old faith) envious of their greater brethren who with no better lineage but a sharper eye to business had risen to wealth and influence on the tide of Tudor favour and the breach with Rome.[2] The immediate objective was to undermine Pembroke's influence both in the Welsh counties and at Ludlow itself, and the factions into which the Council had fallen played into the hands of Essex.

Pembroke did not at first see how things were drifting—or else he was too ill to care. It was at his own suggestion that Essex's ward and personal lawyer, Richard Broughton of Bishop's Castle, had been put on the Council in 1594;[3] Sir Richard Trevor of Trevalun, an old and trusty swordsman of

---

[1] Collins, *op. cit.*, II. 122, 193, 195; H.M.C., *Cecil*, ix. 400, x. 97–8, 166; *A.P.C.*, 1596–7, pp. 340–1.

[2] Mathew, *Celtic Peoples and Renaissance Europe*, chs. xviii–xx; *E.H.R.*, lix. 348–70; *N.L.W.J.*, vi. 190–1.

[3] H.M.C., *Cecil*, xi. 106–7, xiii. 457, *13th R.*, iv. 248; cf. *4th R.*, pp. 334–6.

Essex, who was added a few years later, does not appear to have been a nominee of Pembroke's, but it was the President who by getting him appointed deputy lieutenant had enabled him to " rig " the local musters for his patron.[1] Nor does Pembroke seem to have raised any objection when Meyrick (trading on the Anglesey origin of his own family) made a move towards infiltration into the northern counties by pressing in his master's name the claims of a Caernarvonshire cousin of his as under sheriff.[2] What roused him to denounce the favourite was the discovery in 1598 that in his absence Essex had persuaded the Privy Council to turn down contemptuously his own nominations to the deputy lieutenancy of Radnorshire and to thrust in Sir Gely, a non-resident in the county with no land or kin there but his wife's. " If his lordship cannot endure," he burst out, " that I should recommend any but those only who are devoted to him, I will recommend none at all; and if such without my consent are thrust upon me, I will rather forgo my commission."[3] And there is every sign that he would have suited the action to the word had he been sure of resigning his office to a friend (such as Sidney's son, who was then abroad) and not to a creature of Essex.[4]

The official correspondence of the time shows clearly how far the administrative machine (especially on its military side) had been put out of gear by these distractions;[5] but it was not till after Pembroke was dead that the climax came with Essex's armed insurrection, followed by the execution of the earl and his associates and accomplices, with eddies of the conflict in every Welsh shire where Essex or his ill-fated Welsh steward had had a following.[6] Until the presidential chair was filled, it was the Chief Justice of Great Sessions who had the unwelcome task of cleaning up local administration in Wales; and the Queen took some time to make her mind up about Pembroke's

[1] A.P.C., 1595-6, p. 17; E.H.R., lix. 350, 355-6, 360, 362, 367-8.

[2] C.C.P., p. 121.

[3] H.M.C., Cecil, viii. 233-4.

[4] Collins, op. cit., II. 152, 193, 195.

[5] A.P.C., 1596-7, pp. 389-90, 1597-8, pp. 448-9, 1599-1600, pp. 219-21, 387-8, 551-2, 1601-4, pp. 95-6, 129-30, 156-7, 301-2, 357-9; C.C.P., pp. 43, 47, 54.

[6] E.g., H.M.C., Cecil, xi. 460.

successor. His own son and his predecessor's were both disposed
to look on the post as their rightful inheritance, and at one
time even accommodating Catholics like the earls of Worcester
and Shrewsbury were considered.[1] But Elizabeth had had
enough of the magnates with their feuds, factions and jealousies,
and in the end she reverted to the earlier Tudor practice of
sending to Ludlow experienced officials of good family but
no local territorial ties, in preference to great Welsh or border
aristocrats. A similar swing of the pendulum is to be seen in
the Irish policy of the age. In effect it was a victory for the
bureacratic elements that had given such trouble to Pembroke;
but at least this interval of humdrum but firm and impartial
rule enabled the country to recover from the broils occasioned
by the intrigues of Essex and Meyrick, and with a speed that
bears testimony to the solidity of the work of the Elizabethan
Presidents—though there were times when Pembroke's successor
regretted his acceptance of a task " wherein wise men have
been wearied to seek reformation ". Before the Queen's
death, however, he had the situation in hand, and was re-
asserting the Council's authority in the south;[2] the result was
that the accession of James I and the substitution of a Scottish
for a well-loved Welsh dynasty was achieved without opposition. If there was any breach of continuity in the government
of Wales, it came at the death of Pembroke rather than that of
Elizabeth.[3]

Towards Ludlow it was the Queen's later policy that the
new King followed. Of his four Presidents only one had any
local ties, and his term of office lasted only a year; indeed few
of them stayed at Ludlow long enough to leave any impression
—probably because their fortunes would not stand up to a
longer term of office. The one exception was Spencer Compton,
Earl of Northampton, who had created a sensation by the
magnificence of his investiture to the Order of the Bath before
he began his fourteen-years' reign at Ludlow.[4] But Northampton was a midlander with no personal knowledge of Welsh

[1] Collins, *op. cit.*, II, 122, 124, 152.
[2] McClure, *op. cit.*, i. 166; Tite (ed.), *Diary of J. Manningham* (Camden
Soc., 1868), p. 58; H.M.C., *Cecil*, xii. 341–3, 635–6, 648.
[3] *T.C.S.*, 1948, pp. 11, 15–20.
[4] Burke, *Peerage*, 1949, p. 1504.

society, and largely dependent on the judges in his choice of
local officials; it was he who (with recent Irish parallels in
mind) gave his blessing to the outrageous scheme for " civil-
ising " Wales by planting the crown wastes with Englishmen—
a suggestion the King had the wit to ignore.[1] There is little
sign under the Jacobean Presidents of the pomp of Pembroke's
day; which of them indeed (unless it were Northampton)
could have afforded it on an official allowance of little more
than £1,000 for his own " diet " and that of more than sixty
councillors?[2] The Council was in fact taking on itself more
and more the aspect of a mere court of law (and a pettifogging
one at that), less and less that of a viceregal court. Even in
the routine work of justice and administration the authority of
Ludlow was more circumscribed than it had been under the
great Elizabethans; there was a growing tendency to remove
important cases to the courts at Westminster, while after
Pembroke's death the south-eastern counties were abstracted
from the commissions of his successors for thirty years, and
restored to the house of Raglan, which was thus able to exercise
within its own domain an authority almost co-ordinate with
that of Ludlow.[3] But the duties of the lord lieutenant, embody-
ing the military side of the President's work, sank in importance
during this unwarlike reign, so that the nomination of his
deputies in the shires became a bone less worth contending for.
Ludlow was, in fact losing its metropolitan character; ambitious
young Welshmen were seeking preferment through *Lundain gu*
rather than *Lwydlo deg*, and hardened litigants like Sir John
Wynn took their suits to Westminster if they could.[4]

Its final eclipse, however, still lay in the future. James I,
as tender of Welsh susceptibilities as ever the Tudors had been,
saw to it that the Welsh gentry were well represented at Ludlow
—indeed they now constituted nearly half the Council instead
of barely a third, as when Pembroke took up office;[5] he was
equally scrupulous in consulting the President over all matters

[1] *C.W.P.*, 816; *T.C.S.*, 1937, p. 224.
[2] *The Charges Issuing forth of the Crown Revenue*, 1647, p. 17.
[3] Boyle, *Official Baronage*, iii. 727–8.
[4] Supra, p. 38; *C.W.P.*, 1025.
[5] Cf. lists in Strype, *Annals*, II. ii. 161, Lansdowne MS. 683, fos. 48–9,
H.M.C., *13th R.*, iv. 247, *C.W.P.*, 809.

affecting his domain, and he even tried to check the tendency to call up Welsh cases to London.[1] It may have been the decreasingly border character of Ludlow that brought to a head the issue of the status of the border counties. Even in Elizabeth's day the city of Bristol and the county palatine of Chester had successfully, and Worcester unsuccessfully, contested the jurisdiction of Ludlow; but it was one thing to accept the rule of a predominantly border body, usually presided over by a magnate with local territorial ties and acting primarily as a channel of communications from the central government, quite another to submit to a body largely Welsh in composition, with a head devoid of local influence save in respect of his office, whose primary function seemed now to be that of robbing the borderer of his " birthright to the laws of the kingdom "—especially after the King's own judges had declared all four border shires exempt from the sway of Ludlow. But the attempt of border members, in alliance with the common lawyers, to give statutory force to this judicial finding in two successive sessions of James's first parliament broke against the King's stubborn determination not to allow members to " bandy . . . among themselves " questions pertaining to the royal prerogative, or the Welsh to be " justly grieved by dismembering from them their ancient neighbours ". The only Welsh voice to be raised in debate was one that supported the King; and the borderers had to retire discomfited for another thirty years.[2]

Before Northampton quitted office there had been another change of monarch and another change of policy towards Ludlow. When the presidency became vacant in 1631, Charles I had newly entered into the period of personal government in which he dispensed with parliament and strained every nerve to maintain the royal prerogatives it had dared to challenge. For this purpose the Councils of Wales and of the North, where he could exercise unfettered his discretionary powers, were of capital importance, and he promptly set about strengthening both. Wentworth, the chief architect of the new policy of Thorough, was given the presidency of the North even before

---

[1] *C.W.P.*, 1011.
[2] Skeel, *op. cit.*, pp. 129–50; *T.C.S.*, 1942, pp. 25, 32–4, 55–6.

the dissolution of parliament, and for the corresponding post at Ludlow the King chose the Earl of Bridgewater, a border lord with territorial interests extending into Wales and with nearly fifteen years' experience on the council at Ludlow and five on the Privy Council. Although far below Wentworth (as soon appeared) in weight of character, he carried bigger guns than any of his Stuart predecessors at Ludlow had done. His father had been Bacon's patron and his forerunner on the woolsack, and the son lived up to the family tradition, with a full sense of the dignity of his office; he was also assiduous and methodical, and his steady support of Buckingham gave promise that he would be a faithful agent of royal policy.[1]

The two new Presidents took joint steps towards increasing the prestige of their respective posts, and the King backed them up by frowning on the growing practice of having matters within their jurisdiction decided over their heads by the courts at Westminster—until the conflicting claims of the ecclesiastical courts forced him to support his archbishop and to whittle down further the jurisdiction of Ludlow.[2] Before Bridgewater took up residence (which was not till 1633), fresh instructions had been issued which increased his Council to the unprecedented number of eighty-four, including twenty-four peers and eleven bishops, and restored to him the commission of lieutenancy in the south-eastern counties which Elizabeth had alienated to the house of Raglan. The President himself determined to recover for Ludlow something of its former dignity as a viceregal court. Festivities and hospitalities continued right through 1633, and next year, on Michaelmas night, his formal entry into office was marked by the performance, in a room of the castle still named after the historic occasion, of a masque which has become classic under the name of *Comus*, with words by John Milton and music by Henry Lawes, the rising poet and the rising musician of the day, and the leading parts taken by Bridgewater's own talented family.[3] Milton, whose friend Charles Diodati was probably then living in east Denbighshire,[4]

[1] *D.N.B.*, xvii. 156; Skeel, *op. cit.*, pp. 150–65.
[2] H.L. MS. EL. 7376–7, 7379, 7439, 7480, 7486, 7523, 7527–31; A. I. Pryce, *Diocese of Bangor during Three Centuries*, p. xxii *n.*
[3] Masson, *Milton*, i. 552–89.
[4] *Y C.*, xiv. 45–8; Llewenny MSS. 3.31, 3.47.

may have been present in person; at any rate he gave local colour to the masque by his eulogies of the new President, the "old and haughty nation, proud in arms", over whom he was to rule, and the fair river that formed the central waterway of his province.

It was over a disillusioned Wales that Bridgewater came to rule. "Cymru sy'n ffaelio, mae'r beirdd gwedi'u priddo", lamented an anonymous elegist in 1627;[1] and there were grounds for his despondency. From the earliest times the bards had been arbiters of morals and gentility, as well as of æsthetic standards, for Welsh society, and survivors of the Tudor school were unsparing in their censures on the succeeding age in all three directions. But one by one the pupils of Gruffydd Hiraethog, last of the great Elizabethans, were dying off, leaving the field clear for charlatans who diluted the authentic metres and vocabulary with English importations and stooped for mercenary ends to endow men of straw with virtues as spurious as their pedigrees.[2] It was not from the pageantry of Ludlow, but from the less sparkling air of the London counting-house, that the movement sprang which sought to fill this moral vacuum. From 1629 to 1634 there was a remarkable output from the London press, financed by Aldermen Myddelton and Heylyn, of devotional and instructive literature in simple Welsh. The central product was the *Beibl coron*, which for the first time brought the Scriptures in Welsh to the homes of those who could meet the cost and had learned to read; but with it went translations from standard religious works and short elementary manuals of faith and morals, accompanied by aids to reading in Welsh.[3] The standards of these productions, whether moral or æsthetic, were anything but bardic standards, for the new reformers, intent on a less eclectic public than that for which the bards had written, were content with the diluted Welsh of the market place, and in morals they inculcated the middle-class virtues of sobriety and thrift, humility and self-denial, respectability and Sunday observance, in place of the aristocratic and military virtues favoured by that relic of pagan vanity and vainglory, the bardic order.

---

[1] " Wales is failing, the bards are in their graves " (*N.L.W.J.*, vi. 246).
[2] *T.C.S.*, 1948, pp. 365–78.
[3] *Carwr y Cymry*, 1631 ed. Ballinger, 1930, pp. vii–xiv.

It was among the more earnest of the country clergy that Myddelton and Heylyn found their active coadjutors, and as long as these remained undivided in their allegiance to the established order in religion and politics the movement bade fair to anticipate what was accomplished a century later by Methodism. But the religious and political upheavals that followed divided the ranks of the reformers, till in the interregnum triumphant Puritanism became their residuary legatee; this in turn alienated the gentry and so robbed the movement of its promised national character, leaving its instrument the Welsh press in a state of arrested development and popular literature, in the main, to the tender mercies of the oral ballad. The taint still clung, in spite of the support of four future broad-church bishops, when in post-Restoration days the Welsh Trust attempted (once more from London) to furbish up the same weapons for a renewed crusade, nor had it been dissipated when Methodism resumed the task in the next century.[1]

Of these inner stirrings Ludlow had no inkling; it was in externals only that it touched the life of contemporary Wales, and even here the bright promise of the new president's investiture was not to be fulfilled. He himself soon fell ill—of the same disease (the " stone ")[2] that had laid Pembroke low —and for most of the time he governed Wales from a sick-bed at the Barbican, his London house, by correspondence with his agents and deputies at Ludlow. He had, moreover, the invidious task of enforcing on the Welsh gentry a royal policy which meant heavy demands on their time and their money and constant interference in their personal affairs, till a growing volume of his correspondence came to be taken up with pleas for exemption from local office, and men who had so recently vied with each other for the post of sheriff or deputy lieutenant were now prepared to invoke the aid of powerful neighbours or even to offer bribes to escape the burdensome duties.[3] The

[1] *T.C.S.*, 1904-5, pp. 81-4; *B.B.C.S.*, ix. 71-80; J. Cornish, *Life of . . . Firmin*, 1780, pp. 33-7; W. Wynn, *History of Wales*, 1697, ed. R. Llwyd, 1832, p. 288; N.L.W. MS. 12406, letters of 17 June and 21 July, 1681; *T.C.S.*, 1948, p. 81.

[2] H.L. MS. EL 7308.

[3] *Id.*, 7109, 7139, 7141, 7146, 7175, 7196-7, 7199, 7205-6, 7213, 7227, 7253, 7274-5, 7278, 7295-6, 7318, 7324-5.

policy of Thorough involved not only a tightening of local administration but a degree of military and naval preparedness that devoured money and man-power and re-emphasised the military character of the President's office, till at last the coincidence in time of demands for over £10,000 in ship money and 2,000 men (costing their respective counties between £50 and £1,000 to raise and equip) to fight the Scottish rebels brought the country to the verge of revolt.[1]

Under stress of these crises the promised autonomy for Ludlow went by the board. Ship-money payments, at first sent *en bloc* through the President, became a matter for direct badgering of the sheriffs from London as the financial crisis became too pressing for the exchequer to wait;[2] and in the Scottish crisis Bridgewater (on one of his rare visits to Ludlow in the August of 1640) found himself hampered in distinguishing the loyal sheep from the disloyal goats by the fact that he could not, under his patent as lord lieutenant, issue his own commissions. A month earlier the King had instructed him to charge the deputy lieutenants of Herefordshire and of a group of five South Wales counties stretching as far as Pembrokeshire to place themselves at the disposal of the Earl of Worcester, " who hath been entrusted with some secret service "; and at the same time the Earl of Pembroke was bidden " since he had great power and revenue in Wales, to signify to all his friends and tenants, that they should be obedient to what the Earle of Worcester commanded them ".[3] The character of Worcester's commission will be discussed in another essay;[4] our concern here is with the further diminution of presidential authority. Ever since the King had included in Bridgewater's commission the south-eastern lieutenancies held by Raglan since 1601, the Earl of Worcester's energetic heir Lord Herbert (the future Earl of Glamorgan) had been moving heaven and earth to restore the family prestige; and Raglan was too wealthy and too responsive to the financial demands of the crown to be ignored in these hard times, even though after the fourth earl's

[1] *T.C.S.*, 1948, pp. 34–47.
[2] *Id.*, p. 36.
[3] *C.S.P.D.*, 1640, pp. 631–2; *T.C.S.*, 1948, p. 50.
[4] *Infra*, pp. 92–4.

brief flirtation with Protestantism his son had returned to the
family fold and his grandson become a *dévot*. Worcester, fat
and gouty, hated travel and lived in princely isolation at
Raglan, but his son was constantly at court, receiving from the
King verbal assurances to which only cryptic references were
made in writing, but which issued in a special dispensation to
father and son from the penalties of recusacy, permission to
bear arms (a reward for faithful support in the Bishops' Wars),
and for Lord Herbert a seat in the Council of Wales and a
deputy lieutenancy in his own county.[1] As the star of Raglan
rose, that of Ludlow declined, for the King's financial straits
moved him to economies as well as exactions, and the President's establishment was left " ill besteed "—a sad decline
from the pomp and circumstance with which his rule
began.[2]

It is not surprising that when the Long Parliament met,
these " popish intrigues " became an immediate target of
attack for the opposition, nor that in spite of the zeal with
which Welsh members dissociated themselves from the
manœuvres and joined in the attack, the Council at Ludlow
came once more under fire. Border members had returned to
the issue of the Council's jurisdiction during the brief episode
of the Short Parliament, and in anticipation of a renewal of
the assault the King had urged a full attendance of Welsh
judges and councillors when its successor met. But the tide
was running too strongly against the prerogative courts, and
this time there was no voice from Wales to defend the threatened institution. When a Bill for the exemption of the four
shires was swallowed up in a more comprehensive measure
repealing the clause of the Act of 1534 on which rested the
statutory authority of the court in Wales itself, it was Bridgewater, from his sick-bed at the Barbican, who directed the
campaign for the maintenance of his jurisdiction, insisting that
Richard Lloyd should abandon his duties at Ludlow and on
circuit to put the case before the Commons' committee. The
pressure of parliamentary business enabled Lloyd to use

---

[1] *T.C.S.*, 1948, pp. 40, 43–5; H.L. MS. EL 7433; Dircks, *Life . . . of the
Marquis of Worcester*, 1865, pp. 32–4.
[2] H.L. MS. EL 7364; Salop county archives, (25 July, 1642).

delaying tactics, and as it turned out neither Bill reached the statute book. But that did not save Ludlow; nothing could stop the torrent of feeling against the Star Chamber from sweeping away, in the measure which abolished it " the like jurisdiction " of the Welsh Council in criminal suits.

There followed a period of wild confusion at Ludlow, the court trying to rush through what business it had in hand before the Star Chamber Act took effect (in August 1641), hesitating to take on any new cases and refusing all from the border counties after October; often unable to enforce its decisions and divided among itself as to its surviving powers and the course it ought to follow; till business, already shrinking at the beginning of the year, had become so slack by autumn that less was done in three weeks than formerly in three days. In this attenuated form the Council lingered on as a court of civil justice till the May of 1642, and as an administrative organ till the outbreak of Civil War two months later.[1]

It was at the point when all hope of saving the Council's jurisdiction over the four shires had been abandoned and efforts were concentrated on salvaging its authority over Wales that Richard Lloyd drafted the memoranda to which reference was made at the opening of this study. As a lawyer, he was less interested in the administrative than in the judicial functions of the Council. In his scheme the number of judges of Great Sessions, as well as their salaries, dignities and sitting days, were to be increased, and in the intervals of the circuits they were to sit under a duly qualified President as a central law court at Ludlow (henceforth a part of Wales), with all the powers enjoyed by the courts both of common law and of equity at Westminster. Although nothing came of it all, it may be worth pausing for a moment to consider the arguments by which he supported his plan, since the force of some of them became evident when Ludlow first ceased to serve as a capital for Wales, and some may even have cogency to-day. In the first place he advanced the usual arguments for devolution: the immoderate growth of London, " which is growne monstrous in numbers of People and hard to be governed " (as the Stuarts, who fully appreciated this argument, knew to their

[1] Skeel, *loc. cit.*; H.L. MSS. EL, 7342–7562.

cost), and the advantage of having " several distribucions of the Government, both for the dispatch of the Subiects in their suits and the ease of their Chardge ". Apart from the expense of travelling to London (which gave such an advantage to the rich suitor), Lloyd points out that " the Common people in Wales . . . had rather forgoe their right then travell to London, beinge for want of being able to speake English dishartened to travell farr "—which at least suggests that things were easier for the monoglot Welshman at Ludlow, despite the Acts of Union. Then there was the advantage of having a repository of records accessible to the subject in a central place, instead of dispersed in clerks' houses and " in Contynuall ieopardye of perishinge "—in other words, he would have anticipated Aberystwyth and fixed the manuscript department of the National Library at Ludlow! He also makes a great point of the benefits that accrue when the " extreame oppression of the Contrye " by the " gentlemen and greatemen " is kept in check by " the neighbourhood of such a Courte of Justice ": " by how much more the Gentrye dislike " it, " by soe much the more it will behoove the Prince and Common People, respectively to assert it ". A further consideration he advances is the desirability of having a permanent residence for the Prince of Wales ready to receive him within his own Principality; and finally he urges how much easier it is to pull down such an institution than to build it up again when the need for it is rediscovered.

The author of this memorandum seemed to be the only man of any initiative left at Ludlow. During the two months preceding the outbreak of Civil War he was busy organising, and carrying to the King at the court of York, county declarations of loyalty to the crown and the ancient laws. Meanwhile reports reached Ludlow that one of the arguments he advanced in favour of the Council was about to receive practical demonstration: the King, it was rumoured, had decided to emulate the Tudors by sending the Prince of Wales to hold his own court at Ludlow. The future Charles II was then twelve years old, and already possessed of the personal charm he exploited with such success when he grew up. But a royal court is an expensive luxury, especially when it is liable also to become a military headquarters; and Bridgewater and his subordinates had had too much ado these latter months to wring from the bankrupt court bare provision for a skeleton staff, to welcome the descent of a swarm of locusts on the land. Nothing came of this plan; but a month after the King unfurled his standard at Nottingham he resumed the idea of appealing to Welsh loyalty by taking the Prince with him to the fringes of his Principality. They visited Chester and Shrewsbury, pausing on the way at Wrexham to address a loyal crowd and staying at Esclus as guests of Richard Lloyd, who was honoured with a well-earned knighthood. The Denbighshire trainbands formed the Prince's guard of honour when he returned with his father to Shrewsbury, where they stayed about a fortnight, holding there a rendezvous of the North Wales and border militia. Before leaving Shrewsbury for the first campaign of the war, Charles sent his son through Radnorshire to Raglan, to be greeted once more with every sign of devotion, which he acknowledged in tactful tributes to the " great minds " and " true affections " of the " ancient Brittaines ".[1]

The problem of administering Wales from a single centre did not cease to trouble with the transition from peace to war. Initially the King tried to control the Welsh and border field of action from his headquarters at Oxford, with the Prince of Wales's tutor, the Marquis of Hertford (a west country magnate) as his deputy in the south. Hertford used Cardiff (which had been seized in the King's name from the Roundhead Earl of Pembroke) as his headquarters for South Wales; but after summoning the south-eastern trainbands to meet him there and those of West Wales to rendezvous at Carmarthen, he was fully occupied in holding the border forts and counties for the King. Communications were slow, however, and it was necessary to have a centre of operations nearer at hand. With this end in view—and perhaps with the idea of recapturing some of the enthusiasm stimulated by his personal visits at the outbreak of war, but now rapidly waning—Charles appointed the Prince of Wales as lieutenant governor of North Wales, Shropshire, Cheshire and Worcestershire, in the spring

[1] Phillips, *C.W.*, i. 108–26; *A Loving and Loyall Speech Spoken unto . . . Prince Charles*, 1642.

of 1643, and later captain general of all Wales and the March.[1] He was, of course, too young to exercise personal command, but as representing the crown he would be in a position to co-ordinate (through his advisers) the strategy of his lieutenant generals—Lord Capel (followed by Byron) in the north, Lord Herbert (Worcester's son) in the south, and the Earl of Carbery in the west. But the Prince's journey to what we may call the western front was delayed, and by the following winter the arrival of Roundhead reinforcements on the northern border, followed by Myddelton's temporary break-through into Denbighshire, had made it unwise to entrust to so critical an area the heir to the throne.

Now that the leadership of an experienced soldier was needed on the spot, the King's nephew Prince Rupert was given command, first (like the Prince of Wales before him) in North Wales, and then in the whole area. But the latter still in name held the supreme command, and Rupert, though a prince of the blood, had to rank below him, and yet above lieutenant generals like Byron, Carbery or Herbert. To solve the delicate question of precedence it was proposed early in 1644 to make the new commander President of Wales, exercising the functions of universal lord lieutenant usually attached to the office, but without councillors except such as he might appoint from time to time for councils of war, and without judicial functions other than the exercise of martial law; Bridgewater, who had never resigned the office, was left in convenient obscurity as a permanent invalid at his country house. But Raglan's traditional jealousy of the office was not forgotten even in war time. Among the many opponents of Rupert's appointment was Lord Herbert, who resented an arrangement undermining his promised direct responsibility to the heir apparent (which in effect meant independent action) and reopening the threat of outside interference in his management of affairs among his own people and in his own territory; and it is doubtful if Rupert's title as President was ever formally confirmed.[2] Certainly the suggested vice-president, the Flintshire magnate

[1] Llanfair and Brynodol MSS., bundle 94, letter of Chas. I, 18 Mar., 1643; Carte, *Ormond*, 1851, v. 211–13, 219–20.

[2] Rees, *Studies in Welsh History*, pp. 162–7; Carte, *op. cit.*, v. 230–1, 246, 248, 260; Warburton, *Rupert*, ii. 363, 380.

Sir Thos. Hanmer (a temporising Royalist) never took up office.[1]

Rupert, however, did for a time manage to bring about some measure of unity of control over the Welsh and border campaigns. With no fixed headquarters, he gravitated between Shrewsbury and Bristol, with his brother Maurice to act as deputy in his absence, throwing his weight into whichever theatre of war seemed at the moment to need his presence most, keeping a tight hand on the local commanders and commissioners of array, and replacing the two incompetent commanders in the south by Charles Gerard, a young Lancashire soldier who had seen continental service and had won a reputation in the English campaigns for his mobility as a cavalry leader. Unfortunately both Rupert and Gerard were young men in their twenties whose experience and outlook were those of professional soldiers. Rupert was a foreigner, and at his weakest in dealing with civilians and with problems such as those arising from national sentiment, territorial loyalties or economic conditions; and Gerard, though he came of a race of distinguished lawyers (one of whom was the Elizabethan vice-president at Ludlow who had urged the need for Welsh-speaking judges), was even less happy in his relations with the local gentry. In any case, the period during which Rupert was allowed to give his undivided attention to Wales was a very short one. From the first he was liable to be summoned from his post to retrieve the situation somewhere outside, and before the end of the year of his appointment he was made captain General of all the King's armies under the Prince of Wales as generalissimo. " Your lordship will see Wales abandoned ", was the rueful comment of Arthur Trevor, that prince of early war correspondents who was attached to Rupert's suite, in writing to Ormond in Ireland, " till this game be played out ". The King's brief flirtation with national sentiment was soon over. In the following year the Prince of Wales, after suggestions that he should be sent to Ireland (and replaced in Wales by his brother the Duke of York) had ended in smoke, went to the west country in his capacity of Duke of Cornwall, with a council which had no connection with his Principality.[2]

---

[1] Hanmer, *Parish and Family of Hanmer*, pp. 47–8; Thurloe, iv. 277, 319.
[2] Carte, *op. cit.*, v. 259; Clarendon, *History*, ix. ss. 181–2; *infra*, p. 88.

With Rupert's dismissal in the following October all pretence of unity of control in Wales—or indeed of any coherent royal plans at all—finally vanished.

When the war was over and the monarchy abolished, the new republican governments shared the general propensity of governments arising out of successful revolution to favour centralised administration and to frown on local autonomy; but two experiments were made in treating Wales as a distinct political unit, with what might be called a quasi-colonial status. The Commission for the Propagation of the Gospel in Wales, which was the virtual government of the country from 1649 to 1652, treated Wales as a sort of missionary diocese, with Major General Harrison as suffragan; the rule of Major General Berry in 1655–6, first over North Wales and its border and eventually over an area practically coterminous with the jurisdiction of the old Council of Wales, resembled rather that of a colonial Resident Magistrate. Neither Harrison nor Berry had a capital. The Propagation Commission met peripatetically as two separate bodies, for north and south respectively, each with its own treasurer and officials.[1] Berry, when his province was extended to cover the whole country, pleaded to be allowed Ludlow castle (now rapidly falling into decay) as his official residence. But the request went unanswered; the Cromwellian substitute for the Council of Wales was two small bodies of commissioners for North and South Wales respectively, and Berry had to rest content with meeting the former successively at Shrewsbury and Wrexham, the latter at Hereford, Worcester, Monmouth and Brecon.[2]

Within a year of the King's return Sir Richard Lloyd was back at his old task of preparing memoranda in defence of the court at Ludlow, and this time he was actually backed by a numerously-signed petition from those very border shires that had fought so strenuously against it. The petition accorded too well with predetermined royal policy to go unanswered, but in deference to the prejudices of Lord Chancellor Clarendon (who as Mr. Hyde had taken a leading part in the agitation against Ludlow) the four counties remained outside the revived

[1] Richards, *P.M.*, p. 235.
[2] Thurloe, v, *passim*.

Council's jurisdiction. It existed purely as a court for civil
actions, and the councillors were all lawyers, the administrative
side of its work being confined to the President's personal
commission of lieutenancy over the Welsh counties. For the
first time since Pembroke's day Wales had a Welsh President—
the West Wales Earl of Carbery, of Golden Grove, son-in-law
to his predecessor Bridgewater. Carbery's main duty (which
he discharged with some energy, but mainly by correspondence) was that of safeguarding the Restoration settlement in
Wales by purging local administration of any remaining subversive elements, and enforcing the restrictive political and
religious legislation of the Cavalier Parliament.[1] This, and
the duties of hospitality attached to his office, he carried out
mainly at his own home—which disappointed many expectations at Ludlow castle, now staffed by a paltry household of ten
in place of the swarm of idle lacqueys who had put temptation
in the way of young Richard Baxter a generation earlier. He
did visit his " capital " from time to time, but he was never
popular there, any more than among his tenants and dependents at home. Complaints against him from Ludlow were
investigated and dismissed, but more serious accusations from
Carmarthenshire led to his removal, unregretted, in 1671.[2]

This made possible the achievement of the age-old ambition
of the house of Raglan. At the time of the Restoration the head
of the house was the former titular Earl of Glamorgan, whose
aggressive Catholicism unfitted him for office; but his son, who
succeeded in 1667, had embraced Protestantism under the
Protectorate, and it was on him that the choice of a new
President fell. The status of the Council remained as it had
been in Carbery's day, but Worcester's visits to Ludlow were
still rarer. He conceived himself primarily as an agent for
royal policy in Wales, and his main task as that of preventing
the country from swinging over to the opposition which was
trying to prevent the succession of the King's popish brother.
He contributed towards that end by helping to weed out of
local government any potential friends of the Exclusionists;

[1] Mostyn MSS. (N.L.W. 3071), i. 13, 15, 20, 46, 74, 91, 118, 126, 147,
et passim.
[2] Skeel, *op. cit.*, pp. 166–75.

and his reward was the long-coveted dukedom of Beaufort. On the other hand envenomed attacks were directed against him, both at home and at Westminster, from the few Welsh adherents of the opposition, who cast doubts on the sincerity of his Protestantism, accused him of political and social tyranny, and renewed the old charge of misappropriating the presidential allowance for hospitality at Ludlow. The attack developed into yet another Bill for abolishing the Council, which passed the Commons but was cut short in the Lords by prorogation.[1] There is no evidence that this hostility was shared by the mass of the Welsh gentry; on the contrary the semi-royal tour of his " province ", which was meant to signalise the consolidation of his power and that of the monarchy in Wales, turned into a triumphal progress and one of the high lights in the whole history of the presidency.[2]

His loyalty remained undimmed when the Catholic succession became an accomplished fact; he lent himself, even although his own son was a victim, to James II's policy of getting rid of such officers of militia as stood out against commissions for papists. But he encountered his first check when he tried to assemble the principal gentry at Ludlow and to secure their adhesion there to the new plan of all-round toleration. More than half of those summoned excused themselves, and those who came were non-committal;[3] several were in consequence removed from local office—only to be reinstated when royal policy changed once more a twelvemonth later. Yet it will be shown in a later essay how near he came to success in raising a Welsh army to keep out William of Orange, until the King's own folly cooled the ardour of one after another of the loyal gentry, leaving Beaufort to support his cause in Wales almost single-handed—and to lose his post when it collapsed.[4] In the summer of 1688 King James, after staying with Beaufort at Badminton, was greeted with enthusiasm at Ludlow on his way to Shrewsbury and Chester; only sixteen

---

[1] *N.L.W.J.*, vi. 249–59; H.M.C., *12th R.*, ix. 98–115; *L.J.*, xiii. 721, 727.
[2] Dineley, *Progress of the first Duke of Beaufort*, 1684.
[3] H.M.C., *3rd R.*, p. 259, *5th R.*, p. 414, *7th R.*, p. 504; Richards, " Declarasiwn 1687 " (*Cymdeithas Hanes Bedyddwyr Cymru, Trafodion* 1924).
[4] *Infra*, pp. 228–32.

months later the castle was seized for William, without opposition, by Lord Herbert of Cherbury.[1]

Beaufort's successor, Charles Gerard (now Earl of Macclesfield), was chosen as a warm supporter of the Revolution. His
record in Wales during the Civil War does not suggest that his
rule would ever have been popular; but in any case he was
sent to Ludlow (much as Lord Mountbatten went to Delhi
a few years ago) to wind up an administration and to ring down
the curtain on a long-drawn drama, in which his rule was of
the nature of an epilogue rather than an integral scene.[2]

For Ludlow had long ceased to be a capital in any effective
sense. Like Carbery before him, Beaufort conducted his
correspondence either from his Gloucestershire seat at Badminton (for Raglan lay permanently in ruins after the parliamentary siege and subsequent " slighting "), or from his
London house. When in 1684 he wished to prevent a disputed
election in Denbighshire which might have provoked disorder,
he did not summon the parties to Ludlow, as Pembroke might
have done; instead he called a meeting of the chief county
gentry, most of whom were already in London, to the bishop
of St. Asaph's town house.[3] Sir Henry Sidney's symbolic
direction that his heart should be buried at Ludlow, his trunk
at his Kentish home, would hardly have rung true from
Carbery or Beaufort! Judicial business still went on at Ludlow
during the early months of 1689, but parliament was now
finally resolved to get rid of this unsightly, if harmless, relic
of the royal prerogative, and Wales produced no Richard
Lloyd to write its apologia. Instead, she produced a formidable
petition presenting the court as an oppressive, expensive and
pettifogging anachronism, contravening the spirit of the Acts
of Union themselves by depriving the Welsh of their promised
privilege of common citizenship with the English.[4] No sooner
had Macclesfield taken up his post than the last of the long
series of Bills for abolishing the office and all that pertained to
it came before parliament, and after short debates revealing

[1] Macaulay, *History*, ch. viii; Skeel, *op. cit.*, p. 187.
[2] Skeel, *op. cit.*, pp. 178–9.
[3] Chirk Castle MSS. C. 2–3, E. 51.
[4] *The Case of Their Majesties' Subjects in the Principality of Wales*, 1689.

none of the cleavages of opinion provoked by its predecessors, it became law in July, 1689. The only known Welsh champion of the Council was Sir William Williams, who as a highly-placed lawyer, and the not very popular member for Beaumaris, can hardly be counted a representative of the Welsh gentry. But since Williams had now redeemed his subservience to James II by returning to his earlier political loyalty and helping to draft the Bill of Rights, it must have been on patriotic grounds rather than as a friend to the royal prerogative that he opposed the Bill. Even the high Tory Sir Robert Owen was in favour of abolition, and his brother-in-law the sheriff of Caernarvonshire, declaring that the Welsh were " as ill used as the French subjects " by officials at Ludlow, urged that efforts should be made to persuade his fellow-Tory Halifax (the " Trimmer ") to withdraw his opposition to the Bill.[1] There is no sign that any of the score of Welsh witnesses who came to put their country's case to the Lords found anything to say for the Council;[2] they had long been captured by the lure of London, and if they sought a capital it was there that they found it. It was to London, too, rather than Ludlow (as we have seen), that Wales was learning to look for moral and cultural leadership. When Carbery was petitioned about the need for a Welsh press he had already ceased to be President,[3] and no one even thought of mentioning the matter to Beaufort. Whether in politics or in pageantry, in commerce or in culture, it could no longer be said of Ludlow, as Churchyard had said just a century earlier, " It stands for Wales."

[1] N.L.W., Brogyntyn MS. 1860, Plasgwyn MS. 84; *D.N.B.*, lxi. 457.
[2] *L.J.*, xiv. 195, 209–10, 223, 230–1, 237, 255, 258–60, 294; 1 Wm. & Mary, c. 27.
[3] *T.C.S.*, 1948, p. 87.

III

WALES AND IRELAND
FROM REFORMATION TO REVOLUTION

THE sense of kinship between Welsh and Irish is a modern discovery; in history there has been little of the atmosphere of a Pan-Celtic Congress about their relations,[1] right back to the time when Cunedda established the ascendancy of the *Cymry* over the *Gwyddelod* of Wales, or when Strongbow, seven centuries later, led his Norman-Welsh adventurers across the sea from South Wales (with Giraldus as chronicler of his kinsmen's exploits) to make Ireland their washpot. Another four centuries, and the Reformation came; it is possible that common devotion to the ancient faith might have established between the two peoples the link that common racial stock had failed to forge, had it not been a Tudor who repudiated papal overlordship of the island and declared himself king. But although Welsh and Scottish Catholics might acclaim themselves " the old inhabiters of the isle of Brittany " and the Queen of Scots as rightful queen of Great Britain,[2] in Ireland the Welsh found themselves once more, as in Strongbow's day, on the side of the alien intruder against the native Irish, and Irish loyalty to Rome was a potent factor in turning Wales the opposite way, both by the new perils it engendered and by the new opportunities it created. Unimpeachable Protestants like James Howell or John Owen the epigrammatist, William Vaughan the coloniser, or Sir William Maurice, *penn plaid brytaniaid*,[3] might hail James I's new style of "king of Great Britain" as the fulfilment of historic destiny, but no one

[1] Cf. R. T. Jenkins in *Sociological Review*, xxvii. 170, 177.
[2] *E.H.R.*, lx. 192–7; *T.C.S.*, 1948, pp. 14, 16.
[3] " head of the party of Britons " (Richard Owen in N.L.W., Brogyntyn MS. 3, fo. 177); see also Jas. Howell, *Dodona's Grove*, 1645, p. 31, *T.C.S.*, 1940, pp. 139–9, 1948, pp. 15–16, W. Vaughan, *The Spirit of Detraction*, 1611, p. 323.

suggested that the Irish were part of the family—or indeed anything better than rather disreputable hangers-on who must be
taught their manners. Even when the great revolt of 1641
broke out, Welsh Catholics themselves (whatever their Protestant neighbours might suspect) showed little more sympathy
with their rebellious co-religionists across the Irish Sea than
with the Covenanting rebels north of the Tweed a few years
earlier.

For Wales was on the one hand the natural base for invasion
of Ireland and the nearest depot for recruits, and on the other
the handiest target for Irish retaliation; and when the policy
of plantation began, the prospect of ready-made estates only
eight hours' sail from home (with luck and a favourable wind)
proved far more attractive to the land-hungry Welsh squire
than that of tearing up his roots in exchange for the thankless
labour of hewing a new home out of what Cromwell called the
" howling wilderness " of the New World.[1] These new lords
of the land differed from Strongbow's band in that (as Pollard
points out)[2] they " sought riches rather than sovereign power,
and the desire for commercial monopoly embittered the
political antagonism "—as was soon to appear in the long
struggle of the Welsh cattle trade against Irish competition.
This new phase in the relations between Wales and Ireland
may be said to open with the early years of Elizabeth, when the
two countries were given strategic unity by the appointment of
Sir Henry Sidney to the less congenial lord deputyship of
Ireland while he still remained President of Wales;[3] the same
phenomenon reappears during the Civil War and in the closing
years of the Commonwealth. More significant still is the Irish
rule of his successor Sir John Perrot; no Welshman himself,
Perrot had a wide territorial influence in South Wales (unlike
Sidney, whose abiding Welsh connections were the fruits of
his presidency), and he took to Ireland a substantial Welsh
following, relying on these " Castle Welshmen " for his administration with a partiality outdoing the clannishness later
attributed to John Williams in the management of his English

---

[1] *Supra*, pp. 47–8.
[2] Pollard, *Political Hist.*, vi. 420.
[3] *Supra*, pp. 51–2.

dioceses, and drawing on his head the wrath of the Anglo-Irish settlers, who had their revenge when this " turbulent prototype of Strafford " who had dared to poach on their preserves was sent packing in the Armada year.[1]

It was during Perrot's deputyship that the plantation of Munster drew closer the bonds between Wales and the dominant minority in Ireland. Outstanding among the Munster " undertakers " was Sir William Herbert of St. Julians, great-grandson of the first Earl of Pembroke. As a parliamentary champion of Protestantism against the schemes of the Queen of Scots he had been the first Welshman to make his mark in the Commons,[2] and in the year before Perrot's dismissal he took out substantial allotments of forfeited land in Munster and went to live at Castle Island (co. Kerry). Among the new planters Herbert is conspicuous for his educational and evangelistic zeal and his sympathy with the Irish peasants, whose rents he tried to keep within reasonable bounds, for whom he had parts of the Anglican service translated into Irish (a work the government had neglected), and in whose interests he tried to establish a college on his own lands; but this last scheme met with the same opposition that had wrecked Perrot's more ambitious plan for an all-Ireland university in Dublin, financed out of church property. Herbert also angered his fellow-planters by denouncing both their rapacity and the tyranny of the English garrison, which he would have liked to replace by his trusty Monmouthshire men; they in turn impugned his " Welsh humour " and " fat conceit " and his tenderness for the Irish. Although responsible officials spoke up for him, he returned to Wales in disgust in 1589, with only the first of his three ambitions—" a volume of my writing, a colony of my planting, and a college of mine erecting "—fulfilled to his satisfaction by ephemeral works of controversial theology. But he was kept in touch with the Irish plantation —which fell so far short of his dream of " piety, justice, inhabitation and civility "—by his Montgomeryshire kinsman Charles Herbert of Aston, who was also his neighbour in

---

[1] D. Mathew, *Celtic Peoples and Renaissance Europe*, pp. 220, 224, 226, ch. xi; Pollard, *op. cit.*, p. 434.
[2] *T.C.S.*, 1942, p. 19.

county Kerry; and his name was kept green in the settlement of Gladherbert (*gwlad Herbert*). His educational zeal now found vent among his own people in plans for a college on his estate at Tintern, to be endowed with other lands of his in Monmouthshire and Anglesey, with the aim of combating their " backwardness in religion ". But the fates were against him once more; he died in the very year when the work was to begin.[1] His Welsh and Irish estates passed to another Montgomeryshire Herbert, who as Lord Herbert took his first title from Castle Island before he acquired the better-known name of Lord Herbert of Cherbury. The heir had other uses for the land, but he made his contribution to Welsh education by leaving his library to Jesus College, Oxford.[2]

Perrot's departure was followed, like that of Strafford after him, by a rebellion that soon became nation-wide, backed on this occasion by Spain and the Pope. For the last eight years of the Queen's reign Ireland was taking regular toll of Welsh man-power to the tune of some thousand men a year.[3] The service was naturally unpopular, for it meant on the one hand the chance of a squalid death in an Irish bog, and on the other the threat of meeting, not ill-armed Irish kernes, but the best-trained infantry in Europe, whose musketry was to be met by men far more expert with bow and arrow than with the new-fangled firearm; small wonder that drafts were reported ready to " venture any imprisonment rather than go for the Irish service ".[4] A petition from Anglesey in 1596 got its men exempted on the ground that " having a goodly haven to receave the enemy's shipping " it needed them all at home.[5] But these pressed men were drafted from the rabble who were neither householders nor taxpayers—too often " picked out to disburden the counties of so many vagrant, idle and lewd persons ".[6] For the gentry who led them, the service was not

---

[1] *C.S.P.I.*, 1586–8, pp. 51, 77, 331, 473, 527–39, 575, 1588–92, pp. 62, 119–20, 126, 133–4, 169, 189–92, 210, 221–2; *N.L.W.J.*, iii. 139, 143.

[2] Herbert of Cherbury, *Life*, ed. Lee, pp. 21–2.

[3] *C.W.P.*, 153 ff.; *C.C.P.*, pp. 23 ff.

[4] *C.W.P.*, 174, 181, 201; *C.C.P.*, pp. 47–8; *C.S.P.I.*, 1592–6, p. 313, 1598–9, p. 221.

[5] *C.W.P.*, 178; *C.C.P.*, letter 115 (cf. *T.A.A.S.*, 1947, pp. 26 ff.); *A.P.C.* 1595–6, p. 449.

[6] *C.W.P.*, 183; *C.C.P.*, letter 162.

without its attractions, offering as it did the prospect of knight-hoods and lands. Besides, they had too many friends and kins-men over there to be indifferent to the issue of the struggle. When in August, 1598, a British army was cut to pieces on the Blackwater and the marshal himself, Sir Henry Bagenall, slain, Wales was profoundly stirred.

> Y siwrnai oedd atgas, gwanhawyd y deyrnas,
> marwolaeth a gafas llawer gwr tal,
> sawdwyr Cymru llwyr gwae ni
> o ladd Syr Harri Bagnal,

lamented Evan Lloyd Jeffrey in a popular " carol ".[1] Bagenall was a nephew of Sir William Herbert of St. Julians, his father and Sir William having married daughters of Edward Griffith of Penrhyn, chamberlain of North Wales; and by virtue of this match the marshal had acquired Plas Newydd in Anglesey and represented the county in the parliament of 1586.[2] Among the *sawdwyr Cymru* who suffered in the fray was Sir Richard Trevor of Trevalun doubly a Bagenall " in-law "—having married his eldest daughter to Sir Henry's feeble-minded heir while his younger brother Sackville, with a dis-tinguished naval career before him, became the second husband of the widowed Lady Bagenall.[3] Sir Richard had been in Ireland since 1595, when he led a hundred men from Denbigh-shire and Flintshire to the battlefield with a gallantry that won him a knighthood from the lord deputy two years later; and in the Blackwater fight he was himself wounded and his company suffered heavy casualties.[4] In the punitive force brought out by Bagenall's brother was yet another Trevor, Sir Richard's equally valiant kinsman Edward of Brynkynallt, whose fortunes were to be still more closely linked with English rule in Ireland.[5]

More than this was needed, however, if Blackwater was to be

[1] " Hateful was the journey and crippling to the realm; many a fine man met his death. Soldiers of Wales, woe, woe to us by Sir Harry Bagnal's death " (*N.L.W.J.*, vi. 160).

[2] Griffith, *Pedigrees*, p. 57; Williams, *Parl. Hist.*, p. 2.

[3] *C.S.P.I.*, 1592–6, pp. 313, 318, 326; Palmer, *Grresford*, opp. p. 100; H.L. MS. EL. 7494.

[4] McClure, *Letters of John Chamberlain*, i. 30; *C.S.P.I.*, 1599–1600, p. 113.

[5] *C.S.P.I.*, 1598–9, p. 322, 1600, pp. 217, 530, 1600–1, pp. 30, 40, 1601–3, p. 628 *et passim*.

avenged, and in the following spring the queen sent out as
Governor General (not mere Lord Deputy) the dashing young
Earl of Essex, with an imposing armament of sixteen hundred
foot and thirteen hundred horse. Each of the Welsh counties
except Anglesey sent fifty, although only six months had passed
since Wales shipped her last contingent of nine hundred from
Bristol, Milford and Chester.[1] Now Essex was already the
darling of Wales; not only was he heir to the lands and prestige
of Sir Rhys ap Gruffydd in the south-west, but his prowess had
brought him a considerable following among the restless
younger sons of the North Wales squires, several of whom had
left the ill-paid service of Spain to fight under him at Rouen or
Cadiz or the Azores.[2] Edward ap Raff had welcomed him
home from Cadiz as

Arthur ifanc wrth ryfel;

and his Irish venture was one of the themes of Evan Lloyd
Jeffreys's lengthy " carol " on the year 1599:

Gan Essex Iarll enwog, y carw cadwynog,
  aeth lawer yn llidiog i'r gelyn,
arglwyddi, marchogion, capteiniaid, gwŷr gwychion,
  rhown inneu'n gweddion i'w calyn[3]

Two at least of the Trevors were among the *capteiniaid*—Richard
with Essex's field force, Sackville on convoy duty at sea—and
with them most of the Earl's old companions-in-arms from North
Wales; one of them (John Lloyd of Bodidris) to be knighted on
the field and endowed with lands near Newry which long
remained in his family.[4] From mid-Wales went colonel Edward
Blayney, a younger son of the house of Gregynog in Montgomeryshire, with long experience in continental warfare, and
John Vaughan, head of the clan of Golden Grove in Carmarthenshire. Both eventually acquired lands, knighthoods
and peerages there; Vaughan married the daughter of Essex's
steward, Sir Gely Meyrick, but the knighthood conferred on

[1] *A.P.C.*, 1598–9, p. 543; *C.C.P.*, letter 141.
[2] *E.H.R.*, lix. 357–61.
[3] " A youthful Arthur in the fray " (N.L.W., Llanstephan MS. 124,
fo. 159); " With Essex's earl, the famous reined deer [a popular symbol for
the earl] went many hot in wrath against the foe—lords, knights, captains,
men of renown. Let us send our prayers to follow them " (*N.L.W.J.*,
vi. 160).
[4] N.L.W., Crosse of Shaw Hill MSS. deed 174.

him by his father-in-law's patron was disallowed by the Queen, who was becoming alarmed at her favourite's lavish broadcasting of honours.[1] A further batch of eleven hundred men, including a hundred horse and a complement of carpenters, bricklayers and coopers, left Wales for the same destination early next year, and this time even Anglesey had to send her fifty.[2] Several of Essex's Welsh *capteiniaid* who returned to muster the new levies, seizing the chance to foster their patron's tottering interests at court against the rivals into whose hands he was playing by his follies in Ireland, rallied men who could be trusted to follow him through thick and thin. A few joined him in his mad bid for raising London against the Queen's advisers in 1601; others were his unofficial agents at home. Between them they managed to keep county politics a-simmer for some time after their idol had gone to the block.[3]

Ireland was threatening to become almost as disruptive an influence in Welsh politics as America to the France of Louis XVI; for Essex's henchmen, in so far as they had any aims beyond a love of adventure, were generally men of one or other of the two extremes in religion, in revolt against Elizabeth's middle way. James I's accession (which they favoured), the collapse of the Irish revolt, and the elimination of Spanish interference by the renewal of appeasement, removed the immediate danger; but the Irish service, like the Indian service for later generations, tended to breed a distinctive type, marked in this case by an aggressive Protestantism that made families like the Pembrokeshire Perrots or the Montgomeryshire Herberts, and individual adventurers like Radnorshire's Charles Price of Pilleth, hostile critics of the court whenever it seemed to lean too heavily towards Rome.[4] The Irish Blayneys were more Protestant than the parent stock in Montgomeryshire, which was too closely connected with Powis Castle not to fall under suspicion of being tarred with the same brush, whilst their Irish cousins were in the front of the fight against the

[1] G.E.C., *Complete Peerage*, ii. 186 ff.; *M.C.*, xxi. 275–85.
[2] *C.C.P.*, letters 153, 162, 165.
[3] *E.H.R.*, lix. 362 ff.
[4] *T.C.S.*, 1948, pp. 19, 23, 49, 50; *N.L.W.J.*, vi. 256; *infra* pp. 196–7, 220, 229, 232–3.

rebels of '41 and later against James II[1]; and the otherwise
unaccountable dismissal of Henry Blayney from the Montgomeryshire bench, in company with Lord Herbert of Cherbury, in the " purge " of 1680, may possibly be connected with
obscure and unsubstantiated charges of conspiracy which led
to the arrest of the fifth Lord Blayney in the following year.[2]
Sir Richard Trevor's heirs are found in the Puritan camp under
Charles I and Cromwell, and Edward Trevor's grandson,
although he was later to serve James II only too well, was best
known under Charles II as chairman of the Commons' committee responsible for the harrying of priests in South Wales
during the Popish Plot scare. It was at this time too that the
fourth Lord Herbert of Cherbury explained to his cousin the
admiral (the future victor of Beachy Head) how he had been
moved by his " great apprehension " of popery and arbitrary
rule, and his conviction that " Magna Carta is the standart
we must flourish under or be slaves ", to oppose at the polls
the interests of their powerful popish kinsman the Earl of
Powis.[3]

The liquidation of Elizabeth's wars in Ireland did not
relieve Wales of the burden of the musters, although it was now
for garrison duty and not for field service that the country had
to send its thousand able-bodied men year after year.[4] In
Dublin itself James I's administration was as Welsh in its
upper crust as Perrot's had been at a lower level: Blayney,
Vaughan and Sir Edward Trevor (for he too, like Sir Richard,
had now acquired an Irish knighthood) all sat on the Irish
Privy Council; from 1617 William Jones of Castellmarch in
Lleyn was chief justice there; and even Perrot's bastard son
Sir James, already prominent as a leader of the Protestant and

---

[1] T.C.S., 1946–7, p. 72; Collis, Hist. of Ulster, iii. 17, 83, 216.

[2] N.L.W.J., loc. cit.; M.C., xxi. 281–8; C.S.P.D., 1680–1, pp. 349, 413–5;
H.M.C., Ormonde, n.s., vi. 136–7, 160. The charges were as unsubstantial
as the " Irish plot " for which the primate of Armagh went to the scaffold,
and in which a preposterous attempt was made to implicate Lord Blayney,
nor were any details offered of the treasonable words he is supposed to
have spoken some years earlier.

[3] T.C.S., 1948, pp. 64, 76; infra, pp. 205, 217–18; N.L.W. MS. 9346 B.

[4] A.P.C., 1613–14, pp. 112, 433–4, 1615–16, pp. 90, 228, 516, 1621–3,
pp. 89–90, 1623–5, pp. 472–4.

anti-Spanish party in the Commons, was sent out on a special mission.[1] On the other hand Sir Richard Trevor, although he took out allotments in the plantation of Ulster, retired on a pension from his governorship of Newry (owing to ill-health) and resumed the activity in Denbighshire politics that had been interrupted by his part in the Essex affair, until at nearly eighty he was sent by Charles I to spend his last few years at his old post.[2] Another Denbighshire man who had seen Irish service and now considered the purchase of a residential estate there (as well as a match with the lord deputy's daughter-in-law) was Sir Henry Salusbury of Llewenny, but he died too soon for either this project or his colonial ambitions to mature.[3]

Welshmen were as prominent in the ecclesiastical as in the civil government of Ireland during this century. The three sons of John Wynn ap John who went out there from Merioneth founded a clan of Irish Joneses who won laurels in both fields. Lewis Jones, the eldest son, went to Oxford early in Elizabeth's reign, and with a mere bachelor's degree rose by successive steps in the ecclesiastical ladder to be Bishop of Killaloe from 1633 to his death in 1646, at the reputed age of 104. His marriage to the sister of James Ussher, later primate of all Ireland (whose daughter became the second wife of Sir Edward Trevor) may well have been the first stimulus to the Archbishop's interest in Wales, which he developed by learning the language while he was in exile here during the Civil Wars and Commonwealth and by his long correspondence with Vaughan of Hengwrt.[4] Of the two brothers who joined him in Ireland one became an Irish judge and maternal ancestor to Oliver Goldsmith (whose Christian name perpetuated the family leanings towards Cromwell), the other sat in the Irish parliament and founded a family still prominent in the island to-day. Four of the bishop's sons reached eminence in various fields, two of them as bishops. Henry, the eldest, is described by a

---

[1] T.C.S., 1948, p. 20.

[2] C.S.P.I., 1606–8, pp. 11, 539, 1609–10, pp. 168, 180, 367, 547.

[3] N.L.W., Llewenny MSS. 3.80, 3.87, 3.122, 3.173; supra, p. 34.

[4] Foster, Alumni Ox., I. i. 825; Wood, Athenæ Ox. (ed. Bliss), iv. 805; Aubrey, Brief Lives, 1949 ed., pp. 110, 170; Morrice, Wales in the Seventeenth Century, pp. 20–21; J. F. Rees, Studies in Welsh Hist., pp. 159–61.

contemporary as " a man of great learning " and a pioneer of Gaelic studies; like his father he was a strong Puritan, and when bishops were abolished he served Cromwell as scout-master, to return unruffled to his diocese after the Restoration. It was as a soldier that Henry's brother Michael won fame; he left his studies at the Inns of Court to fight the rebels in '41, but when the King concluded an armistice with them he crossed over to help the Roundheads to reduce Chester and North Wales, returning to Ireland only to die in the hour of his most brilliant victory. His brother Sir Theophilus succeeded him as governor of Dublin and was one of the pillars of Cromwell's rule in Ireland.[1] But not all the churchmen whom Wales gave to Ireland in this age belonged like the Joneses to the left wing in religion and politics. Griffith Williams, the Dean of Bangor who became Bishop of Ossory just before the rebellion and had to flee his diocese almost at once till after the Restoration, used pen and voice with tireless vigour and learning to preach Laudian principles in the church and the indefeasible rights of monarchy.[2]

Trade formed another link. Towards the end of the period with which we are concerned, Ireland was taking some sixty per cent of the small volume of exports that went overseas from Wales—coal from South Wales and from Flintshire, slates from Cardiganshire, cloth, corn and fish from Pembroke-shire.[3] Trade in the reverse direction was not always so welcome. There was strong Welsh support for the measure introduced into the parliament of 1621 to limit the importation of Irish cattle, Sir James Perrot advancing the familiar argu-ment that " by their small Rents there, they will undersell us here, and bring down our Rents ".[4] Even less welcome was the human flotsam that the Irish Sea was apt to wash up at unwatched creeks along our coasts in times of economic stress, to add to the calls on private charity or the poor rates.[5] Yet when normal trade with Ireland was hampered by the pre-valence of piracy (as during Buckingham's maladministration

[1] A. W. M. Kerr, *An Ironside of Ireland*, n.d.
[2] Morrice, *op. cit.*, pp. 205-6.
[3] D. J. Davies, *Econ. Hist. of S. Wales*, p. 53; cf. *supra*, p. 30.
[4] *T.C.S.*, 1942, p. 57.
[5] *Supra*, p. 17.

of the navy), Welsh economy soon felt the pinch.[1] For that reason Strafford's rule as Lord Deputy, which kept the seas safe for shipping and freed the Welsh from the burden of Irish service (save only those officers who were making a career there), was an indirect boon to Wales. But this was forgotten when the rumour got round during the Bishops' Wars that the well-drilled army by means of which he kept order in Ireland was destined to be landed in South Wales to make common cause with a local "popish army" under the Catholic Earl of Worcester (who undoubtedly had some secret commission from the king) and some of his co-religionists, against Scottish Protestants—ultimately perhaps against those south of the Tweed as well.[2]

This was among the causes that made the Welsh gentry rejoice in the early achievements of the Long Parliament and which made Ireland and the " Welsh popish army " the themes of the first contributions of Welsh members towards its debates.[3] The violent courses taken by the opposition cooled off Welsh zeal, but it was revived when the outbreak of the Irish rebellon seemed to give *ex post facto* justification to the rumours of the preceding year. The rebels gave out that the Queen was behind them, and Welsh members—especially those from threatened areas like Pembrokeshire and Anglesey, or from regions where popish influences were strong, such as Montgomeryshire and (later) Monmouthshire—were active in promoting measures against the rebels, for protecting the coasts and for keeping the recusants at home out of mischief. Among the first names put forward by parliament for commissions against the Irish were those of two Welsh M.P.'s with experience in Ireland—Charles Price of Pilleth and Richard Herbert of Cherbury—and two Welsh soldiers who had fought for the Protestant cause in Europe—Sir Gely Meyrick's son Sir John and Charles Lloyd the engineer.[4] With them went fresh drafts levied in the

---

[1] *T.C.S.*, 1945, pp. 23–4, 34–5.
[2] *Id.*, 1948, pp. 34–5, 44–5.
[3] See, e.g., letters in *C.W.P.*, 1672, *A.C.*, IV. iv. 201–2, N.L.W., Llewenny MSS. 3. 23, 3. 30, 3. 39–40, 3. 54, 3. 66, 3. 98, 3. 101, 3. 156, 3. 161, Llanfair and Brynodol MSS., bundle 91 (16 Nov., 1640); cf. *T.C.S.*, 1946–7, pp. 71–3.
[4] *Supra*, p. 36.

Welsh shires—a burden from which Wales had been free for a dozen years, and which was now felt so keenly that when two years later Denbighshire was called on to increase its complement for county defence against the Roundheads, it was reported that the drain of men for Ireland (and later for England) had left barely enough behind for tillage.[1] For the momentary revulsion of feeling produced in Wales by the Irish revolt gave place to a general stampede to the royal standard when civil war loomed in sight.

Charles's armistice with the Irish rebels, concluded in the November of 1643 to free the English forces there for his service at home, opened up yet another phase in Cambro-Irish relations, for it brought to the border campaigns, and eventually to Wales itself, Welshmen seasoned in the Irish wars. Michael Jones, as we have seen, deserted to the other side, but Sir Edward Trevor's son Marcus, who also came over with the " English Irish army " (as Archbishop Williams called it),[2] materially helped the royal cause in the campaigns for Chester and North Wales. His father, after falling into the hands of the rebels, had died in his adopted home, where he cut a much more imposing figure as a Privy Councillor, with estates worth more than twice as much as his original Denbighshire patrimony, than as a Welsh squire of £400 a year, hopelessly outshone even in local politics by the junior branch of his clan at Trevalun with its powerful patrons and its steady advancement at court. Yet his contacts with Wales remained unbroken; it was from Brynkynallt, for example, that he tried to pull strings in 1627 to get his brother-in-law Robert Ussher made provost of Trinity College, Dublin. Marcus, born of his father's Irish marriage, had probably never seen Brynkynallt till he came to Wales on military service, but he readily fell into his place in county society and found a wife there, keeping in touch by occasional visits and exchange of gifts even after he returned to Ireland and as Viscount Dungannon became fourth in the quartette of Welsh squires of this age who acquired Irish peerages.[3]

[1] N.L.W., Crosse of Shaw Hill MS. 1118.
[2] Carte, *Ormond*, 1851, v. 506.
[3] *D.N.B.*, lvii. 224; *C.J.*, ii. 411–12; *C.W.P.*, 1694; *C.C.A.M.*, ii. 1125; *C.S.P.I.*, 1625–32, p. 218, 1633–47, p. 345; *supra*, p. 12.

It was at first intended that the Marquis of Ormond, the new Lord Lieutenant of Ireland, should come over with the troops and take charge of operations on both sides the Irish Sea as a joint theatre—until it became clear that Ireland was not yet settled enough to spare him.[1] When the place designed for him was given to Rupert, whose authority did not extend to Ireland, it became necessary to keep Ormond in close touch with the campaigns on this side, lest his army be cut off from its base and in order that each area should be ready to come to the other's aid in a crisis. Even before the armistice there had inevitably been some joint Cambro-Irish planning. Ten days before the first " English Irish " arrived, Lord Carbery (son of the John Vaughan who had gone to Ireland with Essex, and now commanding for the king in West Wales) was instructed to send victuals from his district to Ireland;[2] but the flow was mostly in the opposite direction. Another Welshman who helped to promote this intercourse was Arthur Trevor, a lawyer son of Sir Edward by his first (and Welsh) marriage; his claim to be " acquainted with the temper of both king-doms " commended him to Ormond as a useful agent at royal headquarters, whence he sent his patron regular and racy dispatches on the progress of the war and frequent requests for men and supplies for Rupert's Welsh campaign. He made periodic trips to the border to see things for himself and to place his local knowledge and influence at the disposal of this alien commander, till at last he became a regular member of his headquarters staff.[3]

Far more important as a co-ordinator of Welsh and Irish effort, however, was John Williams, now a " private and unemployable " refugee from his archbishopric to his native Conway, and without any Irish connection or indeed " any power of command, but that weak one of kindred and good will " undertaking at his own costs the defence of this " ffron-tiere garrison " against the Roundhead menace from the east with what help he could wheedle from Ormond in the west.

[1] Carte, v. 510, 529, 537, vi. 13, 40.

[2] *Id.*, v. 503.

[3] *Id.*, v and vi, *passim*; *T.C.S.*, 1937, pp. 186–200; *Declaration of Sir T. Myddelton*, 1644 (A. Trevor present at council of war in Shrewsbury, 1643).

From the autumn of 1643 to the spring of 1646 he was in constant touch with the Lord Lieutenant, reporting on the progress of the king's affairs in Wales, advising him on the temper and abilities of those engaged on them, and urging with growing vehemence (as the royal cause grew more desperate) the need for men or munitions as the case might be. The Archbishop for his part guaranteed payment for the powder, shot and muskets, helped to organise the clothing, billeting and rationing of the men as they landed, and made strenuous efforts among his neighbours to keep the ports open for their reception —especially Beaumaris, since landings at Holyhead or west of the Conway meant transport over intractable roads and ferries[1].

Ormond was equally insistent on the strategic importance of Beaumaris, and he set great store on having it under the command of a reliable man, with wide enough powers to make it the pivot of a defensive system covering both the vital sea lanes to Ireland and the equally vital passes of Snowdonia, and acceptable to Ormond on the one hand and Williams and the Welsh gentry on the other. His own choice was Colonel Francis Trafford, an experienced soldier of Denbighshire stock who had come to him with warm recommendations from secretary Digby at royal headquarters. After serving in the Bishops' Wars Trafford, a " professed papist ", had fled from the atmosphere of implacable hostility to Rome revealed in the early sittings of the Long Parliament to take refuge among his co-religionists in Maryland, where he sat on the Privy Council and undertook a mission to Virginia to concert measures against the Indian menace; but when the outbreak of civil war offered some prospect of better days for his faith at home, he revisited England and rallied to the crown. He duly came over in charge of another batch of soldiers, and remained as one of Ormond's unofficial liaison officers in North Wales until he finally joined his patron in Ireland when fighting was at an end here; but he was never given the suggested command, doubtless because Rupert (always at cross purposes with Digby) found it inconvenient to make a man of Trafford's

---

[1] Carte, *loc. cit.*; *A.C.*, III. xv. 309 ff. On the tribute of *dillad* and *gwartheg* raised for the Irish in Aberdaron, cf. Gruffydd Bodwrda's *englyn* in *Cynfeirdd Lleyn*, p. 221.

faith so prominent a target for enemy propaganda. The
revised plan did not work well. On the one hand the presence
of a papist with the king's commission, even in an unofficial
capacity, could not be concealed for long; on the other the
post at Beaumaris (with authority over the three shires of
Gwynedd and the title of Governor of North Wales) went to
Sir John Mennes, a seaman with neither the military experience
nor the personal acceptability of Trafford, who returned to
his own element after twelve months of unproductive bickering.[1]

All this meant that much of the brunt still fell on the Archbishop. Captains Bartlett and Wake were kept busy crossing
the sea with dispatches, reinforcements and stores, harried
increasingly by the parliamentary fleet and in constant danger
of leakages of vital information through capture at sea. At
last Williams begged Ormond for the loan of a convoy of
small pinnaces, of which he was given one; this he rigged and
manned as a sort of private mail boat for Ireland. He was
equally in touch with the officers who conducted successive
contingents arriving from Ireland to their new war front,
from Trafford and Captain Cadwgan (who eventually succeeded
Trafford as governor of Antrim) to the Archbishop's neighbour
Roger Mostyn of Gloddaeth, whom he persuaded to go across
and find what men he could to fling into the breach when
Chester was at its last gasp in the early weeks of 1646. He would
have done the same himself, had not Ormond dissuaded him,
for reasons that will soon appear.[2]

For it was at this juncture that there came finally to grief
a scheme of the King's which would have drawn still closer
the strategic ties between Wales and Ireland, but which in the
issue not only put his Irish affairs (as Ormond now explained
to Williams) in confusion and uncertainty, but alienated many
Welsh loyalists and reduced to vanishing point any lingering
hopes of regaining his hold on the country at large. The plan
had been germinating in his mind for two years at least, from
the time when he first concluded the Irish armistice; perhaps

---

[1] Carte, vi. 78, 90, 117; *B.B.C.S.*, xiv. 300–2.
[2] Carte, *loc. cit.* and *Original Letters, passim*: B. D. Roberts, *Mitre and
Musket*, ch. xvi; *A.C.*, II. xv. 339: H.M.C., *6th R.*, p. 96.

its roots must be sought yet further back, in the rôles designed for Strafford's Irish army in the Bishops' Wars and for South Wales in the Earl of Worcester's secret commission of 1639. Worcester himself had the habit neither of body nor of mind for adventures of this type, and with advancing years he became even less attracted to the active life of courts and politics, and more to his patriarchal sway among tenants and dependents and the cultured and courtly ease of Raglan, where a deep personal piety did not preclude tolerance to those of other faiths. It was his son Lord Herbert who became the scheming zealot and the man of affairs. In contrast to his father, who succeeded to the title at a time when parliament was keeping a jealous and unremitting eye on all appointments of papists to posts of responsibility, he was admitted to public life—first as a councillor at Ludlow, then as a deputy lieutenant in his own county—during the years when Charles dispensed with parliament; and he took advantage of his access to court to remind the King of the traditional influence of his house in South Wales and the loss to the public service when that influence was undermined by legal disabilities. In consequence both he and the Earl were given dispensations to wear arms, and he himself a commission in the Bishops' Wars. It was at this time that he was first brought into contact with Irish affairs through his second marriage with the daughter of an Irish earl; but when the rebellion broke out in 1641 he tried to disarm parliamentary suspicions by offering to contribute handsomely towards its suppression.[1] During the months preceding the Civil War he was in frequent communication with the King, and the letters refer in cryptic terms to more secret verbal communications. It is likely that these came to no more than a promise on Herbert's part of the " loans " out of his father's immense fortune which first enabled Charles to put an army in the field at all, with vague but rosy prospects of advancement for the house of Raglan in return; at any rate the position of Lord Herbert as secret agent for the sort of intrigue the King loved so well and handled so ill was already established in Charles's mind.[2]

With the Irish " Cessation " of 1643 Lord Herbert was ripe

[1] Doyle, *Official Baronage*, ii. 7–9; *T.C.S.*, 1946–7, p. 82, 1948, pp. 40, 43
[2] Dircks, *Life of the Marquis of Worcester*, 1865, pp. 33–4.

for further adventures in the King's service, for spring had
seen the *débâcle* of what Clarendon called " that Mushroom-
Army " which he had raised and led for Charles in South
Wales, while the independent command conferred on him
there had so revived and intensified the jealousies of neighbours
(already made clear in the Long Parliament when he had been
first commissioned against the Scots) as to convince him there
was no further scope at home for his restless ambitions.[1] No
sooner had the armistice released an army for the royal
service in England than Charles directed his efforts towards
turning this into a treaty under which the Irish Confederate
Catholics would themselves provide him with another and
larger army, with the possibility of further contingents from
the continental Catholic powers. Even before the Confederates
sent their delegates to negotiate at Oxford in the spring of
1644, Rupert had approached their council at Kilkenny for
arms for his Welsh campaign;[2] and early in April, while
negotiations were still proceeding, a draft commission (irregular
in form, since it had to be concealed from most of the King's
entourage—perhaps too to make it easier to repudiate) was
addressed to Lord Herbert as Earl of Glamorgan—the title
by which the King now generally addressed him, though the
patent of nobility was never formally completed; it named him
Generalissimo and Admiral of a great armament to be recruited
by him in Ireland, on the continent and at home, with power
to raise money for the purpose by the use of some of the royal
prerogatives, including even the creation of peers and baronets.
His promised rewards were the dukedom of Somerset, the Garter
and the hand of the King's youngest daughter for his heir. Glamorgan (as we must now call him) later explained that Irish armies
of ten thousand each were to land in North and South Wales and
a further six thousand from the continent on the east coast.[3]

[1] Clarendon, *Hist.*, bk. vi; H.M.C., *Portland*, i. 134.

[2] Carte, *Ormond*, vi. 14.

[3] Gardiner in *E.H.R.*, ii. 687–708 and *Civil War*, ii. ch. xxvii; Round,
Peerage and Family History, ch. ix. Round's denunciation of this document
as a " preposterous " fabrication of Glamorgan's does not take into account
the copy in the king's private papers (subsequently calendared in H.M.C.,
Stuart, i. 1–2) to which Glamorgan can hardly have had access, nor of the
accompanying patent which shows how soon he began using his new
powers. If this crucial document is authentic, Round's wholesale rejection
of other documents in the case may need reconsideration.

Apart from this last contingent (which a treacherous Round-head governor of Lynn had promised to admit to the port), Wales was thus the keystone to the whole crazy structure. For the North Wales landings Glamorgan seems to have had no definite plans, since the country was still safely in the King's hands; but it was necessary to make sure that the troops disembarking in the south (under an English Catholic in the Spanish service until Glamorgan himself was ready to direct operations) would not march straight into the jaws of the enemy. For at this time the parliamentary forces had subdued all West Wales and even gained some footing in Glamorgan, causing Carbery to resign his West Wales command in despair. Charles Gerard, whom Rupert sent to unite the vacant commands formerly held by Carbery in the south-west and the then Lord Herbert in the south-east, rehabilitated the royal cause in the course of the summer, but without depriving the Roundheads of their crucial control of Milford Haven. He achieved this, however, at the expense of an ominous decline in *moral* among the king's supporters, caused by the tactless and often brutal treatment meted out to the local gentry and peasants by Gerard and his subordinates. The autumn of 1644 saw a serious weakening of the position in North Wales by the great Roundhead victory at Montgomery, and the defection of Monmouth and the surrounding country in the south. Clearly Wales was at the moment no place for the landing of substantial forces from overseas.[1]

Glamorgan's first task then was to do what he could towards removing these obstacles. We know little of his movements at this time, but the indications are that he was with his family at Raglan, and there is no doubt that from this quarter proceeded the initiative that led to the recovery of Monmouth during the winter months.[2] Towards the end of December the King told Ormond, to whom the Irish negotiations had been referred when they broke down at Oxford, that " my lord Herbert having businesses of his owen in Ireland " would use the occasion of his impending visit " in all possible wayes to further the peace there"; for Ormond's unbending Protestantism

---

[1] Cf. Carte, *Ormond*, vi. 203.
[2] Phillips, i. 257–64, 269–73.

was holding up the treaty, and it might be that the presence of a known Catholic with an Irish wife and credentials from court (even if his judgement did not equal his integrity) would inspire new confidence in the English proposals. The King's instructions to this unofficial envoy followed early next year; they empowered him to pledge his own credit and the king's honour to the performance of any terms agreed to by Ormond,

" and if upon necessity anything be to be condiscended unto and yet the lord marquis not willing to be seen therein, or not fit for us at present publicly to own, do you endeavour to supply the same."[1]

What exactly this meant, and what further instructions, written or verbal, may have been given, are still matters of dispute, since so much hangs on the credibility of a confusing mass of disputed documents. Glamorgan himself obviously believed that if he produced the army quickly enough to save the throne there would not be too close a scrutiny of the means by which it was accomplished; and the belief was perhaps justified by Charles's inveterate habit of trusting time, once his primary objective was attained, to resolve any awkward commitments involved in the process.

A few days before making his first (and unsuccessful) attempt to reach Ireland, Glamorgan sent the King through an agent an account of his preparations for the landing of the first detachment of six thousand which he hoped to bring from Ireland by the early summer. The gentry of the counties of Monmouth, Glamorgan, Brecknock and Carmarthen, he declared, had promised to raise and equip " very speedily " another four thousand men, whose main job would be to clear Pembrokeshire sufficiently to enable the Irishmen to land at Milford Haven, which the transports would block to parliamentary shipping as soon as disembarkation was complete. But this undertaking was conditional on the redress of the mounting grievances of South Wales, which Glamorgan had promised to place before the King, and he now urged Charles to bring pressure to bear on Rupert to ease the financial burdens of the southern counties, to remove all free quarter and superfluous garrisons in order to make possible a concentration on the key

[1] Carte, *op. cit.*, v. 7; *E.H.R.*, ii. 697.

points of Chepstow and Monmouth, and to give a guarantee that the local defence force which Glamorgan had helped to bring up to strength would not be removed for service elsewhere (leaving the men's homes, as so often before, exposed to sudden attack) without express order from the King or Rupert. These coasts could then become alternative landing places should Pembrokeshire fail, and in view of this he stressed his own service in composing the " distractions " of Monmouthshire as ground for giving him an appropriate command there. He claimed to have a fund of £30,000 ready for the enterprise and a similar sum promised by the time of his return from Ireland, as well as ten thousand muskets, two thousand cases of pistols, eight hundred barrels of powder and his own artillery; as for shipping, he had " intelligence from his Ships, that divers *Hollanders* and *Dunkirkers* come in daily to him ".[1]

Glamorgan's estimate of the situation was, as ever, absurdly over-sanguine. Arthur Trevor, who heard vaguely of the mission soon after the man he still knew as Lord Herbert first set sail, had little faith in it; he warned Ormond to be on his guard against the possible intrigues of one who bore him little affection, and advised him to procure a copy of the King's new orders (in which he suspected that the Lord Lieutenant was ignored) and to see that he used the intruder as his tool rather than let the contrary happen. With these precautions he believed " good may be made of the Lord Herbert ".[2] But Glamorgan's ship had been driven back by the weather, and June came before he actually reached Ireland. By this time Naseby had struck a fatal blow at the King's power, not only in a military sense, but even more through the moral effects of the publication by parliament of his private correspondence, which fell into its hands with his captured baggage. The letters revealed just enough of the Irish project to raise well-founded suspicions and to alarm Protestant prejudices— not least in South Wales, where Charles now took refuge with

[1] Instructions of Glamorgan to Edw. Bosdon, 11 March, 1644 (*sic, sc.* 1645), found among the captured correspondence at Naseby and printed in *The King's Cabinet Opened*, 1645.
[2] Carte, *Orig. Let.*, i. 76–83.

Glamorgan's father at Raglan while he toyed with alternative plans for retrieving the Naseby disaster. But when he tried to rally the countryside to him, it soon became apparent that nothing had been done to redress the grievances Glamorgan had brought to his notice, and that no effective help would be forthcoming till he had made good the Earl's assurances, and soothed ruffled feelings caused by the open contempt for local sentiment and civilian interests shown by the English commanders Gerard had put in charge of the chief garrisons, over the heads of the county gentry. Most of July went by in these parleys, and in the end Charles had to replace Gerard in his command by the veteran and popular Sir Jacob Astley, whom he left to this thankless task[1] while he looked desperately round for some less slow-footed means of recovery. He reassured Prince Rupert, who was now as urgent in advising him to cut his losses as Archbishop Williams had been fifteen months earlier, by promising to urge Ormond himself to come over with ample supplies from Ireland and to place himself at Rupert's disposal.[2] To Ireland he characteristically sent yet another agent—an English Catholic brought over from France at the Queen's behest—to do precisely the same job as Glamorgan, with whom his relations were as ill-defined as Glamorgan's with Ormond.[3] Charles himself let another precious month slip by in a futile attempt to cut his way through Yorkshire to Montrose and the loyalist Scots.

Meanwhile two developments made largely nugatory even the promises of help the King's concessions had wrung from the malcontents of south-eastern Wales; his captured correspondence, printed in mid-July, was now in everyone's hands, and at the beginning of August the Roundheads had won a resounding victory in the south-west at Colby Moor, enabling them to send captured Royalist arms to foster discontent in the southeast. When the thousand men Astley had raised with such trouble in this area were sent to make good the losses in Pembrokeshire, they promptly deserted to the enemy, and

---

[1] *C.S.P.D.*, 1645–7, pp. 96–7.
[2] Rees, *Studies in Welsh Hist.*, p. 74.
[3] *The King's Cabinet Opened*, p. 20; Carte, *Ormond*, vi. 301; Gardiner, *Civil War*, ii. 260.

Milford Haven was barred to an Irish landing before Glamorgan had even the promise of an army to land there. The alternative plan of a landing in Glamorgan or Monmouth was little brighter, for there the letting of the cat out of the Irish bag had brought back into the Roundhead fold—" under pretences ", as Sir Edward Walker puts it, " of dislike of Popery "[1]—several old henchmen of the Earl of Pembroke who had hitherto declined to follow his political lead; they included Sir Trevor Williams of Llangibby, who only nine months earlier had helped to recover Monmouth for the King. By the time Charles returned in early September, the Earl of Glamorgan had secured from the Confederate Catholics the promise of ten thousand men, but the King could no longer risk waiting for them in what was fast becoming hostile territory.[2]

There remained North Wales, where in spite of steady Roundhead encroachment in the three eastern counties since the autumn of 1644 the harbours so vital to communication with Ireland had been kept open by the resistance of Chester on the one side and the continued efforts of Archbishop Williams and Sir John Owen on the other. In June Sir Marmaduke Langdale, the distinguished cavalry leader sent to replace Mennes in the vacant governorship of " North Wales " (in its restricted sense of Gwynedd), had been summoned to concert measures with Ormond in Ireland for the reception of Glamorgan's promised contingent.[3] Next month the King wrote from South Wales to intervene—without much success—in the ruinous quarrel developing between the Archbishop and Owen, and at the same time to urge the North Wales gentry to emulate those of the south (whose enthusiasm he depicted in colours they would hardly have recognised) in keeping parliament's Scots allies out of Wales, if only to save their lands from being used to foot the Scotsmen's bill, which he declared (and parliament denied) was the Roundhead plan for Wales.[4] The appeal to national feeling came oddly from one whose hopes were pinned on another invading army,

[1] Walker, *Historical Discourses*, 1705, p. 141.
[2] Rees, *Studies*, pp. 72–6.
[3] Carte, *Ormond*, vi. 302.
[4] *A.C.*, IV. vi. 310–11, V. i. 60; *A Declaration of the Lords and Commons*, 8 Sept., 1645.

liable to arouse far more deep-seated prejudice in Wales; but national sentiment, it has been rightly said, was one of his blind spots. In mid-September Charles made his memorable march north through the inhospitable hill country of mid-Wales, with all the men he had been able to assemble in the south, to attempt the relief of Chester—and to suffer the disastrous defeat of Rowton Heath.[1]

South Wales, denuded of troops, was soon overrun by the enemy, and effort was now concentrated on keeping control of the north, especially the key point of Chester, till Glamorgan's Irish army could arrive to restore the situation. Langdale had been called south when the situation became critical there, but soon after Rowton the King sent Sir William Vaughan, a Herefordshire man who had done good service in North Wales and the border ever since he landed with the " English-Irish " army in 1643, in command of a large body of horse and with a wide commission to cover Chester till the Irish should arrive. It was still John Williams, however, who took the chief initiative in rallying Gwynedd for the defence of Chester and Beaumaris and in making preparations for the reception and victualling of the Irish. The prospect of a popish army at his doorstep did not wring his withers as it wrung those of his namesake Sir Trevor and the south-eastern Protestants; churchman as he was, he had as little understanding of religious bigotry as his master had of national prejudice, and he would have been more at home in a full-bottomed wig among the latitudinarian bishops of the next century than he was among the theological heats of his own. Two years earlier he had assured Ormond that " when we shall call upon your Excellencye for Ayde, I shall not trouble my selfe with the professions of the officers, soe they be honest and the King's liege subiectes ".[2] By mid-December he had a firm assurance from Ormond that three thousand foot were ready for shipment, and Welsh Royalists eagerly told each other these would be landed before Christmas. A month later Byron himself, commanding the sorely-pressed garrison of Chester, had word from Ireland that as many as fifteen thousand were now ready to sail—that they

[1] Carte, *Orig. Let.*, i. 90–95.
[2] *A.C.*, III. xv. 311.

would have been with him already, indeed, but for " some miscarriage " which could not be divulged in writing but would soon be put right, making the troops available within twenty-four hours.[1] This was the time when Ormond, in equally cryptic terms, warned Williams, who was growing sceptical of these repeated promises, against crossing the sea to try his own hand at raising a force.[2]

The " miscarriage " was the discovery that the terms on which the Confederates had agreed to send forces involved pledging the king to so complete a surrender to Catholic claims that the papal nuncio himself suspected a trap; and in that very Christmas week when the troops were to arrive, Ormond had put Glamorgan under arrest for exceeding his commission. By the end of January, 1646, it became known that since these terms had leaked out and were causing consternation among friends and sardonic jubilation among foes, the King had decided he must disown his Catholic agent and back up his Protestant Lord Lieutenant.[3] Although this by no means put an end to his attempts to exploit Glamorgan's influence among Irish co-religionists,[4] it rang down the curtain on a manœuvre which in its final results probably did more harm to the royal cause in Wales than any other single factor; indeed echoes of it disturbed the politics of South Wales even after the Restoration, when Glamorgan's son Beaufort, for all his renunciation of Rome, never quite lived down the suspicions of neighbours like Sir Trevor Williams who remembered his father's machinations.[5] Wales had once more felt with telling force the impact of Irish affairs.

With the last hope of reinforcements gone, Chester succumbed in a matter of days, and Byron carried his garrison to make a last stand for the king in the fastnesses of Snowdonia. For a few months Williams went on co-operating with Byron and Owen, but in early May, just after the King had given himself up to the Scottish army, Byron had ruefully to tell

---

[1] Intercepted letters printed in *Sir William Brereton's Letter*, 5 March, 1645 (6); cf. H.M.C., *Portland*, i. 325.
[2] *A.C.*, III. xv. 333–9.
[3] H.M.C., *7th R.*, pp. 236–7, *Egmont*, i. 267, 277, *Portland*, i. 329–30.
[4] See, e.g., *Three Letters Intercepted*, 26 Mar., 1646.
[5] *N.L.W.J.*, vi. 255.

Ormond of the Archbishop's desertion of the cause, followed
(he sweepingly declared—forgetting the faithful Owen) by
that of " all the gentry of Carnarvonshire without exception ";
and once more he had to plead for the speedy despatch from
Ireland of three thousand good men to save Caernarvon.[1]
But Ormond was in no shape to help; his resources almost run
dry and with scant prospect of replenishment, his master a
virtual prisoner, he was between the devil of the Confederates
(with whom he had just concluded a precarious peace) and
the deep sea of a hostile and triumphant parliament. So
Caernarvon too had to yield, and then inevitably Beaumaris
went; there was no longer a port to which Irish men and
supplies could come even had they been available.

With no further prospect of a blow for the King at home,
Welsh Royalists began to turn to Ireland as a field of action
where, without deserting the crown, they could fight their
traditional foe in the forces which parliament sent to Ireland
with Monck and Michael Jones in 1647 (including a " Welsh
brigade" under Captain Kynaston) to renew the struggle after
they had denounced Ormond's peace. Marcus Trevor, for
example, served with Monck (an old Royalist like himself)
and was rewarded with the governorship of Carlingford, not
without head-shakings from the straiter sort of Roundhead.[2]
Before long Ormond himself had yielded Dublin to Michael
Jones as the only means of preserving Ireland for the English
and Protestant ascendancy; but on the King's execution, having
failed to persuade Jones to break with the regicides, he took
up arms against him once more, to be joined by Marcus Trevor,
and from Caernarvonshire by Richard Griffith of Llanfair
Isgaer, who had fought in the operations round Chester till
the city fell. Griffith's old servant sent after him a touching
sheet of laboured penmanship with " praeres to god allmighty
to prosper your jurnney: to gods glory my deare mistres comfort
and innumiabel besides that desier it ", telling at the same time

[1] Carte, *Orig. Let.*, i. 95–6.
[2] *D.N.B.*, lvii. 224; J. T. Gilbert (ed.), *Affairs in Ireland, 1641–52*, Irish
Arch. and Celtic Soc., 1880, I. 294, II. x. 230, 249, 320–1, 344, 367, 388;
T.H.S.L.C., n.s.i. 252; Kerr, *Ironside of Ireland*, p. 99.

how the good lady at home is "in such a passion that she knowes not what to think of" because the "post packes" have arrived at Holyhead with no news of her husband's safe arrival. But Griffith was not really neglectful; he was busy trying to arrange an exchange of prisoners in favour (it seems) of his distracted wife's brother Ellis Lloyd, who as a very young man had left his studies at Barnard's Inn to serve under Hopton in the west, and after being wounded and taken prisoner found himself in London (just before Caernarvon fell) with no means of livelihood save by taking service under the victors. Rather than this he resolved to seek military employment in France or even against the Turks, but eventually drifted to Ireland to serve under Ormond—and to fall once more into enemy hands. It is comforting to find him eleven years later back in his chambers and rejoicing in the near prospect of the fulfilment in the Restoration of his favourite Latin tag, *Dulcia non meruit qui non gustavit amara*.[1]

Five months after Richard Griffith landed in Ireland, Michael Jones's decisive victory over Ormond at Rathmines prepared the way for the Cromwellian conquest, and when Cromwell quitted the island a year later, leaving Ireton to finish his work, parliament sent over four commissioners, headed by the single-minded republican Edmund Ludlow, to represent it in the work of civil government. One of these, John Jones (a Merioneth man, of the same stock on his mother's side as Michael and the Irish Joneses) established a liaison of a new kind between Wales and Ireland during the next few years. Committed to the new republic as one of the two Welshmen to sign the King's death-warrant, he rose high in its counsels at a time when even his old employer, Sir Thomas Myddelton (under whose standard he had enlisted) stood aloof, and the principal Roundheads of the south were actively hostile. For the Welsh Royalists in Ireland the situation had again radically changed; to fight Irish papists was in their blood, but to do it under the banner of a regicide republic offended their deepest instincts. Richard Griffith was back

[1] N.L.W., Llanfair and Brynodol MSS., bundle 91 (letters of 16 Nov., 1640, 14, 25, 28, 30, 31 March, 14 June, 1649), bundle 94 (letter of 5 May, 1660).

home soon after Ormond finally quitted his post at the end of
1650; Trafford is last heard of a month after the King's execution.[1] The case was different with Marcus Trevor; as an
Irish landowner he once more made his peace with the victors,
and was protected from " discrimination " on the part of his
successor in the governorship of Carlingford by his countryman
John Jones, who took occasion to write a homily to the governor
in true Cromwellian spirit on the iniquity of dealing unjustly
with " even one differing in judgement or with little godliness "
and the obligation to " be just to men as men "; soon afterwards
he was offering Trevor (then revisiting Brynkynallt) to redeem
a mortgage on this property.[2] Marcus's half-brother Arthur,
the correspondent of Rupert and Ormond, after a term of
imprisonment, was also in the end reconciled to the Protectorate, accepting the help of Secretary Thurloe in safeguarding
his Irish interests, and returning the favour by putting him on
the track of volumes of Irish records that had gone astray in
the general confusion.[3]

Not long before his Irish appointment John Jones had been
named a commissioner for the Propagation of the Gospel in
Wales; but his attendance at meetings must have been confined
to occasions when he passed through Wales on official visits
to London.[4] On the establishment of the Protectorate, however,
the Rump's Irish commissioners were all recalled (at the close
of 1653) as men too advanced in their religious and political
views to be trusted. But Jones's republicanism was tempered
by a warm admiration for the Protector, whose widowed sister
became his second wife two years later; and so far from con-
demning the new government (like some of his fellow-commissioners) as a " shame and reproach ", he was willing to serve
it as an " active and usefull " commissioner for Wales when the

---

[1] *Id.*, bundle 94 (3 Sept., 1651); Carte, *Orig. Let.* i. 279, ii. 362.
[2] N.L.W. MS. 11440 D (John Jones's letter book), fo. 89. Some of the
letters are printed in *T.H.S.L.C.*, n.s., i. 1861 (see pp. 223–4). The MS.
will henceforth be referred to as " L.B.", the printed transcripts as " L.B.
trans." Cf. Cromwell's speech I, delivered eighteen months after Jones's
letter quoted here: " The judgement of truth, it will teach you to be as
just towards an unbeliever as towards a believer " (Carlyle, *Letters and
Speeches*, ed. Lomas, ii. 292).
[3] *Thurloe*, iii. 550; *C.S.P.D.*, 1657–8, p. 217.
[4] See, e.g., Richards, *P.M.*, p. 97 *n.*

rule of the Major Generals was set up in 1655, to sit on Cromwell's Council of State next year, and to represent two Welsh counties in the second Protectorate parliament, till he was called to the " Other House " as Lord Jones.[1] But Ireland had not yet seen the last of him. There was talk of sending him there in the early months of 1656, and he was mentioned in the summer as a candidate for the Dublin parliament at the same time that he stood for Denbigh and Merioneth— much to the disgust of Henry Cromwell, who as the new Lord Deputy found " saints " of Jones's cast of thought a thorn in the flesh, and tolerated his new " unkel " only so long as his father was alive.[2] Actually it was only just before Oliver's death in 1658 that Jones returned to his old post in Dublin with Ludlow, who had at last emerged from his seclusion to help the hated Protectorate against the common foe.[3]

Within a year of the renewal of his Irish commission the Protectorate was on its last legs, and Ludlow, called away to England for the more urgent task of countering Royalist plots, left Jones in charge, without adequate authority over the troops or even adequate intelligence of the progress of events in London. These new dangers brought about a renewal of the old strategic unity between Wales and Ireland by the concurrent appointment of Jones as governor of Anglesey; and he named as his deputy at Beaumaris (much as Ormond had named Francis Trafford in different circumstances fifteen years earlier) his old associate Hugh Courtney, whose left-wing activities had kept him in disfavour for most of the Protectorate.[4] But the sons of Zeruiah were too hard for Jones. He had the support of his namesake Henry, the episcopal scoutmaster, but by the end of November Monck's declaration for a " free parliament " (which Jones recognised at once as meaning a Stuart restoration) was freely circulating among the troops, with the backing both of " former cavaliers " like Mark Trevor and

[1] N.L.W., Fonmon MS. iii. 1335; Thurloe, i. 639–40, iv. 215–16, 413; C.W.P., 2108, 2116, 2118–9, 2122–3; Harleian Miscellany, iii. 485.
[2] Thurloe, iv. 606, 672. As soon as Oliver was dead his sons spitefully cut off their aunt's annuity (L.B. trans., pp. 297–9).
[3] L.B. trans., pp. 258–62; Thurloe, vii. 154; Firth, Last Years of the Protectorate, ii. 274.
[4] C.S.P.D., 1659–60, p. 28; L.B. trans., pp. 287–9.

H

of those Roundhead moderates whom Jones dubbed " New Royalists ". By mid-December they had seized him and his fellow-commissioners, and the following spring saw him on his way to London to answer articles of impeachment before the restored Long Parliament—the first stage on his road to the scaffold, where his demeanour (in contrast with that of the other regicides) won the reluctant admiration of many who found nothing else to admire in him.[1]

In the Irish career of John Jones we see a new type of Welsh official in Dublin and a new brand of Cambro-Irish landlord. The younger son of a family of small Ardudwy squires, he was bred to trade (with a smattering of the law) in the service of the Myddeltons in London),[2] and the business man he remained —businesslike in his methods (to the extent of keeping duplicates of all important letters in an invaluable letter book), scornful of any suggestion that " to get money by exchange " was " a Crime and a scandall ", yet severe on any departure from the strictest code of business ethics.[3] Like most of his fellow-officers on the victorious side, he used the debentures on his arrears of wages for extensive speculations in crown and church lands in North Wales, and parliament made a further grant of Irish lands to cover his remaining arrears; but there was no suggestion (save from the unfriendly pen of Henry Cromwell) of anything shady about these financial dealings.[4] In any case he did not live to enjoy his new estates, nor were they allowed to pass to his son. His patrimony consisted in the small free-holds he had inherited in Merioneth, increased by what he had been able to buy from the Myddelton estate during his service with the family and what his first wife brought to him in the Wrexham neighbourhood.[5] At heart he remained the

[1] L.B. trans., pp. 262–97; *C.S.P.I.*, 1647–60, pp. 693–4, 716–17; Noble, *House of Cromwell*, 1785, ii. 266–76.

[2] N.L.W., Chirk Castle MS. E. 5602; *C.W.P.*, 1707, 1834; Noble, *op. cit.*, ii. 266.

[3] L.B., fos. 22, 43; L.B. trans., pp. 253–5.

[4] L.B., fos. 39, 87, L.B. trans., pp. 221–3, 227–30, 255–6; *C.S.P.D.*, 1651, p. 583; Williams, *Records of Denbigh*, p. 134; Myddelton, *Chirk Castle Accts.*, 1605–66, pp. 17, 26, 57; *C.W.P.*, 2006. Henry Cromwell may have been confused by reports of the other Col. John Jones (of Nanteos), see *C.S.P.D.*, 1655, p. 66.

[5] N.L.W., Plas Yolyn MSS., Crafnant and Gerddi Bluog deeds; Brogyntyn MSS. (unscheduled), document of 1 Apr., 1664.

Welsh freeholder, in his sympathies and even in his instinc-
tive turns of expression. To a fellow-member of a syndicate
negotiating the purchase of the crown lordship of Bromfield and
Yale he declared himself " not much in love with such interest
as holds up any burthensome power over the people ", and
he preferred to sell at a moderate price to the sitting tenant
rather than " to any other that are soe earnest to interlope
other men's interest for lucar ". These sentiments did not
preclude a wholesome respect for birth and rank—witness the
lengthy pedigree he got Vaughan of Hengwrt to emblazon for
him on the anniversary of the king's death—and he had as
little to say for those who " cutt off the heades of Dukes and
Earles to have them placed on their Shoulders " as for fellow-
officers of his who lined their pockets by juggling with their
men's arrears of wages. His palladium, whether in Wales or
in Ireland, was security for the small freeholder.[1]

It is hardly to be expected, however, that his Irish rule
would be marked by any flights of imaginative statesmanship.
Of devoted industry there was plenty: we catch glimpses of
him at his desk in Dublin, " almost blind with sitting upp "
and unable to write " one sillable more ". But neither his
business training, nor his Welsh heritage of contempt for the
Gwyddel, nor his puritan zeal against the Scarlet Woman, was
an adequate preparation for unravelling the intricacies of the
Irish problem, least of all in " soe criticall a tyme " as one of
what he called (in a letter to Vavasour Powell)

" the Frameing, or Formeing of a Comonwealth, out of a Corrupt rude
Masse, the Deviding of the Countrey amongst the Servants of the lord,
who have Passed through the redd sea, and indured heardshipp in the
wilderness And lastly . . . the pulling downe the workes of Antichrist in
the land, and (by opening a way, for the blessed gospell of Christ to be
preached amongst this people) to expell that Idolitry."

But he had at least the grace to recognise his own inadequacy,
" raised from the dust " as he was " to sit and act in places too
high for me ", with " Qualifications . . . too Narrow for the
Ministers of any Commonwealth, but Sir Th. Mores " save
by special grace from " the Lord . . . with whose Heiffer I
ploughed and laboured ". He candidly admits serious errors
of judgement which wiser men would have avoided, and he

[1] Plas Yolyn MS. 96; L.B. trans., pp. 190–3, 253–5.

does not shut his eyes to the fact that " grase and godliness "
do not always go with " much knowledge in the affaires of
men ".[1]

His whole approach to Irish affairs is conditioned by the
distorted accounts of the massacres of 1641 on which he, like
most other Protestants in England and Wales, had been fed;
indeed it may safely be conjectured that it was Charles I's
supposed complicity or condonation that made Jones a regicide,
and he is obsessed with the conviction that the authors of the
ourtrage must be brought to justice before the island can be
settled. His savage pæan (in the vein of the Song of Deborah)
on the execution of Sir Phelim O'Neill breaks in sharply on
the sweet reasonableness of a letter to Morgan Llwyd, and
stands in startling contrast with the characteristically tender
tone in which he wrote to his family in Ardudwy or his brother
in London or others to whom he poured out his heart. Holding
the " Irish gentry " responsible for the rebellion, he sinks his
respect for pedigree to oppose the return of their lands, being

"perswaeded that the Irish will never be brought to Cohabit with the English
peaceably except all men of Estates be banished, and the Irish ploughman,
and the Labourer admitted to the same immunities with the English"

—in other words, by that undermining of the clan system in
which the English government found its only remedy for unrest
in the Scottish Highlands a century later. This desire to
" breake the Interest of the great men " (which he applies
also to those other thorns in the side of the Puritan republic,
the Scottish Presbyterian lairds) does not, however, suggest
to him a democratic solution, " the Inhabitants universally
being Irish Papists, and Enemyes ". For the present he must
" doe the people good though against their wills ", and this
meant to him a Puritan crusade, preferably from Wales. Like
Sir William Herbert, but by different means, John Jones
would have made Ireland a field for Welsh colonising zeal;
but Welsh Puritans were too busy evangelising their own
country (and some of them, as Jones bitterly comments, too
preoccupied with the fleshpots of church tithes) to be inveigled
to Ireland. Apart from his brother Henry, who became deputy

[1] L.B., fos. 75, 79, 85; L.B. trans., pp. 230–3, 252. Cf. Nobles's estimate
in *Eng. Regicides*, 1798, i. 372–3.

governor of Dublin, Jones had no " Castle Welshmen " like
Perrot's at his elbow; even his personal chaplain was a
Londoner—an ex-stocking footer, men said. No wonder this
Ardudwy Welshman found his Welsh turning rusty on him
when he tried to use it for writing to his country cousins at
home! Cavalier gossip, recorded long afterwards, charged him
also with puritanical tyranny in the regulation of breweries
and beerhouses in Dublin.[1]

Only after the commonwealth had had time to " take root "
in English soil was he willing to see it " grafted on another
stock "; till then military rule must continue, even though he
realises (in one of those flashes of common sense that shoot
across his cloudy political thinking) how few soldiers " knowe
howe to manage the Civell Government persuant to the lawes
of England ". His only immediate constructive proposal for
the settlement of what he alternately calls " poor bleeding
Ireland " and " that Cursed people " on whom " the dis-
pleasure of our great and Just god seemes still to hang ", is

" to set up in each county 2 religious grave knowing men free from corruption and expert in the office of justice of the peace, and give them a good
salary or estate. The Irish being a Quick knowing people, soon discovering
the weaknesses of men, and dexterous to make use thereof, for their
advantage, Butt where they find skill, and knowledge how to order them
They are I thinke the verryest vassalls on Earth."[2]

With that final observation we may leave this honest but not
very imaginative Welsh Puritan administrator of Ireland.
Jones's Puritanism did no more to produce a lasting union of
hearts between the two peoples than Glamorgan's Catholicism,
and Cromwell's plantation of Connaught brought in fewer new
Welsh settlers than James's of Ulster or Elizabeth's of Munster,
because there were so few Welsh Roundheads (except Jones
himself, whose grants perished with him) to take out their back
pay in Irish lands. Yet the whole chain of events did help to
quicken intercourse, not only by the constant passage of troops,
or by the printing of some of Morgan Llwyd's works in Ireland
through the efforts of his ardent but critical disciple John
Jones, or even by Jones's plan for fattening on Irish pastures

[1] L.B. fos. 36, 58, 61, 75, 103; L.B. trans., pp. 190–3, 211, 215; Noble,
House of Cromwell, loc. cit.; *supra*, p. 6.
[2] L.B., fos. 52, 66, 85, 103.

the stock of his Merioneth tenants (in a bad season when they could not meet their rents), but perhaps most of all by the friendly traffic across the Irish Sea in hawks and spaniels to beguile for the Royalist gentry the tedium of political proscription;[1] for here was a step towards making Dublin what it became to the North Wales squires of the next century—a playground and a social capital.

The Cromwellian conquest was effective enough to keep military contacts between the two lands at a minimum for long after the Restoration, which also brought a rude awakening to any Puritan dreams of evangelising the island from Wales; but in other ways the contacts persisted. Griffith Bodwrda, the younger son of a family of small squires from Lleyn, who had risen through the law to lucrative office under Cromwell and a seat in his parliament (as the far from silent member for Anglesey), retired after the Restoration to a post at the Treasury in Dublin, where he found a profitable sideline in developing building sites near the Castle; and Irish lands long remained an important item in the economy of families like the Montgomeryshire Herberts.[2] The old dispute about the Irish cattle trade broke out afresh in the Cavalier Parliament, but with an added element of party strife; for the Welsh M.P.'s who wished on patriotic grounds to check the trade found themselves allies or catspaws of Country Party politicians who supported restriction as a stick with which to beat Ormond, now back at his old post in Ireland and hand-in-glove with their *bête noire* Clarendon.[3] It was under James II that the factors which had so long governed Cambro-Irish relations showed their heads in full vigour for the last time. It will be shown in a later study[4] how by conjuring up once more the spectre of an Irish invasion, as in the days of Strafford and Glamorgan, James helped to provoke a general stampede among the solid phalanx of his Welsh supporters. Welshmen fought on both sides in the Irish wars of James and William,

[1] Richards, p. 97 (cf. L.B. trans., pp. 287–9); L.B., fo. 137; *supra*, p. 20.
[2] *T.C.S.*, 1948, pp. 69–70; N.L.W., Powis Castle MSS.
[3] *N.L.W.J.*, vi. 252; Carte, *Ormond*, iv. 234–5, 259–76; Clarendon, *Life*, 1759, iii. 704–26.
[4] *Infra*, pp. 230–2.

but it was on the side of the Protestant king that the newly-formed Royal Welsh Fusiliers won their first laurels and lost their first active colonel in the land where so many of their Elizabethan and Jacobean forbears had found graves.

In the interrelations between Ireland and Wales, as in so many other respects, the Revolution of 1688 marked the end of an epoch; for the Irish Sea ceased to be a terror to Welshmen and became, in the main, a channel of peaceful intercourse, whether by way of trade or of diversion. Characteristic of the next century are incidents like the provision of milestones along the old Holyhead road through Anglesey in 1752 by the proprietor of the Dublin packet, or twenty years later the subscriptions that flowed in from the Irish parliament and from private citizens of Dublin towards constructing the new road through Sychnant Pass and over Penmaenmawr—or on the other hand the round of social gaieties that Mary Bulkeley of Brynddu enjoyed in the Dublin season of 1735.[1] Even when the railway came, it was for the Irish Railway Commissioners that George Stephenson drew up in 1838 the report which substituted for the earlier plans of a distinguished Irish engineer the present route of the main line through North Wales to Holyhead.[2] Only in the tragic days of the Easter Rising and the Black-and-Tans did Welsh soldiers once more find themselves in Ireland under the shadow of those " old, unhappy, far-off things " that have been the main theme of this study.

[1] *A.C.*, VII. v. 130; B. Dew Roberts, *Mr. Bulkeley and the Pirate*, ch. vi.
[2] Dodd, *Industrial Revolution in N. Wales*, pp. 114–15.

IV

" NERTH Y COMMITTEE "

THE county committee was a characteristic administrative invention of the Puritan *régime*. It was first called into being during the Civil War, as a natural consequence of the fact that parliament organised its campaigns on a county basis until the New Model gave it a national army. In this sense it was the counterpart of the Royalist commission of array; its object was to enlist the influence and resources of the local gentry in an effort to make the county responsible for its own defence and contributory towards the wider strategy. When the victorious party was faced with the task of governing a country, the machinery that had proved so useful in war time was perpetuated on a broader basis and with wider functions. The aim was now to include in the local committees not merely a faction, but a representative selection of the old governing families willing to co-operate and not irretrievably compromised,[1] and to use them (in accordance with what Disraeli used to call our " territorial constitution ") as a principal means of *liaison* between central and local government. The committees were accordingly large—even in thinly-populated Wales their numbers usually ran into the twenties, sometimes into the thirties and forties—and the members' names, by another striking innovation, were included in the body of the Acts they were to administer locally, forming a high proportion of the two bulky volumes of the *Acts and Ordinances of the Interregnum*.

It is proposed in the present study to use these lists, elucidated where possible from other sources, as the basis of an enquiry into the working of the committee system in Wales, chiefly with a view to discovering how far the successive governments of the interregnum were able to elicit the co-operation of the

[1] Firth in *E.H.R.*, iii. 636.

chief county families. The inclusion of a name is, of course, no conclusive evidence that its owner did in fact co-operate, but it does at least argue that he had not shown himself intransigent, and if he was re-elected his goodwill may reasonably be assumed. Even so, identifications are often made uncertain by the English clerks' mangling of Welsh personal and place names and their failure to distinguish between several holders of the same name. English officials must have been driven to distraction when (for example) the Monmouthshire committee failed to identify a man carefully described to them from Goldsmith's Hall as " the John Thomas who is employed about the Excise (there being many of that name in your County) ".[1]

One difficulty in the way of applying the committee system here was the number of Welsh counties that could not produce a sufficient supply of men of wealth and standing, irrespective of party loyalties. It was hard enough in relatively rich areas like the south-east and the south-west, where Monmouthshire, Glamorgan and Pembrokeshire each had between thirty and forty inhabitants of the rank of esquire; but what of West Wales and Snowdonia, where the average number per county fell below twenty?[2] And when even these exiguous numbers were overwhelmingly Royalist in sympathy, leaving only a handful of the smaller squires, yeomen and tradesmen to support parliament, the production of a county committee of the requisite size and weight was indeed a formidable task. In the early war years it was flatly impossible outside Pembrokeshire. Here the Roundhead gentry formed a compact group in the southern part of the county where they could be succoured and sustained by the parliamentary fleet—in spite of which they tended to desert the cause when the fortunes of war went against them. By the summer of 1644 they were strong enough not only to win the adhesion of many who had first declared for the King, but to draw the two adjacent counties of Cardigan and Carmarthen into a short-lived Association with a joint committee named in parliament. In practice, however, the only names of any weight were

[1] *C.C.C.*, i. 753.
[2] *Supra*, p. 2.

Pembrokeshire names (with one, Rice Vaughan, from Mont-gomeryshire); till well after the war Haverfordwest remained the real centre of parliamentary activities for all West Wales.[1] Even John Lewis of Glasgrug, the Cardiganshire squire who " explained " parliament's cause to Wales in 1646, did not come on to any county committee till after the King's execu-tion, and Carmarthenshire bred no Puritans (at least of the bolder brands) before the Propagation Act.[2]

Elsewhere the champions of parliament, if they existed at all, lacked the weight and influence to enable them to make any impression on the solid phalanx of Royalism.[3] In the south-east there were many old clients of the house of Pembroke who might have followed the fourth earl into the Roundhead camp had he been at pains (like his ancestors) to cultivate them; but his main interests lay outside the area, and when his distant connection Henry Herbert of Coldbrook, newly elected for Monmouthshire and drawn towards the Roundhead cause by his wife's business connections in the city, tried to rally his constituents for parliament on the eve of war, he found them solid for the rival house of Worcester and the King—until Charles's dealings with the Irish papists cooled off their affections in 1645. The separatists of Llanfaches (who were in any case socially unimportant) had mostly left for Bristol before the war, and when that city fell to the King they were scattered still farther afield. Their influence did not extend to Brecknockshire, where John Penry had left no following; but soon after the war Vavasour Powell came home to his native Radnorshire, and his preaching began to leaven this staunchly Royalist county—though it was mainly among the smaller gentry, yeomen and peasants that his converts were made.

North-western Wales showed more promise for parliament, for not only was its local commander in the field a man of great wealth and influence in the neighbourhood, but he could draw on the support of a growing body of Puritans centred on Wrexham. These too, however, were mainly of yeoman or trading stock, and could do little without the

[1] *A. & O.*, i. 443; *C.C.C.*, i. 572.
[2] *C.C.C.*, ii. 313; T. Richards in *Hist. Carmarthenshire*, ii. 133–7.
[3] *T.C.S.*, 1948, pp. 52–63.

backing of Myddelton's Roundhead force; while the Myddeltons themselves, though an old enough Denbighshire family, did not easily live down the taunt that their new dignity as lords of Chirkland (conferred in face of opposition from conservative-minded neighbours) had been bought with the profits of " usury ".[1] The Denbighshire gentry who elected Sir Thomas to the Long Parliament declined to follow him in making war on the King, and the war was nearly over before his victorious army gained control there; his borough colleague in the House, Simon Thelwall (who was likewise of local parliamentary stock but more at home in London) served meanwhile with the Pembrokeshire Roundheads in despair of raising a party at home. Myddelton had strong territorial interests in Montgomeryshire also, and here he made an earlier penetration and had support from two old parliamentary families—both, however, broken reeds to rest upon; for Sir John Price kept changing sides, and Edward Vaughan supported parliament merely in order to secure the Llwydiarth estate against his popish nephew, who fought for the other side.[2]

The Llwydiarth estate extended into Merioneth, but Vaughan got no support there from his fellow-gentry either in opposing the King's commission of array on the outbreak of war or in securing the county for parliament in its closing phases.[3] Merioneth, it is true, produced two Puritans of eminence in Morgan Llwyd the mystic and John Jones the regicide, but though both came of old Ardudwy stock neither inherited land there. Jones, as younger son of a small squire, was brought up in the households of his distant connections the Myddeltons in London and Essex,[4] and both he and his friend and mentor Llwyd found their spiritual home in Wrexham rather than in Ardudwy. One of the few Merioneth men to take up commissions for parliament was Jones's cousin Robert Owen of Dolserau, Dolgelley (son-in-law of the antiquary Vaughan of Hengwrt), who shared his regicide

[1] *Supra*, p. 29.
[2] *C.C.C.*, i. 328, ii. 1626–8, iv. 2552: *C.C.A.M.*, ii. 995–6; S.P. 28/251 (Wales), Montgomeryshire, depositions of 3 March, 1648; B.M. Harl. MS. 255, fo. 25 (b); *C.S.P.D.*, 1654, p. 346.
[3] S.P. 28/251, *loc. cit.*; *Cambrian Quarterly Mag.*, i. 65.
[4] N.L.W., Chirk castle MS. E 5602 and pedigree of John Jones.

cousin's attachment to Morgan Llwyd, sat with him as commissioner under the Propagation Act (not without doubts on
John's part of his financial integrity), and ultimately turned
Quaker;[1] but his standing in county society was too humble
to gain him a seat on local committees till after social barriers
had been lowered by Barebone's Parliament. Caernarvonshire
produced three men " ill-affected " enough to the royal cause
to be put under arrest when war broke out:[2] Thomas Glynne of
Glynllifon, an old M.P. who had lost his seat in the Long
Parliament;[3] John Bodwrda of Bodwrda, a deputy lieutenant
of the Bishops' War period whose family had provided the
county (and was to provide it again) with sheriffs;[4] and William
Lloyd, of the Denbighshire Royalist house of Bodidris, who had
married a Caernarvonshire heiress and settled in the county,
to become its sheriff after parliament won the first war and to
lose his life in the Roundhead cause (while still in office)
during the second.[5] But none of the three dared maintain
his opposition in face of the overwhelming sentiment of the
county, and all ultimately joined the King's commission of
array, on which they played ca' canny till parliament got the
upper hand.[6] In Anglesey the real party division lay not
between Royalists and Roundheads but between the factions
of Bulkeley and Cheadle, both of which adhered to the King.[7]

In spite of this lack of local support, parliament went on
hopefully setting down sums for the Welsh counties in its
successive Ordinances for monthly assessments, but except for
the scratching together of three names for Monmouthshire in
August, 1643 (a piece of optimism attributable, no doubt, to
Waller's temporary success there), and another six—three
esquires and three gentlemen—after the betrayal of Monmouth

[1] S.P. 28/251 (Wales), Merioneth, letter of 24 May, 1651; A. & O.,
ii. 209, 211, 661, etc.; Richards, p. 265; N.L.W. MS. 11440D, fo. 43.
[2] C.C.A.M., iii. 1245.
[3] B.B.C.S., xii. 44–8.
[4] N.L.W., Llanfair and Brynodol MSS., bundle 94, letter of 21 May,
1639.
[5] Griffith, Pedigrees, p. 179; A. & O., ii. 247.
[6] Llanfair and Brynodol MSS., loc. cit., petition of 6 Apr., 1644, et
passim; An Exact Relation . . . , June, 1646; The Taking of Caernarven, 11 June,
1646; A Bloody Flight at Blackwater, 15 June, 1646, pp. 2–5.
[7] T.A.A.S., 1931, pp. 101–3, 1945, pp. 25–37.

to parliament in September, 1645,[1] no attempt was made to name any Welsh committees till after the conquest of the country had been completed in 1647. Even the committee of May, 1644, regulating the militia for Gloucester, Hereford and the four adjacent Welsh shires, contained not a single name from Wales because (as the preamble to the Ordinance expressly states) the counties concerned were almost entirely in enemy hands. Yet the exigencies of parliamentary finance made it necessary that as soon as a county had been even temporarily overrun, some sort of local organisation should be set up to collect local contributions. With this end in view the Ordinances commissioning Sir Thomas Myddelton and Rowland Laugharne to their respective commands in North and South Wales in 1643–4 empowered them to enforce the mandates of parliament within their area and to appoint local officials for the purpose, while that of February, 1643, establishing a central committee of accounts, authorised it to appoint county sub-committees financially responsible to it.[2]

From these Ordinances arose two types of county committee: the Standing Committee which was the civil arm of the local military authority, mobilising county resources while the campaign was in progress and enforcing obedience to parliamentary orders when it was won; and the Committee of Accounts, with control through its treasurer of the local war chest. Each was meant as a check on the other, and each was responsible to a different organ of parliament (the one to the Committee of Both Kingdoms and the other to the central Committee of Accounts), though of course final appeal lay to parliament itself. This system of checks and balances, however, in areas where parliament drew its support from so limited a circle, with the major families in opposition or at best of dubious allegiance, was apt to degenerate into friendly log-rolling on the one hand or the promotion of old feuds on the other. Yet no external control could be enforced till the military situation was stabilised and the constitutional issue settled; even then parliament could work only within the framework of a de-centralising tradition which left it with no means of asserting

[1] *A. & O.*, i. 223, 428, 789.
[2] *Id.*, 177, 379, 387, 443.

itself in local affairs save by pinning its faith on one or other of the rival groups of families, without the knowledge to determine the rights and wrongs of their mutual denunciations.[1]

Montgomeryshire provides a case in point. In the summer of 1646 the county treasurer, Lloyd Pierce of Maesmawr (Guilsfield) was imprisoned in Montgomery castle by the local Committee of Accounts for resisting investigation into his handling of county finances. The instigator of the prosecution was Edward Vaughan, whose family had been the principal centre of county feuds since Elizabeth's day,[2] and whose devotion to parliament was with reason doubted by his more zealous neighbours. Pierce himself—an old sheriff of ship-money days and a descendant on his mother's side of Sir Griffith Vychan (the county's Agincourt hero), though his father was a Shropshireman—was deemed so indispensable to the cause by the Standing Committee that they offered bail to the tune of £40,000 for his release, which Vaughan refused. The matter went up to the Lords, with counter-claims by Pierce, and it was with the utmost difficulty that he was rescued from Vaughan's clutches for further service to parliament.[3] Denunciations on similar grounds of parliament's agents in Wales are painfully common: in Brecknock and Carmarthen, for example, the county treasurers (Thomas Games and John Lewis) were accused of defrauding their respective counties of more than a thousand pounds between them.[4] But such charges must be read against a background of old family antagonisms sharpened by more recent religious and political divisions; indeed they bear a strong resemblance to the charges and counter-charges that used to enliven the evidence when the Star Chamber was the chief clearing house for family feuds.

[1] A report on the South Wales committees in August, 1647, praises those of Monmouth and Brecknock, but has little to say for those of Glamorgan, Carmarthen, Cardigan, or Montgomery (H.M.C., *Egmont*, i. 450–1).

[2] *A.P.C.*, 1588, pp. 357–9, 419, 1588–9, pp. 97, 178–9, 267–8, 291–3, 1590–1, pp. 109–10.

[3] Lloyd, *Sheriffs of Montgomeryshire*, pp. 521–33; *M.C.*, ix. 104, xxvii. 173–5; S.P. 28/251 (Wales), Montgomeryshire, 2 May, 20 June, 1646; *C.S.P.D.*, 1645–7, pp. 97, 441, 455, 459, 461, 491; *L.J.*, viii. 352. The committee had still not put into force in 1647 the ordinance for weekly assessments passed in 1644 (H.M.C., *Egmont*, 1.361).

[4] N.L.W., Fonmon MS. 1/57 (ix–xi); cf. H.M.C., *Egmont*, i. 450–1.

The most delicate and invidious task that fell to the county committees was that of putting into force the parliamentary policy, announced in the Ordinance of March, 1643, of making the enemy pay for the war. For this purpose *ad hoc* organisations, with a staff of salaried officials, were set up to hold in trust for parliament the estates of such delinquents as had been condemned to sequestration—collecting rents for transmission to London, granting leases subject to parliamentary consent, and so on. No committees for Wales were named in the Ordinance, but provision was made that where no county committee existed that of a neighbouring shire should act—a clause under which the Pembrokeshire committee began the work of sequestration in Carmarthenshire in 1646; and the Ordinance of 1644 for the militia of South Wales and the border was administered by a body with powers of deprivation and sequestration over the whole area.[1] It was probably under military authority, however, that the earliest sequestrations were carried out—ultimately that conferred in the Ordinances appointing military commanders for North and South Wales. We catch glimpses of such local organisations at work in parts of Monmouthshire as early as 1643, in Montgomeryshire by 1644, Brecknock and Denbigh by 1645, Glamorgan, Radnor and Flint by 1646; while the Pembrokeshire members of the West Wales Association of 1644 seem to have acted as sequestrators in their own county, and in Carmarthenshire as well until a three-county committee for the purpose came into existence by 1645.[2] In Snowdonia, the last part of Wales to be subdued by parliament, sequestration did not begin till the war was over; the principal delinquents had been named in Ordinances securing on their estates the loans raised by Myddelton for the prosecution of his campaigns, and when the time came for repayment parliament raised the sums by proportional fines on the earmarked estates, leaving the smaller fry to be dealt with at leisure.[3]

We know very little about the composition of the war-time

[1] *A. & O.*, i. 106, 531; *The Earle of Carberyes Pedegree*, 1646, p. 3.

[2] *C.C.C.*, i. 644, ii. 1460, 1568, 1632, 1719, 2132; *C.C.A.M.*, i. 77, 201, 449, ii. 729, 1024, iii. 1446: S.P. 28/251 (Wales), Radnorshire treasurer's accts., 1646; Williams, *P.H.*, p. 29.

[3] *A. & O.*, i. 514–5; *C.C.C.*, i. 57–8, 63; *C.C.A.M.*, i. 434, ii. 733; N.L.W., Brogyntyn MSS. (unscheduled), 10 Feb., 1646.

sequestration committees, but it is clear from surviving indications that the limited circle of parliamentary supporters shared between them in rotation, or even held concurrently, such posts as sequestrator, agent or solicitor, commissioner for sequestration, assessment or militia, and committeeman for any of these purposes, playing into each other's hands when they were not denouncing each other to the higher authorities. Sometimes, indeed, the process can have been little more than an example of

> . . . the simple plan
> That they should take who have the power
> And they should keep who can.

There is reason to believe that a powerful inducement to the low-born John Poyer to take up arms for the King in the second Civil War was the fear that his better-class colleagues were going to make him disgorge the revenues of Carew castle, which he had kept in his own hands since he seized it in the course of the fighting in 1644;[1] and in Brecknockshire Howell Gwynne was accused by the extruded Bishop of Llandaff of having forcibly annexed the profits of certain episcopal rectories while still fighting for the King in 1645, refusing to relinquish them even after the Bishop had compounded. Nor was he the only Royalist to wring what personal advantage he could from his party's defeat. In Carmarthenshire that "subtle ambo-dexter" Roger Lort of Stackpool, after serving the King for two years, got himself made solicitor for sequestration for the express purpose (it was alleged) of saving his own estate and those of his friends, thereby defrauding the Commonwealth of a sum estimated at £100,000; John Jones of Nanteos was credited with a similar performance in Cardiganshire.[2] Such accessions to the ranks of the county committees no doubt gave added weight, but without contributing either to their integrity or to their effectiveness.

It was only after the second Civil War that statutory sequestration committees were set up, for South Wales in the Ordinance of February, 1649, for North Wales in that of the following August. Their immediate purpose was to levy the

---

[1] A. L. Leach, *Civil War in Pembrokeshire*, pp. 83, 103, 129.
[2] *C.C.C.*, ii. 1537, iii. 1881; *C.C.A.M.*, ii. 1019–21; *C.S.P.D.*, 1655, p. 66.

collective fines incurred by the two areas for their recent delinquency, but the North Wales committee was expressly empowered to deal with fines and sequestrations still outstanding from the first war. Provision was made in both Ordinances for county organisations to work under the area committees, but these can hardly have got into harness before there was another change.[1] The Lords had always disliked the county committees as savouring too much of a policy of expropriation; as early as 1646 they had vainly tried to persuade the Commons to agree to their abolition, but now a compromise was arranged under which from the beginning of 1650 all existing sequestration committees were abolished and their powers taken over by the central committee (representative of both Houses) at Goldsmiths' Hall, which under the new Ordinance now proceeded to nominate three subordinate committees for Wales, covering respectively the North, the South and Monmouthshire. The members acted as commissioners for their own counties, and the other paid officials were appointed from Goldsmiths' Hall, though often in response to local suggestions. The South Wales committeemen were mostly new to the work, but nearly two-thirds of the much larger North Wales body had already sat on the Composition Committee of 1649; the new members were generally more partisan and of lower social standing—approximating in these respects to the pre-1649 county committees, on which many of them had sat. Nearly all the North Wales members, and two from the South, were future commissioners under the Propagation Act. This suggests that the motive behind reorganisation was a desire to discount the local pull of powerful delinquents with friends at court by a change of local personnel and an increase of central control. The local committees were renewed from time to time, but with little material change in membership except for a gradual contraction in size as business slackened off.[2] Central control was further tightened at the beginning of the Protectorate, and the worst evils were alleviated—expenses reduced

[1] *A. & O.*, ii. 14, 207.
[2] C. Hill in *E.H.R.*, lv. 224–7; *L.J.*, viii. 474; *C.J.*, iv. 475, 482, 664; *A. & O.*, i. 329, ii. 829; *C.C.C.*, i. 172–3, 673, 691, 694.

and officials bullied into producing their accounts.[1]   In
Caernarvonshire Colonels Madryn and Carter, the two harpies
who had run the county committees from the start, were
restrained from using their public position to further private
feuds and private greed;[2] in Denbighshire the notorious
Cneifiwr Glas, Edward Davies of Llangollen, had at long last
to account for his stewardship of Valle Crucis Abbey—but
not to resign his office of sequestrator, which he continued to
exercise in a widening area for another five years.[3]

Changes in policy, however, were of little use without more
radical changes in personnel than were possible among such a
restricted circle of partisans as Wales could produce.   Lewis
Price, owner through marriage of a small property in Montgomeryshire, became a North Wales sequestrator only four
years after he had been fined for misconduct as solicitor for
sequestration in his own county;[4] Lloyd Pierce's brother-in-law
Gabriel Wynn of Dolarddyn (Montgomeryshire) went on
helping to administer the affairs of his county till the eve of
the Restoration in spite of accusations that on Myddelton's
first conquest he had detained and claimed as his own inheritance lands he was handling as a county sequestrator;[5] and
a running fire of accusations failed to dislodge William Watkins
of Llanigon from the widespread control he exercised (with
powerful backing) in most of south-eastern Wales. It was within
Watkins's sphere of influence that a general rising of the
Glamorgan gentry against the whole committee system was
provoked in 1647 and that the Brecknockshire solicitor for
sequestration became the object of an armed attack two years
later.   In the " heads of grievances " of the Glamorgan insurgents the parliamentary faction is accused of egging on servants
and retainers to " insult over the Gentry " by " making all

[1] *C.C.C.*, i. 113, 313, 449, 492–4, 543, 569, 574, 577–8, 592, 644, 689,
691–2, 709, 723, 726–7, ii. 1460, 1537, v. 3301; *C.C.A.M.*, i. 77, 107–8,
ii. 1100.
[2] *C.C.C.*, ii. 1511, 1600; N.L.W., Brogyntyn MS. 63; H.M.C., *2nd R.*,
p. 87; *T.C.H.S.*, p. 14.
[3] *C.C.C.*, i. 727; Pennant, *Tours*, 1883 ed., ii. 1; *C.W.P.*, 2195.
[4] S.P. 28/251 (Wales), Montgomeryshire, 6 Nov., 1646: *C.S.P.D.*,
1645–7, p. 491; *M.C.*, xxvii. 186–8.
[5] *C.C.C.*, ii. 1460; *Montgomeryshire Pedigrees* (Powys-land Club), p. 64.

men of considerable estate Delinquents " and liable to sequestration, of refusing to account for the " vast summe " lying in
their hands, and of introducing into the county committee
partisans from outside " meerely out of faction to out-vote the
rest of the Gentlemen ".[1] Examination of surviving records
shows that there was substance in the charges. Only a few of
the sequestration commissioners and other officials whose
names have come down to us were eminent enough to have
borne the office of sheriff, fewer still were of the standing of
M.P.'s; of six Brecknockshire sequestrators accused in 1650
of misappropriating £5,000 worth of delinquent estates, only
one could be styled " esquire ", and not one of the twenty-two
members of the three sequestration committees appointed for
Wales that year was a man of any considerable estate, about a
third of the North Wales contingent being military adventurers.[2]

To men of this stamp the handling of sums of money amounting to several years' yield of their own estates, with the excellent
pretexts afforded by pestilence, shortage of transport, intractable roads and unsettled conditions, for repeated postpone-
ments in the despatch of money or accounts to London,[3] was
a direct incentive to corruption, while the inducement of a
ten per cent commission on what they sent was almost as
direct an invitation to extortion—unless, indeed, Stephen
Hughes's brother (a South Wales committeeman) was right
in saying that the bonus did not cover the cost of conveyance.[4]
These sources of revenue might be supplemented by profitable
deals with the victims or favourable leases of their lands to
friends and relatives, who could also be gratified with one
of the many subordinate posts at salaries of the order of
£100 or £200—a tempting sum for the times. No wonder
" a Committy feast " became a popular byword![5]

Perhaps the most notorious of all the traffickers in Welsh
sequestration was Philip Jones of Swansea, who founded a

[1] A Full Relation . . . , 2 July, 1647; A Declaration of the Proceedings . . . ,
26 June, 1647; The Heads of the Present Grievances, 1647.
[2] C.C.A.M., ii. 1100; C.C.C., i. 172–3.
[3] C.C.C., i. 272, 277, 364, 450, 475, 572, 616, 676.
[4] A. & O., i. 329–35; Richards, P.M., p. 236.
[5] A. N. Palmer, Holt, p. 161.

new county family on the fortune he made during the inter-regnum. As a member of the central committee at Goldsmiths' Hall he was able to influence the composition of all the South Wales committees, on each of which he seems to have had friends or dependents with whom he kept in touch through his agent William Watkins, an ex-M.P. already deprived of his seat in the Long Parliament as a " projector ". Jones was believed to have the treasurers of three counties in his pocket, and the whole " ring " had an unsavoury reputation through-out the neighbourhood, especially in Carmarthenshire, where the dearth of local parliamentarians left them a clear field; among their alleged devices for cozening poor men out of their rights was that of examining monoglot Welsh witnesses in English. It is true, as Dr. Richards points out, that the attacks on Jones come mainly from crypto-Royalists or disap-pointed rivals, and reach their height in the last years of the Rump, when the Propagation Commission, of which he was a prominent pillar, was under heavy fire; it is also true that Watkins's accounts did eventually pass the audit. But the Fonmon fortune speaks for itself; Philip's own heir felt qualms about his heritage after the Restoration, and had to be re-assured by the faithful Watkins.[1]

The few men of substance engaged in this traffic, however, enjoyed no better reputation. Edward Vaughan of Llwydiarth, supposed to be " one of the wealthyest persons in all Wales, that is childlesse ", was also charged with peculation as principal sequestration agent in Montgomeryshire. Since the charges originated with his old enemy Lloyd Pierce they no doubt owed something to personal and political animus; but he carried heavier guns than Pierce, and despite his avowed sympathy with the ejected clergy and his persistent defiance of orders from Goldsmiths' Hall when they clashed with the prosecution of his own claims, he kept his position right through the interregnum.[2] Henry Williams of Caebalfa in

[1] *C.C.C.*, i. 135, 492–5, 512–3, 517, iii. 2177–80; *C.C.A.M.*, ii. 799; Thurloe, ii. 93; Fonmon MSS., 1/40, 47, 57; Richards, *P.M.*, pp. 98–9, 249–52.
[2] *C.C.C.*, i. 290, 562, 707, 751, ii. 1626–8; *C.C.A.M.*, i. 75, ii. 995–6; Richards, *R.D.*, p. 285; Williams, *Welsh Judges*, p. 102: *C.S.P.D.*, 1645–7, p. 491.

Radnorshire (and other estates in Brecknock) was an old sheriff whose son was to represent both counties in post-Restoration parliaments; yet he too was accused of detaining public moneys in his hands as commissioner for sequestration in 1653;[1] and we have seen something of the reputation of Roger Lort, whose family had given to Pembrokeshire a whole succession of sheriffs.

Sequestration was a war-time expedient which the successive governments of the interregnum, in their chronic financial straits, made the capital error of prolonging into more settled times. But parliament also provided Wales, as soon as its subjugation was complete, with county committees for more normal administrative purposes, and the membership of these was generally drawn from a less narrowly partisan circle and used for less invidious ends. The first lot to cover the whole country was appointed under the Assessment Ordinance of June, 1647;[2] and as a nucleus of members in almost every county continued to serve in this capacity until the Restoration, an analysis of these initial committees, and of the re-shufflings that took place under subsequent Ordinances, will serve as some sort of barometer of Welsh reactions to the changing political atmosphere. Naturally the solid core of each group came from the few county families who had adhered to parliament during the war. Half of the Pembrokeshire committee had already served on the joint committee of 1644 for the associated counties, including some who, like Philipps of Picton and a junior Barlow of Slebech, were originally for the King. Sir Hugh Owen of Orielton was not included, for his prolonged absence from his seat at Westminster had aroused suspicions which were confirmed by reports of his flight from Roundhead Pembrokeshire to his estate in Royalist Anglesey;[3] and the "ambodextrous" Lorts were omitted on similar grounds. But about a third of the whole body came from the families from which M.P.'s and sheriffs were normally drawn, and less than a third were below the rank of esquire.

[1] *C.C.C.*, i. 636; *N.L.W.J.*, vi. 254.
[2] *A. & O.*, i. 958.
[3] *C.J.*, iv. 551; *C.C.A.M.*, ii. 875–6.

By the end of the war Henry Herbert was no longer the solitary Roundhead among the major families of south-eastern Wales. Charles's negotiations with the Irish Catholics through the Earl of Glamorgan had alienated from him (and from the Earl's father, the pillar of the Cavalier cause in this area) many of the local gentry, especially those of the Pembroke connection, like Sir Trevor Williams of Llangibby (son of the deceased county member) and his son-in-law Roger Williams of Cefnheyley, both of whom now sat on the Monmouthshire committee, with Herbert's ex-Royalist father.[1] Pembroke's own heir headed the Glamorgan list, which also included a more distant clansman, almost certainly the son of the member for Cardiff who had fallen for the King at Edgehill.[2] None of the major county families, such as those of Margam, Ewenny or St. Donats, had been involved in the great defection of 1645, but some of their cadet branches were now represented on the parliamentary committee; for example Bussy Mansell of Britton Ferry, with the prestige attaching to a distinguished name and a fortune of over £1,000 a year, had commanded the local Roundhead forces after serving the King till September, 1645, and he served the Puritan cause not only on a succession of county committees, but as a commissioner under the Propagation Act and a member of Barebone's Parliament, supporting the Protectorate even after Oliver's death and ending as a Country Party politician under Charles II.[3] Edward Pritchard of Llancaiach, though not quite so well-to-do as his friend Mansell, was substantial enough to entertain the King and all his retinue at his house on the morrow of Naseby, and reaped the reward of his subsequent desertion in the governorship of Cardiff.[4] From a somewhat lower social grade again came small squires like Bassett of Broviskin and Windham

[1] *N.L.W.J.*, vi. 255–6; *C.S.P.D.*, 1645–7, pp. 250, 386–9, 1654, pp. 271–2; *C.C.A.M.*, ii. 1022; *L.J.*, viii. 293; Thurloe, iv. 545.

[2] He appears as "William Herbert" *sans phrase* till 1649, when the designation "de Cogan" is added in the same context. If they are not the same person, the first must be Wm. Herbert of Friars, also worth £1,000.

[3] Clark, *Limbus Patrum*, pp. 374–8, 439; *N.L.W.J.*, vi. 254–5; *C.C.C.*, i. 747; Symonds, *Diary* (Camden Soc., 1859), p. 216: *C.S.P.D.*, 1645–7, p. 186; *infra*, pp. 193, 196, 202–3, 209.

[4] Symonds, pp. 205, 216; Thurloe, i. 637.

of Dunraven, or lawyers like Evan Seys of Boverton, younger
son of a local family whose disinherited elder brother became
an itinerant preacher under the Propagation Act, while he
himself accepted high legal office under the republican
governments and represented his county in the Protector's
parliaments.[1]

Far more influential on the south-eastern committees than
any small squire or country lawyer, however, were those two
Puritan soldiers of fortune Rowland Dawkins of Cilfriw and
Philip Jones, who from small beginnings raised themselves,
the one to military eminence and an estate of £250 a year,
the other to the far more dazzling rewards of political dexterity.
Even Henry Herbert did not disdain to co-operate with the all-
powerful Philip in packing with their friends the local sequestration committees;[2] and the Puritan wing was further strengthened by the inclusion of Jones's brother-in-law (and fellow-
trafficker in tithes) John Price of Gellihir, an early Baptist.
This wing, if we include in it all those who later sat with
Mansell, Jones and Dawkins as commissioners under the
Propagation Act, was pretty extensive in Gwent and Morgannwg, where the two county committees of 1647 contributed
between them over a sixth of the total commission. In Monmouthshire the two Herberts of Coldbrook come into this
category, but religious as distinct from policital Puritanism is
better represented by their fellow-commissioners Rice Williams
(a lay preacher of some repute) and William Blethin, both of
whom stuck to their principles in the ensuing days of persecution.[3] The rest of the Monmouthshire committee was made
up of other connections of the Herbert clan, together with a
selection of local Morgans and Bakers and Gloucestershire
immigrants like Thomas Pury and John Hanbury the ironmaster, whose family was so long to be connected with the
industrial development of the neighbourhood.

Sir Thomas Myddelton was the inevitable pillar of the six
North Wales committees. In Denbighshire he had the support

---

[1] *N.L.W.J.*, vi. 255–6.
[2] Fonmon MSS. 1/47, 57 (xii–xiii), 59; *C.C.C.*, i. 517; Richards, *P.M.*,
p. 421.
[3] Richards, *P.M.*, pp. 146, 238.

of his cousin Sir William (son of Sir Hugh the goldsmith), who had fought under him, as well as of two sons, his borough colleague Simon Thelwall, his steward Watkin Kyffin, and Sir John Trevor of Trevalun, with his son the future Secretary of State. The elder Trevor was a more advanced Puritan than Myddelton, as appears in his membership of the Propagation Commission (which Myddelton opposed) and his later protection of local Dissenters under the lash of the Clarendon Code. Although heir to a far older Denbighshire family than Myddelton's, he too had been brought up in London and (unlike Myddelton) generally lived there; but the Commonwealth governments found him a useful *liaison* with the North Wales counties at times when the zeal of the ex-Roundhead general was cooling off. He too brought to the committee his steward, John Peck, a younger son of a Yorkshire county family who had come into the district (apparently as tenant on the Chirk Castle estate) shortly before the war, but who soon won his way into the ranks of the local magistrates and sequestrators and even on to the Propagation Commission (though at this stage he was inclined to boggle at the parliamentary oath), founding a new family of Peck of Cornish Hall which kept its place in county society after the Restoration.[1] The Wrexham Puritans, many of whom had fought with Myddelton and now attached themselves to Morgan Llwyd, were well represented, notably by John Jones of Maes y garnedd (a local man by marriage only) and Robert Sontley of Sontley, who came of an old bardic family now enriched with lands forfeited by their distant kinsman Edwards of Chirkland when he refused the oath of allegiance imposed on Catholics after Gunpowder Plot; this and a personal quarrel with the church authorities turned him towards the more uncompromising wing of Puritanism, though his private life was apparently anything but puritanical. The grandson of a sheriff, he had himself been considered for the office before the war, and filled it as soon as Myddelton and Mytton had subdued the land; in these campaigns his kinsman Roger (grandson of an aggressively Protestant vicar

---

[1] Palmer, *Older Nonconformity of Wrexham*, pp. 8–9, *Gresford*, pp. 105–7, *Holt*, pp. 159–63; *C.C.C.*, i. 592; Thurloe, iv. 277; *C.S.P.D.*, 1649–50, p. 42; N.L.W. MS. 1595 E, fos. 123, 151, Chirk Castle MS. E. 6087.

of Wrexham) had served as captain from the first successful invasion; and the pair continued to play important parts in the civil, military and ecclesiastical government of the area throughout the interregnum[1]

Myddelton's attempt to win the adhesion of his non-Puritan neighbours had only a limited success; a letter from Kyffin to his master later in the year shows many of them sharing Peck's scruples about the oath and waiting for each other to make the first move.[2] A surprising recruit to the Denbighshire committee was Owen Salusbury of Rûg, son of the gallant defender of Denbigh castle for the King, but primarily a Merioneth landlord; it also included Owen Thelwall, a younger son of the loyal house of Plas y ward, whose mother was a Vaughan of Llwydiarth,[3] Owen Brereton of Borras (of distinguished lineage but indeterminate politics) and John Edisbury of Marchwiel, an ex-commissioner of array who had recently become steward of Myddelton's lordship of Chirk.[4] Less surprising is the inclusion of Sir Robert Needham of Pool Park, Ruthin, whose father (younger son of a Shropshire house with an Irish peerage, and grandson of a vice-president at Ludlow) had acquired the estate by marriage, and whose parliamentary sympathies appear in his election during the war to replace the Royalist M.P. for Haverfordwest, on the recommendation of Laugharne himself.[5] Altogether about half the Denbighshire committee was drawn from families of the grade of M.P. or sheriff.

Much the same proportion of the upper gentry was to be found in the Flintshire committee. Sir John Trevor and his son were there by virtue of the Flintshire property on which they normally lived when they visited Wales; their colleagues were drawn from a wide range of county society and political

---

[1] *C.S.P.D.*, 1611–18, p. 191, 1625–49 (Addenda), p. 661; H.L. MS. EL. 7161; Richards, *P.M.*, p. 190 *n.*, *Cymru a'r Uchel Gomisiwn*, pp. 51–3; *Camb. Quart. Mag.*, i. 72; Lloyd, *Powys Fadog*, ii. 140–8, iii. 136, 155.

[2] Chirk Castle MSS., *loc. cit.*

[3] Griffith, *Pedigrees*, pp. 59, 274.

[4] Palmer, *Old Parish of Wrexham*, pp. 227–8. The houses of Plas y ward and Borras were both in the anti-Llewenny faction after the Restoration, though the former had been an ally in Elizabeth's day (*infra.*, pp. 205, 215).

[5] Williams, *P.H.*, p. 167; Burke, *Peerage*, pp. 1122–3; *M.C.*, ix. 104, xiv; N.L.W., Haverfordwest MS. 246.

colour. They included the ex-Royalist head of the ancient
house of Salusbury of Bachegraig;[1] Roger Hanmer of Gredington, representing a junior branch of an illustrious but temporising family, who was himself now ready to accept parliamentary nomination as sheriff,[2] his neighbour Thomas
Dymock of Willington, whose family had given the county
three sheriffs since Mary's reign, and whose house had been
garrisoned for parliament;[3] Ralph Hughes of Dyserth, a ship-
money sheriff;[4] and Thomas Ravenscroft of Hawarden, an old
parliamentary hand who had served the King in arms but
deserted him on the first Roundhead invasion.[5] Perhaps the
only enthusiastic supporter of the cause among them, apart
from Trevor, was the small squire Luke Lloyd of Bryn, who
had commanded the garrison at Willington and ultimately sat
on the Propagation Commission, remaining a staunch Puritan
even after the Restoration, which he supported.[6] Most of
these came from a limited area in English Flintshire and many
were closely bound by ties of kindred; it was they who provided most of the county's sheriffs during the interregnum.

The early conquest of Montgomeryshire had given time for
building up a substantial body of parliamentary supporters
whose proven zeal gave a solid foundation to the local committees. Sir John Price was still distrusted, but the military
services of Vaughan of Llwydiarth could not be ignored, whatever his coolness towards the dominant Puritanism; and among
the sons of minor county families whose political sympathies
qualified them for membership were John Price of Parke,
Gabriel Wynn of Dolarddyn (whose claims on the estate of
a wealthier Royalist neighbour gave him a personal stake in
the victory of the other side), and Matthew Morgan of
Aberhafesp, descended from four sheriffs and himself an early
choice of parliament for the same office when it had the
choosing. All these were among the first to rally to Myddelton

---

[1] *A.C.*, I. i. 328. He seems to have been fully in the confidence of the
Godly party (Thurloe, v. 491).
[2] Thurloe, iv. 277, 319.
[3] *C.S.P.D.*, 1644–5, p. 182.
[4] *T.C.S.*, 1948, pp. 38–9.
[5] Williams, *P.H.*, pp. 85–6, 92, 134; Carte, *Original Letters*, i. 31–2.
[6] Richards, *R.D.*, p. 128.

in September, 1644. The inclusion of Charles Lloyd o Dolobran may have been due to his blood relationship to the Vaughans of Llwydiarth, but the Quakerism of the following generations, who were to give lustre to the name on both sides of the Atlantic, suggests the direction in which the family sympathies probably lay.[1]

For the preaching of Vavasour Powell was now beginning to leaven the lower reaches of county society, enabling parliament to add to its local agents a few men of strong Puritan convictions. Foremost among these must be placed Richard Price of Gunley, who had fought since 1645 as a Roundhead officer and served on the local committee of accounts at the end of the war. A steadfast disciple of Powell, he became in turn a commissioner for the Propagation of the Gospel, a parliamentary sheriff and one of the six Welsh members of the Parliament of Saints.[2] Three of his fellow-Propagationists —Rice Vaughan of Gelligoch (Machynlleth), Evan Lloyd of Llanwnog and Edward Owen—were with him on the committee of 1647; Vaughan was a jurist of some note who had helped to organise the West Wales Association of 1644 and reaped his reward as registrar to the central body of sequestrators in London and ultimately as an assistant Welsh judge, but failed to secure election for Merioneth in the first Protectorate parliament; Lloyd was also an old Roundhead captain, of old family but small estate, who became sheriff after the King's execution and remained an active magistrate throughout the interregnum; about Owen little is known.[3] To strengthen this wing two Puritans were imported from Shropshire: Rowland Hunt and Thomas Nicholl, both active Roundheads and Presbyterians in their own county and both inheritors of land in Montgomeryshire through descent from the old local family of Heylyn (indeed Alderman Rowland Heylyn, joint producer with Sir Thomas Myddelton's father of the *Beibl coron* of

[1] *Camb. Quart. Mag.*, i. 62; *N.L.W.J.*, vi. 256; *M.C.*, ix. 104, xiv. 390.
[2] *M.C.*, xxvii. 175–81; Richards, *R.D.*, p. 178, *P.M.*, pp. 39, 90, 96; *C.S.P.D.*, 1645–7, p. 156; N.L.W., Rhual MSS., deed 143, Carreglwyd MS. iii. 143; *Camb. Quart. Mag.*, i. 73.
[3] *C.S.P.D.*, 1653–4, p. 34, 1659–60, p. 12; Williams, *Welsh Judges*, pp. 101–3; Lloyd, *Sheriffs of Montgomeryshire*, pp. 517–21; *C.S.P.D.*, 1654, pp. 299–30.

1630, was their common grandfather), by virtue of which both served as sheriffs of Montgomeryshire—Nicholl just before, and Hunt just after the war.[1] The Hunt family continued to befriend Welsh Puritanism long after the Restoration, providing trustees for the Presbyterian chapel at Wrexham and employing as chaplain its first settled minister before he was called to the pastorate.[2] But the Montgomeryshire committee as a whole was of rather lower social standing than those for the two neighbouring counties, almost a sixth of its members being below the grade of esquire.

Caernarvonshire, as we have seen, was the only county of Gwynedd with a Roundhead nucleus. The three " ill-affected " spirits who had been arrested when war broke out were still regarded as parliament's only firm friends in the county even after their enforced desertion of its cause.[3] But when Archbishop Williams abandoned the King in 1646 there was a general stampede in the same direction;[4] in consequence the local committee included a high proportion of old commissioners of array, and half its members came of old parliamentary families. Glynne was accompanied by his brother Edmund and Bodwrda by his son Griffith—the one destined to retain a tepid Puritanism after the Restoration, the other to identify himself closely with the Cromwellian *régime* but to secure his retreat with cynical dexterity when it fell.[5] Griffith Jones and his son-in-law Sir William Williams of Vaynol (who had an old family quarrel with the episcopate) may well have found the parliamentary committee more congenial than the royal commission of array; the accommodating Wynns of Gwydir supplied it with three members, two of whom had been named commissioners of array, though they seem to have shown their usual skill in taking avoiding action;[6] and Richard Anwyl of Penmachno represented a younger branch of the Merioneth Anwyls. William Foxwist, the only other important member, was a lawyer of Yorkshire

[1] *M.C.*, xxvii. 156–9, 165–73.
[2] Palmer, *Older Nonconformity*, pp. 55 *n.*, 58.
[3] *C.W.P.*, 1811.
[4] *A Bloody Flight at Blackwater*, 15 June, 1646, pp. 2–5.
[5] *T.C.S.*, 1948, pp. 69–70; *B.B.C.S.*, xiv. 44.
[6] *C.W.P.*, 1720, 1764, 1811A, 2099.

extraction who became a Welsh judge and M.P. under Cromwell.[1]

Despite the absence of a parliamentary party in Anglesey, the fact that on Caernarvon's surrender the island had made its submission without fighting made it possible to include on the committee most of the old commissioners of array except Bulkeley and Cheadle. This meant that civil government on the island was still in the hands of the middle range of gentry (mostly clients of the Bulkeleys) who had normally given it its sheriffs; they included the interrelated families of Owen of Bodeon, Wood of Rhosmor, Bold of Tre'rddol and Lloyd of Lligwy (with fortunes ranging from £500 to £700 a year), Griffith of Carreglwyd, Holland of Berw, Meyrick of Bodorgan, and the sadly shrunken Tudors—now styling themselves Theodore—of Penmynydd (with £200 to £400 each), as well as Bagenall of Plas Newydd, who could have bought them all up, but from sources of wealth outside Wales.[2] It was among these families that parliament had chosen deputy lieutenants for the island on its surrender,[3] and they continued to provide its sheriffs during the interregnum. Merioneth was equally at a loss for local Roundheads—excepting of course John Jones, who was naturally put on this first county committee; but here too some of the ruling gentry were ready to sink political differences and to co-operate with the new ruling powers. Salusbury of Rûg was thus kept in countenance by Robert Anwyl of Park, head of the principal clan of the county (with an income of £1,000 a year),[4] who diverged from the principles of his brother-in-law Owen of Clenennau to the extent of serving as sheriff even after the King's execution. The committee also included Howel Vaughan of Glan y llyn—one of John Jones's canvassers in the by-election of that year—who ranked among the smaller gentry, but through his son's inheritance of Llwydiarth became an ancestor of one of Wales's great political dynasties, the Wynns of Wynnstay.[5] Edmund Meyrick of Ucheldre was another member[6] and so in all

[1] Williams, *P.H.*, p. 4.
[2] H.L. MS. EL 7155.
[3] *L.J.*, viii. 748.
[4] H.L. MS. EL. 7150.
[5] Griffith, *Pedigrees*, p. 253; *A.C.*, VI. iv. 319.
[6] Brogyntyn MS. 3059; *Journ. Merioneth Hist. Soc.*, i. 134.

probability was John Vaughan of Caer Gai whose father (the poet, translator and pre-war sheriff) had suffered so heavily in the cause of throne and altar.[1]

Parliamentarians were also at a discount among the county families of Cardigan and Carmarthen, Brecknock and Radnor. The weightiest name on the Cardiganshire list is that of Sir Richard Pryse of Gogerddan, who for the past twelve months had represented his county in parliament in place of the expelled Royalist member; his political views may have been influenced by his marriage into the Myddelton family, as his son's were by his marriage to the daughter of the Cromwellian Bulstrode Whitelock.[2] His cousin and fellow-committeeman James Lewis of Abernant Bychan had sat in five parliaments and fought for the King till he was captured and changed sides, when he helped parliament to gain one of its decisive victories in West Wales, and served as local sequestrator, but without living down the suspicion that his sympathies were still with the side he had deserted. To the same family group belonged a third member, Thomas Wogan, who had entered parliament for the borough at the same time as Pryse was elected for the county, but unlike him stayed on to try the King.[3] The nucleus of the Carmarthenshire committee consisted of ex-Cavaliers (including most of the governing families) who had negotiated the surrender of the county in October, 1645. The Earl of Carbery, having commanded for the King in the whole area, was too deeply compromised, but his cousin Sir Edward Vaughan of Tor y coed was included, in company with Sir

---

[1] The name is given in 1647–9 as "John Vaughan of Trowfoot" obviously a misreading of "Trawscoed", but pretty certainly not the Cardiganshire Trawscoed, whose owner was still unco-operative. In 1657 the name appears in the same context as "Trawscoed"; but from April, 1649 to Dec., 1652 the place of "John Vaughan of Trowfoot" is taken by "John Vaughan of Caergay". May it not be that the poet's son was temporarily living at the farmstead of Trawscoed (under three miles from Caer Gai) while the family mansion was being repaired after the Roundhead sack of September, 1645 (Phillips, *C.W.*, i. 342)? Local tradition (I am informed by my friend Mr. Thomas Roberts of the Normal College, Bangor) points to a different farm as the temporary refuge of the family. See also Griffith, *Pedigrees*, pp. 217, 241.

[2] *Cf.* Thurloe, v. 112.

[3] Williams, *P.H.*, pp. 28–9; *C.C.A.M.*, ii. 1020; *Cambrian Register*, 1795, p. 166.

Rice Rudd of Aberglasney (who was linked by marriage with the dominant Cardiganshire group) and the two Gwynnes, Rowland of Taliaris and Howell of Glanbran, both of old families with a standing in the county out of proportion to their income level of £200 to £400 a year; the one connected by marriage with Carbery himself, the other with Windham of Dunraven in Glamorgan. Howell Gwynne's classic outburst, "Heigh god, heigh devil I will be for the strongest side" is probably an adequate summary of the politics of this group.[1] Yet little as they might be trusted, parliament had to use them if its committee was to have any local weight; as it was, more than two thirds of the members were men of no standing in county affairs.

The position in Brecknock and Radnor was somewhat different inasmuch as neither county had seen any fighting to speak of. The one military incident in Radnorshire had been the capture of Abbey Cwmhir by Myddelton's forces in 1644. Its defender, Richard Fowler, came of a Staffordshire family whose purchase of the property made him (by repute) the county's only " squire of five hundred a year "; his name headed the new county committee, and he later accepted nomination as sheriff under Cromwell.[2] Another co-operator among the principal gentry was Henry Williams of Caebalfa, who had already served as county treasurer and was later to become commissioner of militia and of sequestration and knight of the shire in Protectorate parliaments; he may also have been one of the two members of that name on the Propagation commission.[3] The only other substantial members came from

[1] *Major General Laughorns Letter*, 28 Oct., 1645; *The Earle of Carberyes Pedegree*, 1646, p. 4; *C.C.C.*, iii. 1826–7; *C.C.A.M.*, i. 212; *C.S.P.D.*, 1645–7, p. 455; H.L. MS. EL. 7218; *W.W.H.T.*, i. 73–5. I assume that the Rowland Gwynne described as of Taliaris in the committee of March, 1659, is identical with the Rowland Gwynne *sans phrase* of earlier committees; but Howell Gwynne also had a son Rowland, who became sheriff in 1660.

[2] Williams, *Radnorshire*, 1905 ed., p. 267; Rhys and Brynmor Jones, *Welsh People*, p. 450.

[3] Identification is again uncertain: the sequestrator was certainly of Caebalfa; one of the Propagation commissioners and the county committeeman may have been his namesake of Ysgafell, who was Vavasour Powell's right-hand man and suffered imprisonment in the cause at the Restoration. (Richards, *R.D.*, pp. 228, 293; *C.C.C.*, i. 636; Williams, *P.H.*, p. 173; Radnorshire treasurer's accts. in S.P. 28/251 (Wales)). On his unsuccessful candidature for Brecknockshire, 1654, see *C.S.P.D.*, 1654, pp. 271–2.

Herefordshire: Sir Robert Harley of Brampton Bryan, quon-
dam patron of the early Welsh Puritans, whose son had just
been elected to parliament for New Radnor in place of the
extruded Royalist member, and Edward Broughton of Kington,
who had been offered a parliamentary commission at the very
beginning of the war. But the committee included one zealous
Puritan from among the smaller local squires in John Williams,
a captain of militia who had been busy in county affairs on
parliament's behalf since the war ended and became an
assiduous field preacher (in close association with Vavasour
Powell), eminent enough among his brethren to be chosen
not only as sheriff and sequestrator in his county and Propagation Commissioner for Wales, but to sit in the Saints' Parliament and on Cromwell's first Council of State.[1]

The Brecknockshire committee revolved round Sir William
Lewis of Llangorse, whose grandfather had made a fortune as
mercer in Brecon, and who had himself served two turns as
sheriff of his county. He lived mainly near London and sat
for an English constituency in parliament, where his son had
just been returned for Brecon. As a leading light of the Presbyterian moderates in the House, he was able to exert a decisive
influence over the composition of his county committee, which
included his own brother (the county treasurer), two *protégés*
of his (Edward Rumsey and Charles Walbeof) belonging to
old but not pre-eminent county families, and Howell Gwynne
from Carmarthenshire, together with two members of the
Elizabethan parliamentary family of Games, which had since
declined in importance. The whole management of county
affairs was believed to be in the hands of this group under
Lewis's direction, whether as magistrates or as sequestrators,
and another kinsman of his was solicitor for sequestration.
They were assailed with the familiar charges of peculation
and underhand Royalist activities, but Rumsey at least maintained that he had always been a champion of parliament and
had suffered in its cause.[2]

[1] Williams, *P.H.*, pp. 4,179; H.M.C., *Portland*, iii. 100; *C.C.C.*, v. 3301;
S.P. 28/251 (Wales), Radnorshire, 17 Mar., 31 July, 1646; Richards,
R.D., pp. 178, 208, 233.

[2] Williams, *P.H.*, pp. 17, 23; *A Particular Charge or Impeachment in the
name of . . . the Army . . . against . . . Sir W. Lewis, . . .* 1647, pp. 5, 10, 12;
C.C.C., i. 577–8; *C.C.A.M.*, i. 77, ii. 1100; H.M.C., *6th R.*, p. 165.

It appears from all this that the immediate effect of the Civil War was to widen the social basis of Welsh political life rather than to bring about any revolutionary shift in its centre of gravity. Although many honoured names disappeared for a time from public affairs, about a quarter of the members of the first parliamentary committees were men who would in any case have taken the lead in county politics; what was new was the size of the committees, which inevitably brought in a lower social stratum. Parliament was obviously unsure of the authority that some of its Welsh committees would be able to wield, and wherever possible it added a stiffening of trusty and influential outsiders with some sort of local connection. Thomas Mytton, the Shropshire leader who had completed the parliamentary conquest of North Wales, was included in the committees not only for Montgomeryshire (where his family had ancient connections) but also for Anglesey, Flint and Merioneth, while the Recorder of London, John Glynne, a leading light among parliamentary lawyers ever since the Strafford trial and now a prominent member of the Presbyterian group in the Commons, was elected to join his elder brother Thomas on the Caernarvon and Anglesey committees. The Montgomeryshire lists were repeatedly headed by the name of Sir John Wittewronge, an Essex knight (of Flemish descent) who by marriage into the Myddelton family had acquired the manor of Talerddig, on the strength of which he became sheriff of the county after the Restoration.[1] Wittewronge's numerous London committees must have kept him too busy to pay much attention to Montgomeryshire affairs; and the same may be said of Robert Coytmor of Coetmor—secretary to the Earl of Warwick (commanding the parliamentary fleet) and later to the Commonwealth's Admiralty committee, as well as a speculator in Flintshire lead mines—who was included in the Caernarvonshire list as younger son of a local family and brother-in-law to Lord Bulkeley.[2]

In South Wales Arthur Annesley, the future Earl of Anglesey,

[1] *M.C.*, xxvii. 342–7, xxxii. 69.
[2] Griffith, *Pedigrees*, pp. 42, 277; *C.S.P.D.*, 1644–5, pp. 221, 615, 1649–50, p. 36; Rhual MSS., deed 304; *C.W.P.*, 774. He corresponded with John Jones in Ireland in 1651 (N.L.W. MS. 11440 D, fo. 9).

was added to the committees for Carmarthen and Pembroke; he was the son of the Lord Mountnorris who had quarrelled so bitterly with Strafford in Ireland, and who on the strength of his marriage with a daughter of the house of Picton had snatched the representation of Carmarthen borough from Vaughan of Derwydd in Charles I's first parliament. The son was in turn elected to take the place of Price of Pilleth as member for Radnorshire just before his inclusion in the county committee, and he later returned to his father's old seat of Carmarthen in the Convention Parliament. His sympathies were no doubt influenced by his mother's Puritanism as well as his father's Irish experiences; he employed a Presbyterian chaplain and his sister continued to frequent Presbyterian worship under Charles II.[1] The Glamorgan committee was strengthened by two outside appointments. The first was that of Algernon Sidney, the republican " martyr " of 1686, whose father the Earl of Leicester (son of Sir Henry Sidney, the Elizabethan President of Wales) had married a Glamorgan heiress and represented the county in two of Elizabeth's parliaments, while Algernon himself a few weeks after his election to the county committee was returned for Cardiff in parliament to replace the elder Herbert of Cogan.[2] The other, Walter Strickland, was the Long Parliament's agent with the Dutch and became a prominent public figure under the Protectorate; his Glamorgan connection arose from his marriage with the heiress of Sir Charles Morgan of Pencarn, born to that adventurous warrior's Dutch wife while Sir Charles was on service in Holland, and subsequently naturalised.[3] These names, of course, must have been added for moral effect rather than with a view to adding to the working strength of the committees.

Even the limited success attained by parliament in expanding its war-time local machinery into something more representative of county society was short-lived, for the growing republicanism of the army, which split the ranks of the victors, made any hope of reconciliation with the vanquished slenderer

[1] Williams, *P.H.*, pp. 52–3, 173; H.M.C., *11th R.*, vii. 15.
[2] Williams, *P.H.*, pp. 96, 106.
[3] *D.N.B.*, lv. 54; *T.C.S.*, 1945, p. 17; Thurloe, iv. 17; *supra*, p. 36.

than ever. A week before parliament elected its county assessment committees for 1647 the army had drawn up articles of impeachment against eleven Presbyterian M.P.'s, including Sir Robert Harley's son Edward (the first parliamentary governor of Monmouth), Sir William Lewis and John Glynne, who were working for accommodation with the King and disbandment of the army. Among the charges against Lewis and Glynne was that of helping Welsh delinquents to evade the law; and indications are not wanting that for such as could afford a fat fee Glynne was a valuable friend at court, though without it there was little hope of a " favourable countenance, ... much lesse a Courtesie ".[1] The impeachment never materialised, but most of the eleven thought it wiser to withdraw from the House, and the rest (including Glynne) were expelled. When therefore another batch of county assessment committees was elected in February, 1648 (to raise money for the Irish war), Glynne's name was missing from the Caernarvonshire and Anglesey lists and Lewis's from that for Brecknockshire. Apart from prestige, the omissions can have had little more effect than the addition to the Flintshire list of the name of John Puleston of Emral, the future Commonwealth judge, who was obviously too busy with legal ploys for parliament to be an effective member.

Apart from these minor changes, the Welsh committees remained substantially unaltered until after the second Civil War. Sir Robert Harley still sat on the Radnorshire committee in spite of the charges against his son, and if Lewis was left out in Brecknockshire, two of the ex-Royalists whom he was accused of favouring were actually added to the committee for Radnorshire. With them came Robert Martin, a Cornishman who had commanded the county forces for parliament in the closing stages of the war and was put on the county bench soon afterwards, only to disappear from local affairs from the King's execution till the eve of the Restoration.[2] In Pembrokeshire the main difference lay in the admission, with the three

---

[1] U.C.N.W. Library, Baron Hill MS. 5386; N.L.W., Llanfair and Brynodol MSS., bundle 94, Ellis Lloyd to Richard Griffith, 15 May, 1646.

[2] *C.S.P.D.*, 1645–7, pp. 199, 440, 496; S.P. 28/251 (Wales), Radnorshire, 19 Apr., 15 Oct., 1647.

notorious Lorts, of two Perrot brothers—deserters from the
royal cause since 1644—whose violent quarrel with John Poyer
had landed them in prison in 1647 and was to be a powerful
factor in precipitating the second Civil War in Pembrokeshire.[1]
The agitation in Glamorgan, which developed under Judge
Jenkins's inspiration into an attempt to use the anti-republican
section of the army to rescue the King from the extremists,
had missed fire as badly as the more peaceful efforts towards
the same end at Westminster, without affecting the *personnel*
of local administration; for although the agitators were often
drawn from the same family groups—Stradling and Bassett,
Seys and Walter—the committees as a whole held aloof.[2]
But the spring and summer of 1648 brought more significant
changes. The extension of the Pembrokeshire committee to
include Poyer's bitterest enemies was a symptom of that
closing of the net around him which drove him to desperate
courses, until he had rallied to his cause not only waverers
from his own county and the Glamorgan malcontents, but
Laugharne himself, now commanding for parliament in the
whole area, and with him a host of hitherto trusty Roundheads.
The victory of St. Fagans in May restored parliamentary
authority in south-eastern Wales, and a few days later a new
Ordinance regulating the militia for the counties of Gloucester,
Monmouth, Brecknock and Glamorgan set up county committees which showed only slight variations from those of the
preceding February, the names having evidently been chosen
before the backsliders had fully revealed themselves.[3]

By this time the flame had spread to North Wales; it was
extinguished in Caernarvonshire in June, and although it
flared up still later in Anglesey, Cromwell's victory of Preston
had meanwhile deprived it of all chance of being fed from
outside. It was in August, shortly after this victory, that

[1] *A. & O.*, i. 1072; Leach, *Civil War in Pembrokeshire*, pp. 125–7; *C.C.A.M.*,
ii. 1019–20.

[2] A possible exception is the John Walter who signed several of the letters
from the disaffected gentry to Laugharne (*A full Relation of the whole Proceedings* . . . , 2 July, 1647, pp. 6–7), if he is identical with the John Walter
who was elected to the Monmouthshire assessment committees of June,
1647 and Feb., 1648, and the South Wales militia committee of May,
1648—which seems unlikely.

[3] *A. & O.*, i. 1136.

parliament grouped the North Wales counties (excepting the still unsubdued Anglesey) into an Association after the pattern of the West Wales Association of 1644, with a committee in each county to organise defences. In the choice of these bodies military experience and stout partisanship were bound to count for more than social prestige. Thomas Mytton, as area commander-in-chief for parliament, added Caernarvonshire to his civilian sphere of influence, and was joined by his active lieutenant John Jones both here and in Montgomeryshire. Colonels Carter and Twisleton, governors of Conway and Denbigh, had almost as wide a sway; they were English officers in Myddelton's army, and although they acquired a more permanent footing in Welsh county society by marriage and by the acquisition of land, it was as victorious soldiers that they ruled in their adopted land now and during most of the interregnum. To the same category belongs Thomas Mason, governor of Ruthin, but his influence was less widespread and his status less enduring. So too in Montgomeryshire it was the military virtues of Hugh Price of Gwern y go (Llanwnog)—probably brother of Lewis Price the county sequestrator—that gave him his seat on the county committee, as they had already raised him from the humble bailiff of Llanidloes hundred (with a small estate but a long pedigree) to the powerful governor of Powis castle; eight years later he was to represent his county in Cromwell's second parliament.[1] Lloyd Pierce had now sunk his feud with Vaughan of Llwydiarth sufficiently to help him in rallying the county against the Royalist *coup* and to join him on the county committee; the next few years saw him serving as commissioner of militia and a second term as sheriff.[2] These three, with Gabriel Wynn, Edward Owen and Lloyd of Dolobran, Matthew Morgan as sheriff, George Devereux as borough member, and the Puritan preachers Ambrose Mostyn and Vavasour Powell, had been chief promotors of the county's declaration of loyalty to parliament in May.[3]

---

[1] *M.C.*, xxvii. 186–8; Williams, *P.H.*, p. 144.
[2] Phillips, *C.W.*, ii. 373–4; Rees, *Studies in Welsh History*, p. 109; S.P. 28/251 (Wales), Montgomeryshire, 3 June, 1651.
[3] Phillips, *C.W.*, ii. 370–2.

Although the Royalist revolt in North Wales, unlike its southern counterpart, had been limited to a relatively small group of irreconcilable Royalists, all who had not actively identified themselves with the victors lay under suspicion of having " privately countenanced " it—especially in the shires of Gwynedd, which had evaded committing themselves to declarations of loyalty to parliament like those that came from Powys.[1] Apart from a strengthening of the military element, therefore, the new committees were marked by a retreat of the older county families. In Denbighshire the names of Needham of Pool Park, Brereton of Borras and Edisbury of Marchwiel are among those we miss, in Flintshire those of Salusbury of Bachegraig and Hughes of Dyserth. In Caernarvonshire the most serious loss is that of the three original Roundheads, Glynne and Bodwrda having died before the revolt reached a head and Lloyd of wounds received in action;[2] but the houses of Glynllifon and Bodwrda were still represented, and Recorder Glynne, now restored to his seat in the House and raised to the rank of serjeant, was put in as makeweight. Merioneth lost the services of Anwyl of Park and Meyrick of Ucheldre, but (somewhat surprisingly) gained that of the head of the house of Nannau, who had been declared a delinquent by the Commons on the eve of war and whose uncle had helped to resist the Roundhead invasion of 1645.[3] The Montgomeryshire committee was reduced by more than a quarter, but the reduction did not entail the disappearance of any important names. Over the five counties, however, there was a net loss of about a dozen representatives of the older ruling families.

Defections were more serious in South Wales, where more of the major gentry who had identified themselves, early or late, with the parliamentary cause were involved in the revolt. It was not until the end of the year, nearly five months after the final rounding-up of the insurgents at Pembroke, that parliament,

[1] C.W.P., 1811; Rees, loc. cit.

[2] C.W.P., loc. cit. The date of the document (calendared " ?1646 ") is obviously some time in 1648 before the Roundhead victory of 5 June. Although news of Lloyd's death reached the Commons within a few days his name was left on the committee list. Cf. Camb. Quart. Mag., i. 69.

[3] C.J., ii. 689; Camb. Quart. Mag., i. 65; Griffith, Pedigrees, p. 200.

in one of the last Ordinances it passed before the elements hostile to the King's trial had been "purged" by Colonel Pride, undertook the reorganisation of the militia in all Wales except Anglesey and the three south-eastern counties already dealt with in May.[1] The composition of the Pembrokeshire committee shows what a blow the revolt had dealt to the hope of reconciling Welsh county opinion with the new *régime*. Almost all the members of previous committees with any experience in public affairs had been in some way involved, from the Laugharnes, Cuneys, Rice Powell and Arthur Owen, who had never wavered in their parliamentary principles during the first war, down to such recent and unreliable converts from rabid Royalism as the Lorts.[2] Accordingly only five undistinguished names survive from over thirty in the last committee, and to these are added three (equally obscure) from Pembrokeshire itself and two of greater eminence from Cardiganshire: Thomas Wogan, M.P., and James Phillips of Tregibby, husband of the poetess (" the matchless Orinda "), who, after a chequered career in the war identified himself with the winning cause to the extent of sitting on the Propagation Commission, the High Court of Justice of 1651, and in Cromwell's parliaments and army committees—though contemporaries saw in him more of the administrator than the partisan.[3]

It was a strange reversal of the wheel of fortune when Pembrokeshire, after maintaining the parliamentary cause single-handed in West Wales for most of the first war, had to be brought back to the fold by the new-born zeal of its neighbours; but in the second war the Earl of Carbery had deserted the King and withheld from him the powerful and pervasive influence of Golden Grove. Even so, Cardiganshire lost the services of Pryse of Gogerddan and nineteen less eminent committeemen, and had to make shift with a body less than half the size of its predecessors. Much the same is true of Carmarthenshire, but here parliament, having given *congé* to

[1] *A. & O.*, i. 1233.
[2] Leach, *Civil War in Pembrokeshire*, p. 39; *C.C.A.M.*, ii. 1020.
[3] Williams, *P.H.*, p. 30; *Cambrian Register*, 1795, p. 167; R. T. Jenkins, *Orinda*, pp. 5–10.

fifteen members of the last committee (headed by Sir Rice Rudd and Sir Edward Vaughan) thought it well to give moral support to the six nonentities who replaced them by adding the name of the Earl of Northumberland, heir to much Devereux property in the neighbourhood through his father's marriage to the daughter of the first Earl of Essex, for which reason he had been named in the Militia Ordinance of 1642 as lord lieutenant of Pembroke.[1] The Radnorshire committee was also buttressed up from outside by the addition of Arthur Annesley (already serving for two other Welsh counties), of Essex's son Viscount Hereford (whom the Lords made lord lieutenant of Monmouthshire in 1646) and of Silvanus Taylor, a city Presbyterian, with property at Tal Beddwyn in Radnorshire, who had fought for parliament. A financier rather than a politician, Taylor kept his seat on successive county committees with one slight interruption till the eve of the Restoration, and became a commissioner for the Propagation of the Gospel in Wales; but as he was also on county committees in the metropolitan area as well as an active administrator of Commonwealth finances, it is unlikely that Radnorshire—or Wales—saw much of him.[2]

The Anglesey revolt had been quelled in October, but the island remained under military rule, with no pretence at a local committee, for another seven months, in spite of a petition to the Committee of Both Kingdoms towards the end of 1648 from eleven " well-affected " islanders. The signatories were evidently not deemed weighty enough to undertake the displacement of the Royalist gentry and the religious and political reorganisation of the island for which they pleaded. The only man of substance among them was Thomas Williams of Llanfihangel Ysceifiog, and even he had never been considered for posts in county administration in pre-war days; most of the rest were nonentities or recent immigrants like the Lancashire Boultons, with one illiterate; but Williams's lawyer cousin Thomas Michael (or Michael Thomas)—one of two brothers who signed the petition—received some satisfaction

---

[1] T. Richards in *Hist. Carmarthenshire*, ii. 134; *C.J.*, ii. 426.
[2] *L.J.*, viii. 546; *A. & O.*, *passim*; S.P. 28/251 (Wales), **Radnorshire**, 31 July, 1646.

by being included in the North Wales composition committee of the following August and in the area sequestration committees that succeeded it.[1]

In the rest of North Wales the final royalist *débâcle* tended to strengthen the county committees by securing the restoration or adhesion of important families that had kept (or been kept) at arm's length while the issue was still in doubt. Salusbury of Bachegraig came back to the Flintshire committee, and was joined by Lloyd of Halghton[2] (another ex-sheriff), though to balance this the name of Roger Hanmer was omitted. Edisbury similarly returned to the Denbighshire committee, and Maurice Wynn and Simon Thelwall were added to that of Merioneth. For moral effect the name of John Glynne was also included in the latter and that of Sir Thomas Trevor (cousin to Sir John, son of the ship-money judge and auditor of the duchy of Lancaster) in the former; Trevor, whose election to the Long Parliament for Monmouth borough had been disputed and quashed, had found a seat after the war in a Cornish borough.[3] On a more exalted plane the Earl of Denbigh, having justified his nomination under the Militia Ordinance as lord lieutenant of Denbighshire and Flintshire by coming to Myddelton's aid in the border campaign of 1644, was now put on both county committees.[4]

After so considerable a purge of the less pliable elements, the King's execution led to fewer changes in Welsh local administration than might otherwise have been expected. Reference has already been made to the two committees appointed to administer the Ordinances of February and August, 1649, imposing collective fines on South and North Wales respectively for their delinquencies in the second Civil War. Ranging as they did over whole areas instead of single counties, these bodies were naturally more selective than the normal county committees, especially in the south, with its

[1] Llanfair and Brynodol MSS., bundle 94, undated draft petition of 1648; Griffith, *Pedigrees*, pp. 107, 362; *A. & O.*, ii. 207; *C.C.C.*, i. 173, 686, 689; *C.W.P.*, 1709, 1759–62, 1880, 1872, 2868.
[2] Lloyd was proposed as a trusty magistrate by the " godly " of Flintshire in 1656 (Thurloe, v. 491).
[3] Williams, *P.H.*, p. 135.
[4] *A. & O.*, i. 1233.

committee of twenty as against fifty-two for the north. Most were experienced committeemen who had shown consistent zeal for parliament; several became shining lights of the Propagation Commission and two were in the Saints' Parliament. A few of the Pembrokeshire gentry such as Roger and Sampson Lort (now active supporters of the republican government),[1] Sir Erasmus Philipps and Walter Cuney, who had been left out of the last militia committee, were now adjudged repentant enough to join in the game of fleecing their less prudent neighbours whose names appear in the Ordinance as excluded from the benefits of composition. This " black list " includes old committeemen who were prominent in the rising, a few steady Royalists who had flocked to them, and some of the West Wales weathercocks who had failed to veer round in time (like Sir Hugh Owen and Sir Rice Rudd), together with some from the south-eastern counties who had been caught out in Royalist intrigues after reconciliation to parliament. Prominent among these last were Sir Trevor Williams, his son-in-law Roger Williams of Cefnheyley, and William Morgan of Pencrûg, sheriff of Glamorgan, who had let the Royalists into Chepstow; Robert Thomas of Llanvihangel (Cowbridge), probably owes his proscription to this or some similar intrigue.[2]

The old Roundheads of North Wales had remained staunch, and so the composition committee, though so much larger than its South Wales counterpart, was more completely dominated by them. The Puritans of the Wrexham area were strongly represented, for in addition to those who had already sat on the Denbighshire county committee we find the names of two neighbouring yeomen (Daniel Lloyd of Abenbury and William Wynn of Ruabon) and a Wrexham draper (Gerald Barbour), who became active members of Morgan Llwyd's congregation, together with two other Roundhead captains, Thomas Ball and Hugh Courtney—the one a recent immigrant from Cheshire to Gresford, the other a Cornishman who came to fight and remained to govern, first as a member of the Anglesey county committee, then as one of four militia commissioners for North Wales, and finally as a member of Barebone's

[1] *C.S.P.D.*, 1649–50, pp. 39, 181–2.
[2] *A. & O.*, 11, 14.

Parliament.[1] When the Propagation Commission was appointed next year, it drew over a dozen of its members from this committee. Lloyd, who became treasurer to the local sequestrators, died during the Protectorate, but the Puritan zeal of several of his colleagues was still very much alive after the Restoration. Richard Anwyl, Roger Hanmer, Owen Salusbury and Griffith Nanney were almost the only members of the composition committee representing non-Puritan county families, but a good half of the list consists of names otherwise unknown to fame; the North Wales committee certainly went lower in the social scale for its members than that of the south.[2]

These two committees are no criterion of Welsh reactions to the King's execution; it is to the county assessment committees appointed under the Ordinance of April, 1649, that we must turn for any indication of the extent to which the leaders of county society were prepared (or permitted) to co-operate with the infant republic.[3] Obviously the disappearance of names like those of the Earls of Northumberland and Denbigh, Viscount Hereford and Arthur Annesley, has no significance for Wales; similarly the renewed non-co-operation of Recorder Glynne is an interesting incident in an aspiring Welsh lawyer's career but has little bearing on Welsh opinion or the effectiveness of the Welsh committees. As an offset to these defections Oliver Cromwell himself, in virtue of the lordships of Raglan, Chepstow and Gower allotted to him by parliament in 1648, was put on the Glamorgan committee with his son Richard. It was in Radnorshire that the most sweeping changes took place: with the omission from the list of Harley and Fowler and most of the few other representatives of the local gentry who had hitherto co-operated, the county was left with a committee of ten, none of whom except Williams of Caebalfa and the absentee Silvanus Taylor carried any weight and few with any previous experience on a county committee. There was less change in the other counties of the south-east; Glamorgan lost nobody but gained other recruits besides the

[1] Palmer, *Older Nonconformity*, pp. 6, 30–31, *Parish Church of Wrexham*, p. 131; Richards, *P.M.*, pp. 90–99; Llanfair and Brynodol MSS., bundle 94, order of 9 March, 1651; *T.H.S.L.C.*, n.s.i. (1861), pp. 235–6, 246–8.

[2] *A. & O.*, ii. 207.

[3] *Id.*, ii. 24.

Cromwells, including Edmund Gamage, an obscure scion of the eminent house of Coyty.[1] This was the only southern committee that could compare in size with those elected for the north. Most of the Monmouthshire names had already appeared in the South Wales sequestration committee earlier in the year; several acted also for Brecknockshire, now given a very small committee on which Howell Gwynne, Edward Rumsey and Edward Games were the only survivors from 1647. In West Wales similarly the Pembrokeshire committee (which partly overlapped that for Carmarthenshire) contained the old hands who had rediscovered their parliamentary principles in February and a few other representatives of the families blackballed after Poyer's revolt; Rowland Dawkins was added as military stiffening to the Carmarthenshire committee. Cardiganshire had only six members allotted to it, headed by James Lewis and James Phillips.

Anglesey was again omitted from the original lists, but a supplementary Ordinance a few weeks later gave it a committee in which Thomas Williams, the chief petitioner of 1648, was accompanied by a Boulton and three other men of no standing on the island.[2] The Merioneth committee, on the other hand, was strengthened not only by the return of Anwyl and Meyrick, but also by the addition of two important recruits from county families: William Wynn of Glyn Cywarch, and John Lloyd of Caerau, one of the three militia commissioners for his county a few years later. Robert Coytmor had gone out of public life with his patron the parliamentary admiral when republican principles began to prevail, but his brother (and Anwyl's brother-in-law) Richard now took his place in Caernarvonshire until Robert returned with the Protectorate.[3] There was a net addition of nearly a dozen names in Montgomeryshire, but the only notable ones are those of John Pugh of Mathafarn (whose elder brother had served and suffered in the royal cause) and of Charles Lloyd of Garth, a member of an old local family who had gone into business in the city and who later served county and borough successively

[1] Clark, *Limbus*, p. 396.
[2] *A. & O.*, ii. 120.
[3] Richard was possibly Robert's (and therefore Anwyl's) nephew.

in the Protectors' parliaments.[1] The few additions and subtractions in other northern counties left the position substantially unchanged; with the exception of Anglesey each had a membership of some twenty or thirty.

The county assessment committees set up towards the end of 1649 are notable for two main features: the bringing up to strength of those for Anglesey and most of the southern counties, and the addition to each list of the name of Major General Thomas Harrison, who was to become virtual dictator of Wales for the next three years through his presidency of the Propagation Commission.[2] The restoration of committee government in Anglesey was brought about by giving Thomas Williams and his humbler supporters the backing of trusty soldiers from other counties (such as Carter, Madryn and Twisleton) and of some of the local Owens, Lloyds, Bolds and Woods who had been temporarily displaced; but over a third of the new committee were strangers. The use of good party men (especially soldiers) from one county to buttress up the parliamentary cause in another—the very expedient that had helped to provoke the Glamorgan rising of 1647— is now becoming general. Richard Price of Gunley, after having his authority extended in April from Montgomeryshire to Caernarvonshire, now comes on to the Merioneth and Anglesey committees as well; Thomas Ball of Gresford is on five of the six North Wales committees; and in the south Rowland Dawkins and Philip Jones are spreading their tentacles from Glamorgan to Pembroke and Carmarthen respectively. But some counties are now able to find local support for the dominant faction, even if from a lower social stratum—as for example in Radnorshire, where at least three of Vavasour Powell's adherents are brought into the county committee: John Dauntsey of Glascwm, an elder of Vavasour's church who came of Herefordshire stock, had been active in local politics since the end of the war and became a magistrate, sequestrator and Propagationist; Richard King, associated with Dauntsey in most of these activities; and Dauntsey's

---

[1] *C.S.P.D.*, 1644–5, p. 181; *Camb. Quart. Mag.*, 1.63; Phillips, *C.W.*, ii. 219; *T.C.S.*, 1948, p. 69.
[2] *A. & O.*, ii. 285.

neighbour Peter Price, who like him became a Quaker.[1] John
Lewis of Glasgrug, author of *The Parliament explained to Wales*,
was added to the Cardiganshire committee, and David Morgan,
a burgess of Carmarthen who was making himself obnoxious
to the close corporation of the borough by his championship
of the rights of the commonalty, to that of Carmarthenshire;[2]
nothing is known of the religious or political views of John
Lloyd of Vaerdref, who was put on both committees. On the
whole, county committees were becoming less representative
of county society than of the Saints—especially the Saints in
arms—and with the duplication of membership, control was
passing into the hands a narrowing circle of partisans.

These tendencies were emphasised when in the following
month the Commission for the Propagation of the Gospel in
Wales came into being. The Commission was not organised
on a county basis; in fact, as Dr. Richards points out, in his
valuable analysis,[3] Gwynedd supplied not a single member,
and Cardigan and Carmarthen only two each, while nearly a
sixth came from the border. But most of the rest had already
served on Welsh county committees, and it was on these men
that parliament continued to rely for its hold on the Welsh
counties until the Protectorate; for whatever success it might
have in gaining support from among the unattached local
gentry, it was from the Propagation commission that the key
posts in county administration (treasurers, militia commissioners, receivers of taxes and the like) were almost invariably
filled.[4] Until it received its *coup de grâce* in 1653 the Propagation
remained the real government of Wales. Generally, of course,
commissioners were chosen from among men of approved
Puritan piety, preferably such as had attested their convictions on the battlefield; but the " conversion " of some
was of suspiciously recent date, and the contemporary jibe
about Sampson Lort—" he can pray as long as there is profitt,
no penny, no pater noster "[5]—would no doubt also fit others

[1] Duncomb, *Herefordshire*, i. 102; S.P. 28/251 (Wales), Radnorshire,
23 Oct., 1647, 16 May, 1651; Richards, *R.D.*, pp. 219, 221, 265; Thurloe,
ii. 128.
[2] Glyn Roberts in *Hist. Carm.*, ii. 17.
[3] *P.M.*, ch. vii.
[4] S.P. 28/251 (Wales), *passim*.   [5] *Camb. Reg.*, 1795, p. 165.

whose Puritanism, like the Protestantism of some of their ancestors, amounted to little more than greed for the Church's wealth.

Military infiltration into county government was again in evidence, in North Wales at least, in the committees appointed under the next Assessment Ordinance (November, 1650),[1] when the regicide Robert Duckenfield, governor of Chester (who acquired a few years later the old crown lordship of Bromfield and Yale)[2] was included in the lists for Denbighshire and Flintshire, John Jones for Caernarvonshire and Anglesey, and for the latter his friend Hugh Courtney. As some slight offset, the representation of the Denbighshire county families was increased by the inclusion of Philip Eyton of Eyton, younger son of a staunchly Royalist house and younger brother of a future Welsh judge, but apparently a Roundhead himself; while the Anglesey committee gained the support of Sir Hugh Owen of Orielton—who had considerable estates there— although he was still under a cloud for his support of Poyer and had his Pembrokeshire lands sequestered the following year.[3]

It is in South Wales that the most significant changes occur in the assessment committees appointed two years later, when the Rump was on its last legs. The most notable feature is the growing ascendancy of Philip Jones; not only does he add Brecknock, Cardigan and Pembroke to his two previous committees, but in all five counties there are extensive changes in membership in some of which his hand may be directly traced, in others readily inferred. This was his *riposte* to the attack on the Propagation Commission generally and himself in particular which had begun with the South Wales petition of March, 1652, and continued to agitate parliament till the end of 1653.[4] Jones's own county of Glamorgan, hitherto marked by a rare continuity in the structure of its local committees, now sheds five of its more experienced members, including some like Herbert of Cogan and Bassett of Broviskin, whose names had appeared in almost every list for the past five years;

[1] *A. & O.*, ii. 456.
[2] W. M. Myddleton, *Chirk Castle Accts.*, *1605–66*, p. 78 *n.*
[3] Lloyd, *Powys Fadog*, ii. 161–3; Williams, *Welsh Judges*, pp. 104–5; *C.C.C.*, i. 146, ii. 1236, iv. 2787–8.
[4] Richards, *P.M.*, ch. xvii.

they are replaced by a much larger number, but most of the
new names are obscure ones, and only one can be definitely
connected with Philip Jones.[1] The Brecknockshire list is also
swollen in size, but Walbeof and Howell Gwynne—two survivors of Sir William Lewis's ascendancy—are left out, and
among the newcomers are Philip Jones's agent Watkins and his
protégé Edmund Jones. The latter was a Glamorgan lawyer of
obscure origin who had married into the Brecknockshire family
of Games of Buckland (his father-in-law being treasurer to
the South Wales sequestrators), and after serving Charles I
on the county commission of array (and it was alleged as one
of the garrison of Raglan Castle) had courted the conquerors,
receiving as his reward first the recordership of Brecon and
the county seat in the parliament of 1654 (in face of local
protests), and later the attorney generalship of South Wales—
a post from which the leader of the attack on Philip Jones
had been dismissed.[2] Two of the new members had their
roots in Radnorshire: Richard Williams of Caebalfa, whose
father we have already met on the Radnor committee, and
John Williams, the Vavasourian preaching captain, whose
influence, like that of so many others of his kind, was now
spreading beyond his own county.

Cardiganshire lost five old committeemen and gained five
new ones, including Philip Jones himself, with Henry Vaughan
and Hector Phillips. Vaughan could be either Carbery's
cousin—son of the fiery Royalist Sir Henry and future M.P.
for Carmarthenshire—or (more probably) Vaughan of Trawscoed's brother, both were associated in popular gossip
(Roundhead in the one case, Cavalier in the other) with the
machinations of Philip Jones. Hector was James Phillips's
brother and fellow-sequestrator, treasurer to the militia since
1651 and future borough member.[3] This committee was now by

[1] Evan Lewis, a *protégé* of Price of Gellihir, who had fought for parliament
and speculated extensively in sequestered lands. He later sat on the Poor
Prisoners and Scandalous Ministers committees, as M.P. for Brecknockshire
in Cromwell's first parliament and on its assessment committees of 1657
and 1660 (Williams, *P.H.*, p. 17; Fonmon MS. 1/59).

[2] *C.C.C.*, ii. 1524; *C.S.P.D.*, 1651, p. 287; Williams, *P.H.*, pp. 16–17.

[3] Thurloe, ii. 80; *Hist. Carm.*, ii. 25, 476; Fonmon MSS. 1/55, 57;
Williams, *P.H.*, pp. 30, 38; S.P. 28/251 (Wales), Cardiganshire, 6 Aug.,
1651; *Camb. Reg.*, 1795, p. 166.

far the smallest in Wales, for its counterpart in Carmarthenshire
was brought to a level with the rest by a net increase of eight;
and Philip Jones's hand may be traced in at least four of the new
appointments, including those of the county treasurer, John
Lewis, and of the ardent Baptist Jenkin Franklyn of Carmarthen, who had come into prominence since 1650 as a threefold
commissioner—for the Cardiganshire militia, for sequestration
in South Wales, and for all Wales under the Propagation
Act.[1] The Pembrokeshire committee was also restored to
something like its strength before the Poyer revolt, but mainly
by bringing back members of old county families (such as
Wogans, Perrots and Cannons) who had then compromised
themselves but were not among the leaders; and although
Philip Jones was credited with adherents among these old
delinquents also, his influence cannot be directly traced in the
new appointments. The North Wales lists remained unchanged
excepting for Montgomeryshire's, which by the accession of
sixteen new members regained its original lead in point of
size; but the new members, except for a local Mytton, were
mostly men of humble standing (only three could style themselves " esquire "), and doubtless represented county Puritanism rather than county society. Among them were Lewis Price
the sequestrator and Thomas Lloyd of Trawscoed (Guilsfield),
younger son of the Lloyd Pierce who had twice been sheriff,
and himself a future sheriff in the days of the Major Generals;[2]
Edward Vaughan, on the other hand (whose delinquencies
were under investigation at Goldsmith's Hall) was eliminated.

The one contribution of Barebone's Parliament towards the
committee system in Wales was the appointment of small local
bodies (generally not more than five to each county) to administer its humanitarian legislation for the relief of poor prisoners.[3]
It was natural that the Parliament of Saints should look to
like-minded men to carry out its plans in the shires; well over
a third of the members had been commissioners under the
Propagation Act; these were especially numerous in the committees for the north-eastern and south-eastern counties. In

[1] Fonmon MSS., *loc. cit.*; *C.C.C.*, i. 512–3; *Hist. Carm.*, ii. 150.
[2] *M.C.*, xxvii. 189.
[3] *A. & O.*, ii. 753.

South Wales the committeemen were mainly experienced hands, but several new names appear in the north; for example Hugh Pritchard of Brymbo and Andrew Ellis of Bangor Iscoed (governor of Hawarden and a man of some consequence in virtue of his recent marriage with the daughter of the Puritan peer Lord Saye and Seele), who sat for Denbighshire and Flintshire respectively, were both men whose administrative experience had been gained on the Propagation Commission. Three out of Montgomeryshire's exceptionally high complement of six members belong to the same category: Lewis and Hugh Price of Llanwnog, those stout Vavasourians who clung to their leader even in the ensuing days of persecution, and their neighbour Thomas Lloyd.[1] Where no sufficient nucleus of eminent Puritans was to be found on the spot, as in Merioneth or Carmarthen, recourse was often had to Propagationists from other shires or to local Saints of lower social status like Robert Owen of Dolserau (Dolgelley)—already a militia commissioner for his county[2]—or Richard Boulton in Anglesey. Thomas Edwards, governor of Wrexham and the only Denbighshire member who was not an agent of the Propagation, was of Cilhendre in Salop, and up to now had served on his own county committees; but he was also a close friend of Sir Thomas Myddelton and of John Jones the regicide, whom he sheltered at his home on the eve of his trial and execution in 1660.[3] Anglesey, Cardigan and a few other counties where Puritanism was still a negligible force, made up their contingent from the usual circle of unpolitical small squires and yeomen.

The first purpose for which the county machinery in England was brought into play under the Protectorate (in August, 1654) was to complete the work of ejecting " scandalous " ministers; but in Wales this task was delegated to two area committees—a group of twenty-three for North Wales and nearly twice as many for the south (excluding Monmouthshire, which on this occasion ranked with the English counties, though Barebone's Parliament had grouped it with Wales).[4]

[1] Palmer, *Older Nonconformity*, p. 7; Richards, *P.M.*, pp. 90–91, 96; N.L.W. Plymouth deeds, 1738–43.

[2] S.P. 28/251 (Wales), Merioneth, 24 May, 1651.

[3] N.L.W., Plas Yolyn MSS.; Palmer, *Older Nonconformity*, pp. 7–8; Phillips, *C.W.*, ii. 307–8, 312–3, 332–3.

[4] *A. & O.*, ii. 968; Richards, *R.D.*, p. 268.

Just about half the members had sat on the Propagation Commission, and nearly all the rest were men whose names had appeared year after year on county committees. An important exception was Sir Hugh Owen of Orielton, who had now been allowed to compound for his delinquencies, and in view of his previous services to parliament was too important a man to be passed over, even though his " reservedness " left men unsure of his real opinions and suspicious that he was " too sparing or too prudent to bear the burthen of the affairs of his country ". He was accompanied by his brother Arthur of New Moat, a much more consistent Roundhead in the first Civil War but involved with Poyer in the second and out of office ever since.[1] It is likely that the Robert Thomas of this committee was the Glamorgan insurgent of 1647, who had been excluded with Sir Hugh from the benefits of composition in 1649 but had since been allowed to compound for his own sins by sitting in judgement, as county sequestrator, on those of his neighbours. His later appearance as a witness of Philip Jones's will and an adherent of the Country Party tend to confirm the impression that he had now thrown in his lot with the triumphant Saints.[2]

A few weeks later another committee, this time of thirty-three for all Wales, was appointed to examine the finances of the Propagation, which had been under constant fire for the last two years. Naturally the Saints themselves were less in evidence here, though Roger Lort gave one more display of " ambodexterity " by helping to investigate his brother Sampson's conduct as commissioner. The list is headed by two judges and Sir Hugh Owen; most of the rest are old committeemen. It seems likely that the commissioners had a more sympathetic hearing from the northern members than from those representing the south, the scene of the activities of Philip Jones; he might perhaps expect to receive a friendly

[1] *Camb. Reg.*, 1795, pp. 164–5; Leach, *Civil War in Pembrokeshire*, pp. 33, 39, 52, etc.

[2] *N.L.W.J.*, vi. 254; *C.C.C.*, i. 522; Williams, *P.H.*, p. 107. The name is too common for identification to be certain; for example the Robert Thomas of Tregos (Glam.) who was recommended by Bussy Mansell for the South Wales sequestration committee after Booth's rebellion of 1659 was clearly not the future baronet; but he may have been the sequestrator of 1652, and possibly (though not probably) the committee member of 1654.

judgement from Edmund Thomas of Wenvoe, his newly-elected colleague as knight of the shire for Glamorgan, but hardly from the Pembrokeshire Owens or Robert Thomas, who had been in active opposition to the rule of the armed Saints ever since the crisis of 1647–8, or from Roger Williams, who had till now been out of politics since the King's execution.[1] The North Wales contingent showed a much higher proportion of Puritans who had consistently supported the " good old cause ", including two of Morgan Llwyd's congregation and Thomas Critchley—Edwards's successor as governor of Wrexham, Duckenfield's steward of Bromfield and Yale, and deputy receiver for North Wales—who like Roger Lort had a close relative among the commissioners.[2] However this may be, the verdict in the end was favourable.[3]

The Protectorate had been established more than three years before Cromwell's second parliament elected county committees to assess the taxes voted in June, 1657, for the war with Spain.[4] These give us our first insight into Welsh reactions to the more settled *régime* brought about by the Instrument of Government. There are some striking changes. In the first place a halt is called to the military encroachments on county government which had begun under the Rump and reached their climax under the Major Generals in 1655. Mytton was dead, and the disappearance of Thomas Harrison from all the county lists and of the Cromwells from that of Glamorgan were only to be expected now that the Propagation Commission (over which Harrison presided) was gone and that Oliver ruled the land; and we may attribute to the anti-militarist reaction against the Major Generals the fact that soldiers like Dawkins in the south, Carter, Twisleton, Ball and Price of Gunley in the north, who had been taking whole groups of counties under their wings, now had to confine themselves to their own. On the other hand that " supreme Cromwellian "[5] Philip Jones now lorded it over South Wales with all the prestige of a member of the inner circle of government.

[1] Williams, *P.H.*, p. 97.
[2] Palmer, *Older Nonconformity*, pp. 4, 6; *C.W.P.*, 1932.
[3] *A. & O.*, ii. 990: Richards, *P.M.*, p. 272.
[4] *A. & O.*, ii. 1058.
[5] Richards, *R.D.*, p. 219.

These men, however, were not only soldiers but agents of the Propagation; and the subversive activities of Harrison with his coadjutors Morgan Llwyd and Vavasour Powell had made this once powerful group as obnoxious to supporters of the Protectorate as the soldiers were to its critics. It is hardly surprising that the Cheshire Propagator and military governor Robert Duckenfield should have been removed from his North Wales committees after writing to upbraid the Protector with allowing his piety to wilt under " abundance of temptation and flatteries "! He was one of some twenty old commissioners who forfeited their places on one or more county committees. John Williams and Hugh Pritchard were weeded out of Radnorshire and Denbighshire respectively as adherents of Powell and Llwyd who had signed the latter's anti-Cromwellian *Word for God*, although little more than two years had passed since both Pritchard himself and his leaders had earned the Protector's gratitude by prompt measures for scotching a Royalist attempt on Shrewsbury;[1] Hugh Courtney, Williams's colleague in the Saints' Parliament, was still more deeply involved in opposition and only just out of gaol, so he disappeared from the Anglesey list in company with his fellow-Propagationists Thomas Swift (brother-in-law of Walter Cradock and governor of Holyhead) and Thomas Mason, an intimate of Courtney's who had served on Caernarvonshire committees ever since he helped to complete the military reduction of the county.[2]

It was in the upper Severn valley, the main seat of Vavasour's influence, that these left-wing malcontents were most thickly spread—especially in Radnorshire, where he was believed to " rule the roast " from sheriff and magistrates downwards.[3] Almost a clean sweep was made of the county committee, hardly any old hands remaining except the Vavasourian Dauntsey and the easy-going Williams of Caebalfa.[4] Even Silvanus Taylor was left out (presumably for his part in the

[1] Thurloe, iii. 207, 252.
[2] *Id.*, iii. 294, i. 639; Lloyd, *Powys Fadog*, iii. 209–11; Palmer, *Parish Church of Wrexham*, pp. 74–5.
[3] Thurloe, ii. 124: Richards, *R.D.*, ch. x.
[4] Possibly his namesake of Ysgafell, but the latter's close association with Powell makes that unlikely.

Propagation), as well as Powell's disciple Peter Price, to be replaced by Robert Curtler, an early member of the Committee of Accounts, and John Yardley, a more recent magistrate and sequestration treasurer,[1] with a throng of still obscurer names and two of greater moment: Sir William Lewis (now on terms with the republic) and George Gwynne, of the ancient local family of Llanelwedd (once accomplices in the Essex plot of Elizabeth's reign), who as M.P. for his county in 1654 had helped in the enquiry into Propagation finances, and whose son was to achieve some notoriety as a Whig politician in the days of the Glorious Revolution.[2]

Montgomeryshire lost nearly a score of members, including two Propagationists (Rice Vaughan and Edward Owen), together with Lloyd Pierce, who like them had been in county politics ever since the war, and John Kynaston of Plas Kynaston, who had first appeared on the committee for Poor Prisoners in 1654 and had just completed a turn as sheriff.[3] The great majority of those now eliminated, however, were among the big batch elected in 1652; only one (John Griffith) can be definitely connected with Vavasour Powell, and even he (like many of the " richer sort " in Powell's congregation) had not signed the *Word for God*.[4] The gap was filled mainly from the old governing families. Vaughan of Llwydiarth returns to county politics after an absence (save for his perennial activities as sequestrator) of six years; Rowland Hunt, the Shropshire Presbyterian, is back for the first time since the King's execution, and Sir John Price (who had sat in the first Protectorate parliament) makes his first appearance on a county committee. Still more significant is the emergence from retirement of magnates like Lord Herbert of Cherbury and his son (reputed *protégés* of Philip Jones);[5] of George Devereux (grandfather of the ninth Viscount Hereford), who had supplanted

[1] S.P. 28/251 (Wales), Radnorshire, 23 Oct., 1647; *C.C.C.*, i. 534, 577, 587; Thurloe, ii. 128.
[2] Mathew, *Celtic Peoples and Renaissance Europe*, p. 427; Williams, *P.H.*, pp. 173-4.
[3] *M.C.*, xxvii. 190; Palmer, *Older Nonconformity*, p. 8. The main stock of the Kynastons was strongly Royalist, with a recent record of recusancy (*infra*, p. 197).
[4] Richards, *R.D.*, p. 219; Thurloe, ii. 124, 226.
[5] Fonmon MS. 1/57, appendix.

Lord Herbert as borough M.P. after the war and now represented the county in Cromwell's parliament;[1] and of a selection
from such families as Purcell and Juckes, from which the
county had traditionally drawn its sheriffs and parliamentary
representatives. The effect of left-wing disaffection on the
eastern fringes of North Wales was clearly to swing county
committees over to the right; but there were balancing elements.
James Berry, the Shropshireman who had ruled all Wales
during the era of the Major Generals, remained on the
Montgomeryshire committee in spite of all the anti-militarist
prejudice, and William Wynn of Ruabon, Dauntsey of Glascwm
and Price of Llanwnog all went on acting for their respective
counties even after they had put their names to Vavasour's
manifesto; Robert Sontley, who signed it, was replaced on the
Denbighshire committee by his kinsman Roger, a Propagationist and an adherent of Morgan Llwyd but a militia captain
of proven loyalty.[2] Indeed in the north-eastern committees
most of the experienced Puritans and Propagationists continued
to serve, with a few who had not appeared on any lists since the
composition committee of 1648, and a new recruit in John
Manley of Wrexham, a younger son of a Royalist family who
became a parliamentary major and later sheltered a conventicle
in his house in contravention of the Clarendon Code.[3] They
were reinforced, as elsewhere, by members of county families
hitherto solid for the King, such as the Wynnes of Melai and of
Voelas, not long weaned from Catholicism, and the Prices of Giler.

The purge of Propagation agents extended to the south-
eastern counties, with the result that Henry Herbert, once the
sole prop of the parliamentary cause in this area, disappears
from the county committees of Monmouth and Brecknock and
his fellow-commissioner Catchmay the lawyer from the former.
But other factors enter in here; one may perhaps detect the
hand of Philip Jones in the elimination from the Brecknockshire
list of Edward Rumsey, last survivor of Sir William Lewis's
nominees, and from Glamorgan of Edmund Gamage, a critic
of Propagation finances;[4] on the other hand it is more likely

[1] Williams, *P.H.*, p. 149; *M.C.*, xxvii. 191–214.
[2] Richards, *Uchel Gomisiwn*, p. 53, *R.D.*, p. 235.
[3] Palmer, *Older Nonconformity*, p. 3; *C.S.P.D.*, 1664–5, p. 205.
[4] Fonmon MSS. 1/57 (iii), 58.

as right-wing plotters or suspects that Robert Thomas (who had spent much of the two preceding years in durance in Cardiff castle) and Roger Oates were left out of the local committees. The rising star of the south-east is now Edmund Thomas of Wenvoe, a firm Cromwellian (though rumour accounted him anything but a " zealot ") and a member of Cromwell's "Other House".[1] He figures in the lists for both Glamorgan and Monmouth with James Berry to strengthen his hands in the latter. In West Wales some of the ex-delinquents who formed the nucleus of the first Carmarthen-shire committee are eliminated, as well as Roger Lort, who had joined them later; but Howell Gwynne returns after seven years' absence from county politics, and still more important is the accession of Sir Edward Mansell, whose family (excepting the junior branch at Britton Ferry) had been firmly loyal to the old order in church and state. Pryse, the second baronet of Goderddan, succeeds his dead father on the Cardiganshire committee, and the Pembrokeshire list includes not only the Owen brothers, but one of the Laugharnes who had been on the county committee as far back as 1646.[2] There is no sign of Philip Jones's influence here—indeed few had greater cause for hating him than the Mansells, who had been among the victims of his sequestrating zeal.[3] The general tendency in South Wales as well as along the eastern border is towards the moderating influence of the old families; but the Propaga-tion is doubly represented (in Pembroke as well as Cardigan) by James Phillips, a firm enough Cromwellian to be included in the national committee set up to watch over the personal safety of the Protector.[4]

In Gwynedd, which had no part or lot in the Propagation, the situation is different, for here the rise of new men favourable on principle to the Protectorate and its aims was beginning to undermine the preponderance of the older and more eminent families accepting it from expediency. Anglesey is a case in point. The small knot of yeomen and tradesmen who had

[1] Richards, *R.D.*, pp. 416, 420. Oates had served since Dec., 1649 (cf. *B.B.C.S.*, vi. 250).

[2] Leach, *Civil War in Pembrokeshire*, p. 103.

[3] Fonmon MS. 1/57 (vii).

[4] *A. & O.*, ii. 1040.

joined Thomas Williams in petitioning for Puritan rule in 1648, with accretions from the minor gentry like Owen of Llanfaethlu and Lewis of Cemlyn, Wynns of Llangoed and Penhesgin, now bade fair to become a counterpoise, both socially and politically, to the established families (Owens, Woods, Bolds, Lloyds, Theodores, and Porthamel Bulkeleys) to which the republican governments still resorted for sheriffs. But although the new men were not of this standing, all except Thomas Michael could put " esquire " to their names; and a far more important change in the opposite direction was the return of Baron Hill to county politics in the persons of the future Lord Bulkeley (who served as both sheriff and committeeman) and his close kinsman Rowland Whyte of Friars, brother-in-law to the Denbighshire Royalist colonel Robert Ellice, and himself of a family that had often provided the island with sheriffs.[1]

The Caernarvonshire committee is reinforced by Richard Edwards of Nanhoron and John Williams of Meillionydd—the one a steady, the other a fair-weather Puritan—and by Morris Griffith, an elder and lay preacher of Vavasour's flock; Jeffrey Parry of Rhydolion, a fellow-sequestrator with Edwards and Williams since 1652 and later reputed " a great Heaven-driver in Llyn, and a zealous maintainer of Conventicles ", would doubtless have been with them but for his support of the *Word for God*. All four, with Griffith Jones of Castellmarch, were among the score of political suspects from Lleyn and Eifionydd lodged in Caernarvon gaol soon after the Restoration.[2] At the same time two lawyers whose names had last appeared eight years ago now reappear in the character of M.P.'s and placemen of the Protectorate: William Foxwist (now a judge) and Griffith Bodwrda (who also served for Anglesey), with his elder brother the heir to the estate.[3] There are a few other new names, but none of them can be identified with the post-Restoration separatists of Lleyn, who came mostly from the labouring classes and were therefore ineligible.[4]

[1] Griffith, *Pedigrees*, pp. 38, 53, 64, 130, 194.
[2] *C.W.P.*, 1998; Richards, *R.D.*, pp. 208, 218, 228, 306; W. Gilbert Williams in *Y Genedl Gymraeg*, 5 June, 1923; *A.C.*, suppt., 1917, p. 309.
[3] Williams, *P.H.*, pp. 4, 10, *Welsh Judges*, pp. 60–61; *T.C.S.*, 1948, pp. 69–70.
[4] Bob Owen in *T.C.H.S.*, vi. 32–5; N.L.W. MS. 1564 E (ii).

Sir William Williams, a survivor of the earliest county committee and sheriff in the first year of the Protectorate, is
temporarily out of the picture, but this loss is balanced by
the accession of a Hookes of Conway, and the Wynns of Gwydir
are there in force, including (for the first time since the death
in 1649 of Sir Richard, the Long Parliament member) his
brother and successor Sir Owen, who boasted that he had
eschewed " public assemblies " since the downfall of the
monarchy, but nevertheless had proclaimed Cromwell as
Protector when he was sheriff of Caernarvonshire and had
later served in the same capacity for Denbighshire.[1]

The return of Robert Coytmor, who had just petitioned—
apparently with success—against the return of Madryn to
parliament for Caernarvonshire,[2] to his own county committee,
is doubtless due to the fact this his master the Earl of Warwick,
out of politics since the King's death, had now come back to
public life and married his grandson to the Protector's daughter.
As a counterpart to Berry in Monmouth and Montgomery,
John Glynne (now the Protector's chief justice) and Henry
Lawrence (the President of his Council) are added to that of
Caernarvon. Glynne, of course, was a native, and was included
also in those of Denbigh and Flint, where he had acquired the
Earl of Derby's estates; Lawrence, although he had no known
connection with Caernarvonshire, was now its representative
in parliament.[3] Merioneth, which only six years earlier had
been unable to provide three trustworthy commissioners to
supervise its own militia without borrowing a Sontley from
Denbighshire,[4] was also feeling the first impact of the Puritanism which Hugh Owen of Bronclydwr organised into Dissenting
congregations after 1660. This new element may well have been
represented by the five unidentified recruits to the local committee, although the only recognisable Puritan name on the
county list is that of Robert Owen of Dolserau, a county commissioner of militia since 1651.[5] Higher in the social scale the

---

[1] *C.W.P.*, 1993, 2024, 2110, 2119, 2144.
[2] *Id.*, 2131.
[3] Williams, *P.H.*, p. 61.
[4] S.P. 28/251 (Wales), Merioneth, 24 May, 1651.
[5] R. T. Jenkins, *Hanes Cynulleidfa Hen Gapel Llanuwchlyn*, p. 25; *C.W.P.*,
1998.

names of Nanney of Nannau and Vaughan of Caer Gai are no longer to be found, but there is still an Anwyl; and from Cardiganshire has been added the far more eminent name of John Vaughan of Trawscoed, the future judge and former member of the Long Parliament, emerging at last from his retirement since the parliamentary victory after making his peace with Philip Jones (if rumour is to be trusted) with the customary *douceur*.[1]

It may safely be said that the county committees of 1657 were the most representative Wales had had since the war—representative not only of the new Wales that had sprung up during the Commonwealth (and which was naturally overweighted), but also of the pre-war Wales that was being tempted back into political life by the apparent stability of the Protectorate and the slackening of the activities of the sequestrators. The small supplementary committees elected later in the same month, for four counties of the south and two of the north, to rake in the rest of the assessment, illustrate chiefly the growing authority of Philip Jones in West Wales. Seven of the eight Carmarthenshire members and two out of five from Brecknockshire—most of them old delinquents—were all commonly ascribed to his circle of dependents.[2] On the other hand the reappearance of Robert Thomas and Edmund Gamage on the Glamorgan committee, to which Sir Edward Mansell was also added, was a balancing factor in the south-east. In the north the return of the pre-war county families continues: Sir William Williams is back on the Caernarvonshire list, with Twisleton's brother-in-law Glynne of Lleuar (who was to represent the county in Richard Cromwell's parliament) and the William Griffith of Cefnamwlch who became its fiercest Puritan-hunter after the Restoration, but was now ready to serve as sheriff had he been chosen;[3] while Denbighshire includes in its quota Judge Jeffrey's father, who had been sheriff when the Major Generals were in power.[4]

[1] *T.C.S.*, 1948, p. 56; *Camb. Reg.*, 1795, p. 166.

[2] Fonmon MSS., *loc. cit.*; *C.C.C.*, i. 512–3; *C.C.A.M.*, iii. 1339. One of them, Jenkin Dawkins, was the younger brother (or nephew) of the more famous Major General, but never seems to have been more than, at most, a lukewarm supporter of Philip Jones (*C.C.C.*, i. 557, 660, 691; Clark, *Limbus*, p. 583; *Hist. Carm.*, ii. 150).

[3] Williams, *P.H.*, p. 61; *C.W.P.*, 2146; *T.C.H.S.*, xi. 37–9.

[4] *A. & O.*, ii. 1234.

Over two years passed before county committees were elected again, and by then the political wheel had made a complete turn. Oliver was dead, Richard had come and gone, Royalist hopes of an early restoration had risen high, and among those known to be plotting for it were old moderate parliamentarians as well as rabid Royalists. When Sir Thomas Myddelton, Sir Hugh Owen and Edward Vaughan (now sheriff of Denbighshire)—all of them key men in the last lot of county committees—were denounced by the government's spies at the exiled court as ready to lead an armed rising for Charles II, the faction in power had no option but to lean on the zealots who had been so extensively weeded out of local administration two years earlier, but who were ready to cooperate now that the Protectors no longer stood in the path of the rule of the Saints.[1] These conditions are reflected in the committees elected by the restored Rump in July, 1659, for the ordering of the county militias on which its effective authority must largely depend.[2] In South Wales the committees were elected on the usual county basis, though with numbers reduced by nearly a third; but the whole of North Wales was placed under a single committee less by almost two-thirds than the sum of its predecessors of 1657.

Inevitably the name of Sir Thomas Myddelton is left out of the latter, although up to the last month he had been living in quiet retirement at Chirk and another month was to pass before he was openly in arms with Booth and declared a traitor and rebel.[3] His steward Watkin Kyffin went out with him, and Flintshire lost three old members in Judge Puleston and Salusbury of Bachegraig (whose sons were believed to be engaged in the plot)[4] and Ravenscroft of Hawarden. Sir John Trevor and his steward remained, with most of the Wrexham group of Puritans—including even Hugh Pritchard, who had been excluded from the last committee. Indeed, when Booth's rebellion was scotched and the engine of sequestration brought back into gear, it was Pritchard, with Andrew Ellis, Gerald

[1] Thurloe, i. 749; Richards, *R.D.*, p. 234.
[2] *A. & O.*, ii. 1320.
[3] Myddelton, *Chirk Castle Accts., 1605–66*, p. 72; *C.S.P.D.*, 1659–60, pp. 94, 154, 170.
[4] *C.W.P.*, 2193.

Barbour and Thomas Ball, who operated it for the two north-eastern counties. In Caernarvonshire, on the other hand, Jeffrey Parry was the only representative of the new Puritans to be associated with veterans like Madryn and Twisleton in control of the militia, though Edwards of Nanhoron seems to have been added later; Cromwellian officials like Foxwist and Bodwrda, and even so old and influential a Roundhead swordsman as Carter (now flourishing a knighthood conferred by Oliver before his death) are all left out,[1] while Robert Coytmor is penalised for his patron's too great intimacy with the Protector, and takes his brother Richard with him. Price of Gunley, Vavasour's chief lieutenant in Montgomeryshire, becomes king-pin not only of his own county committee but of the whole area, for to him is entrusted control of the six-county militia after he has earned official thanks for his energetic measures against the Booth faction. There could be no ques-tion of electing so prominent a suspect as Edward Vaughan, though as it turned out he took no active part in the revolt and by September was back at his old post of sequestration commissioner, helping Price to take punitive measures against his less canny neighbours;[2] but three Puritan zealots who had been turned out in 1657 (Kynaston and the two Propaga-tionists Rice Vaughan and John Griffith) were re-admitted, and Lewis Price helped to complete the dominance of left-wing Puritanism. Owen of Dolserau stands almost alone in Merioneth, and Anglesey supplies not a single name of note, unless we count strangers like Courtney, who was back in favour and restored (through the intercession of John Jones) to his post as governor of Beaumaris, and his friend Thomas Swift; no more is heard of the small coterie of island Puritans that had collected after the second Civil War, with a conven-ticle of their own at Beaumaris.[3]

The ex-Royalists and "neuters" among the country gentry who had entered public life in such numbers at the height of Oliver's power (and even some who had dropped their opposition

---

[1] *Id.*, 2151, 2203; N.L.W. Brogyntyn MS. 2955.

[2] *C.S.P.D.*, 1659–60, pp. 93, 96, 99, 159; *C.C.C.*, i. 751, 758.

[3] *C.S.P.D.*, 1659–60, p. 28; *Arch. Camb.*, 1917 suppt., p. 300 (cf. Richards, *R.D.*, p. 158).

at an earlier stage) were mostly swept away. In the north-east this means not only new recruits like Price of Giler, Wynnes of Voelas and Melai, but old hands like Thelwalls, Salusbury and Hughes of Dyserth; in Montgomeryshire Roundheads with as long a record as Price of Parke and the Shropshire Rowland Hunt, no less than Herbert of Cherbury and other old delinquents who had tardily come to terms; Sir John Price was dead. Maurice Wynn of Gwydir is the sole survivor of the major families of Caernarvonshire. He had been sheriff of Merioneth soon after the war and was now Receiver of North Wales; as a business man with early Puritan leanings he may well have found the *régime* more congenial than did the rest of his family.[1] His nephew, the future fourth baronet (just emerging from a year's reluctant service as sheriff) had not been quite astute enough to avoid suspicion of being among Booth's Caernarvonshire adherents; he spent part of the autumn of 1659 in Carnarvon gaol and avoided sequestration only by assiduous (and no doubt costly) court-ship of Madryn, as he had previously courted Carter.[2] None of the other old families of Gwynedd remained in power.

About a third of the North Wales committee were unknown men, and not many even of the rest could style themselves " esquire ". This made outside support more necessary than ever; but neither Berry, a Cromwellian Major General, nor Lawrence, who had presided over the Protector's Council—still less Glynne, who had argued so strongly in favour of his acceptance of the crown—was congenial to the ultra-republican temper that prevailed in the Rump. One substitute was found in John Bradshaw, who had presided at the King's trial and now had joint custody of the Great Seal. A second was Sir Richard Saltonstall, a Cheshire man with property in Brymbo and in close relations with the extremer wing of the local Puritans, and a signatory of the *Word for God*.[3] The third, who had no discoverable connection with Wales, was Thomas Cooper, a London Independent who had left the counter for

[1] *C.W.P.*, 1132.

[2] *C.W.P.*, 1952, 1965, 2032, 2146, 2152, 2161, 2167, 2195, 2198–9, 2201. For another Royalist appeal to Madryn (Davies of Gwysaney) see N.L.W. MS. 1595 E, fo. 293.

[3] Palmer, *Old Parish of Wrexham*, p. 113 *n*: Richards, *R.D.*, p. 235.

a colonelcy in Cromwell's army and eventually a seat in his "Other House", but apparently without shedding his republican convictions—in this resembling John Jones, whom he was now supporting in Ireland in what proved to be a vain attempt to save the island from a Stuart restoration; so perhaps it is to Jones that we must attribute his nomination.[1] Since Cheshire was the destined centre of revolt, the co-operation of Duckenfield as governor of Chester (and a critic of Cromwell to boot) was an obvious necessity, so he was brought back to the committee.

There was less change in South Wales. It is true that Sir Hugh Owen and his brother, having been denounced as privy to the conspiracy, could no longer appear in the Pembrokeshire list, but two of the three Lorts were there, with Philipps of Picton, Herbert Perrot, Wogan the regicide and most of the other familiar names. The remaining West Wales committees were more drastically reduced in size, the most striking feature being the complete elimination, for the first time since the war, of the whole Golden Grove connection; Howell Gwynne went out with them, but *en revanche* Rowland Gwynne of Taliaris was back on the committee for the first time since the second Civil War. A different reason must probably be assigned to the omission of Phillips of Cardigan Priory and Lewis of Glasgrug: the former was doubtless too good a Cromwellian for the taste of the Rump, while Lewis may have been too outspoken in the criticisms of the Welsh religious settlement which had appeared in his *Evangeliographa* a few years earlier. On the other hand Pryse of Gogerddan was still co-operating.

In the south-east the outstanding factor is the ascendancy of Bussy Mansell (even though, like James Phillips, he had been one of the Protector's civil bodyguard) over Philip Jones the Cromwellian "Lord". Mansell displaced Jones on the Brecknockshire committee; when the South Wales militia was mustered it was he and not Jones who commanded it and kept the country "free from insurrection"; so it was to his advice that those now in power listened when the time came for choosing new sequestrators to deal with the estates of the few

[1] Firth, *Last Years of the Protectorate*, i. 150, ii. 15; Firth and Davies, *Regimental History of Cromwell's Army*, i. 125–6, ii. 477, 668; *T.H.S.L.C.*, n.s., i. 284–5.

southerners who had slipped away to join Booth and Myddelton. In May Jones had to defend himself in the Commons
against a whole Newgate Calendar of charges brought by his
enemies in Carmarthenshire and referred to a committee
which included Thomas of Wenvoe, Bussy Mansell, Evan Seys
and Edmund Gamage—no friends of his.[1] In Glamorgan
itself he lost the company of his agent Watkins and of his old
associate Dawkins, and his dependents Edmund Jones and
Roger Games disappeared from the Brecknock committee.
Radnorshire, though not grouped with the north for militia
purposes, is still, under the influence of the Vavasourian
missions, alligned with it rather than with the south politically,
and so the new committee is marked, on the whole, by a return
of left-wing and Propagationist elements. Only four of the
1657 committee remain, with Dauntsey among them; even
the adaptable Williams of Caebalfa is turned out, though
Gwynne of Llanelwedd is kept on, while Silvanus Taylor
supplants Sir William Lewis, and John Williams the preaching
captain is brought back. Ten new members, only three of
them of the grade of esquire, take the place of those eliminated;
the only recognisable name is that of Thomas Tunman, a firm
friend of Vavasour Powell.[2]

By the end of the following January the political climate had
changed once more. The Rump had again been dissolved by
military force—to be restored soon afterwards at the bidding of
Monck, who was now closing in on the defenceless capital with
the army that came down with him from Scotland. The shape
of things to come had not yet revealed itself, and this uncertainty is reflected in the composition of the county committees
elected by the Rump to administer the assessment it voted a
month after its reinstatement.[3] They are marked in general
by the return to power of the moderates—especially those who
had had to yield to extremer elements under the threat of
Booth's rebellion—rather than any influx of avowed Royalists.
James Phillips's Cromwellianism was no bar to his return to

---

[1] Williams, *P.H.*, p. 99; *C.C.C.*, i. 747; Fonmon MSS. 1/56, 57; Richards,
P.M., p. 272.
[2] Thurloe, ii. 114.
[3] *A. & O.*, ii. 1355.

the Cardigan and Pembroke committees; even the two regicides, John Jones and Thomas Wogan, were re-elected for
their respective counties, and no attempt was made to bring
back Booth's neo-Royalist associates, save only Edward Vaughan
in Montgomeryshire. Vaughan's neighbours, however, were
not as readily convinced as the higher authorities by his
protestation that he had been " utterly ignorant " of the plot,
and the two Denbighshire militia captains Sontley and Manley
had taken on themselves, soon after the rising began, to arrest
him (sheriff as he was) and put him safely under lock and key
in Shrewsbury castle, where he remained untried for weeks.[1]
Captain Edward Taylor, a staunch Dissenter of local yeoman
stock, had first appeared on a Denbighshire committee in 1649.

It was probably Vaughan's complaints that procured the
exclusion of these two over-zealous spirits from the January
committee; and with them went most of the original nucleus
of fighting Puritans in north-eastern Wales who had attached
themselves to Morgan Llwyd: Taylor of Wrexham, Ball of
Gresford, Wynn of Ruabon, Peck of Cornish Hall; Lloyd of
Abenbury was already dead, leaving Barbour the Wrexham
draper and Pritchard of Brymbo (somewhat surprisingly
added to the Flintshire committee) as the last survivors of the
Propagation in this area. In their place came Sir William
Meredith of Stansty, who generally lived outside Wales and
whose background was the milder Puritanism of an earlier
day; for it was his grandfather who at the very beginning of
James I's reign had left money for the wages of a preacher at
Wrexham as a step towards reforming " the most desperate
and lamentable estate of all the churches of North Wales."[2]
Ralph Hughes, who had never identified himself with the
Saints, was brought back to the Flintshire committee and Sir
Owen Wynn of Gwydir and his son to that of Caernarvonshire,
after their omission from last year's militia committee. The
most striking change in the north-west is the exclusion, as a
potential trouble-maker, of the all-powerful Thomas Madryn,
while Edwards of Nanhoron and Williams of Meillionydd,
the other Caernarvonshire Puritans left out in July, were

[1] C.S.P.D., 1659–60, pp. 159, 190, 193, 241; C.W.P., 2193.
[2] Palmer, Old Parish of Wrexham, pp. 195–7.

restored, in company with Griffith Bodwrda, and even the
" Heaven-driver " Parry of Rhydolion kept his place. In
Anglesey and Merioneth and in most of West Wales the new
committees simply reverted to the last Protectorate lists,
omitting the names added and restoring those removed in 1659.

Much the same happened in Montgomeryshire, except that
Lord Herbert of Cherbury did not return to the committee
and the deceased Sir John Price appears to have been now
replaced by his son Sir Matthew, the sheriff for the year and the
post-Restoration persecutor of Vavasour Powell and his
disciples.[1] This was an ominous sign, but its significance lay
in the future; so far the Vavasourians were still in force in the
two committees covering the upper Severn valley, which for
the last time included John Williams and Dauntsey, Yardley,
Curtler and Tunman (but not Peter Price or Richard King)
in Radnorshire, and in Montgomeryshire Richard and Hugh
Price (but not their fellow-Propagationists Lewis Price—now
commanding Caernarvon castle—Edward Owen and Evan
Lloyd). Charles Lloyd of Dolobran was dead, but his place (like
Sir John Price's) was filled by his son and namesake, newly
down from Oxford and already attracted by the preaching of
George Fox. This, and his later marriage with Sampson Lort's
daughter, ranked him with the advanced wing of the Propagationists and lost him his seat on the county committee when the
next elections were made.[2] The zeal of the more advanced
wing was balanced by the more cautious Presbyterianism of
Silvanus Taylor and the two Shropshiremen Nicholl and Hunt,
and by the more secular outlook of old Roundheads like
Matthew Morgan and Price of Parke and of more recent co-
operators like Devereux and Purcell. But those who favoured the
Restoration noticed that all the stronger castles of North Wales
—Beaumaris, Caernarvon, Conway, Denbigh and Powis—were
still in the hands of men of " unsound and desperate principle ".[3]

---

[1] M.C., xxvii. 331–2; Richards, R.D., p. 318. The " Sir Nathaniel
Peircie, Bart." whose name is at the end of the Montgomeryshire list cannot
otherwise be traced; but a transcription of the clerk's hasty notes might
easily turn " Price " into " Peircie " and " Math: " into " Nath: ". The
transcriptions are everywhere full of the grossest inaccuracies.

[2] Williams, Montgomeryshire Worthies, pp. 169–71.

[3] H.M.C., Leyborne-Popham, p. 162.

In West Wales the house of Golden Grove reappears but not that of Glanbran. It is in the south-eastern counties, however—especially Monmouthshire—that the reaction of the early months of 1660 is most marked. There Philip Jones's foes succeeded in elbowing him out of his remaining committees. To the Brecknockshire committee was added John Gunter of Tredomen, a lawyer of local origin but practising in London; as sequestration commissioner in Brecknockshire he had violently attacked the conduct of Jones, who had him dismissed and imprisoned and even (on Gunter's testimony) tried to silence him by having him shipped to Jamaica. He retorted by organising the attack on Propagation finances in the closing years of the Rump, and missed no chance of denouncing those concerned with it under the Protectorate; and the attack was resumed in force early in 1659. Edward Freeman, who was put on the Glamorgan committee, had been Gunter's associate from the outset, losing thereby his attorney generalship of South Wales to Philip's nominee Edmund Jones.[1] John Hagget, an old Somerset Roundhead whom Cromwell had made chief justice of the West Wales circuit and who was now added to the Carmarthenshire committee, had been a fellow member with Gunter of the investigating committee of 1654.[2]

The Monmouthshire list is an almost completely new one, in which virtually the only survivors of the original Roundhead nucleus were those who had had no share in the Propagation. The list is headed by Sir Trevor Williams of Llangibby—his first appearance in public affairs since he had been excluded from composition after the second Civil War; James Berry's urgent warnings to the Protector against him and other fair-weather friends who " played with both hands " had not fallen on deaf ears.[3] He was accompanied by Thomas Morgan of Machen, one of his fellow " hinderers " of the royal cause in south-east Wales after Naseby, but like him in retirement during most of the interregnum, and another Thomas Morgan who was an unpolitical soldier of fortune, of Monmouthshire

---

[1] Fonmon MSS. 1/55–9; *C.C.C.*, i. 492–4, 507, 827; Thurloe, ii. 93, 129.
[2] Williams, *Welsh Judges*, pp. 171–3; *A. & O.*, ii. 992.
[3] Thurloe, iv. 545.

origin and once instrumental in the parliamentary conquest of
his native soil, but now in the public eye as Monck's lieutenant
in Scotland who had just been publicly thanked for his part
in bringing Monck's army across the Tweed to settle the fate
of England.[1] A third name was that of Walter Rumsey of
Llanover, one of Charles I's South Wales judges and one of
his commissioners of array for Monmouthshire, who remained
faithful to the crown when the Rumseys of Crickhowel (his
brother's family) courted Philip Jones.[2] Here then the stage
was already set for the Restoration as in no other Welsh county;
it would not be far from the truth to say that in the whole area
county administration had been swept clean not only of Puritan
zealots but of more wordly politicians likely to prove " hinderers " to the second Charles as they had been to the first. No
wonder Thomas of Wenvoe on hearing the list wrote to his
" dear brother " the republican Ludlow in Ireland lamenting
that parliament was proscribing its best friends in Monmouthshire, leaving the field clear for " cavaliers or at best neuters,
who will never engage against the enemy if decision were ".
But far from awaiting, like Ludlow, the " ruin " he foresaw if
this drift became general, he hastened to secure his retreat,
and was soon helping Bussy Mansell to organise the militia that
was to safeguard the King's return.[3]

It was some five weeks later that the crucial county committees for this purpose were elected.[4] The issue was no longer
in doubt now that the members ejected in 1648 had been
recalled and the country was once more ruled by the Long
Parliament, which had never assented to the abolition of the
monarchy; and the composition of the other Welsh committees
now followed the pattern already set in Monmouthshire. As in
the preceding year, there was one for each county in South
Wales and one (a little further reduced in size) for the whole
of the north. The members may be divided into three main
categories: those drawn from the old governing families that
had been out of public life during the interregnum; those who

[1] Walker, *Historical Discourses*, 1705, p. 141; *C.J.*, vii. 808.
[2] Williams, *Welsh Judges*, pp. 132–3.
[3] *C.S.P.I.*, 1647–60, p. 718.
[4] *A. & O.*, ii. 1425.

had supported the monarchy as long as the issue hung in the balance but had come to terms with its supplanters either with Howell Gwynne's cynical determination to be "on the strongest side" or when the Protectorate reached a stage of stability that made collaboration seem almost a patriotic duty; and those who, having identified themselves completely with the Puritan *régime*, were now led by self-interest or disillusionment to lend themselves to a restoration of the dynasty they had helped to dethrone—a restoration, however, envisaged at that stage in terms which did not mean the complete abandonment of old religious loyalties, at least for those who belonged to the Presbyterian wing of the movement.

Philip Jones is a shining example of the last category. His old foes reappeared in force on their various county committees, and they had in Brecknockshire the additional backing of William Thomas, bailiff of Brecon, who had supported with his pen their nine-years' campaign against the men of the Propagation.[1] Shortly afterwards, too, some of them were nominated by the Council of State to a committee (ordained under the very last Act of the Long Parliament before it dissolved itself) to reopen the investigation into the use made by Jones and his associates of the vast resources they administered under the Propagation Act. It was a formidable body including, as well as Freeman and William Thomas, a few early committeemen like Evan Seys the judge and Windham of Dunraven and more recent ones like Gwynne of Llanelwedd and Edmund Gamage, with some independent local magnates like Mansell of Margam and Lewis of the Van who had suffered under Jones as sequestrator—and only William Watkins to put in a word on the other side. But nothing came of it, and meanwhile Philip had somehow got himself re-elected to the Glamorgan committee with his son-in-law Price of Gellihir, his faithful henchman Watkins and his old comrade-in-arms Rowland Dawkins.[2] Bussy Mansell and Stradling of Roath (a colourless "yes-man") were the only other local remnants of

---

[1] Richards, *P.M.*, pp. 249-53.

[2] Price's client Evan Lewis was also on the Glamorgan committee but that did not save him from a spell of imprisonment after the Restoration; Robert Thomas denounced him as a dangerous and disreputable character and opposed his liberation in 1662 (Williams, *P.H.*, p. 17).

the Propagation—once so firmly entrenched here—left to co-operate with old committeemen like Seys of Boverton and Bassett of Broviskin in preparing the overthrow of the *régime* they had helped to build up. Their West Wales brethren, always less numerous, were now whittled down to the two Phillipses, of Picton Castle and Cardigan Priory respectively. Algernon Sidney, whose adhesion to the Puritan state had been dictated by political rather than religious motives, was too unbending a republican to be associated with a Royalist restoration on any terms, so he drops out of the Glamorgan committee.

The theocratic or millenarian character imposed by Vavasour Powell on the Puritanism of Powys, to which a Stuart monarchy was even less acceptable than a Cromwellian, made it inevitable that county administration in Radnor and Montgomery should be swept clean of the last relics of the Propagation and the more militant Puritan elements in general. In north-east Wales the decisive factor was the return to power of Myddelton, with his steward Kyffin and the few old Puritans and Round-heads associated with him in Booth's *attentat*. The more un-compromising Puritans among Morgan Llwyd's followers who had been active in resisting it had already been for the most part eliminated, and Hugh Pritchard now followed them. The Propagation in this area was now represented by a few more pliable spirits like Andrew Ellis in Flintshire, and in Denbigh-shire Sir John Trevor (with his son, his cousin Sir Thomas and his steward Peck) and Sir John Carter, the Philip Jones of the north. Ralph Critchley, another local Propagationist, had been out of county politics since the Protectorate, but his kinsman the ex-governor of Wrexham (whose part in the financial investigation of 1654—his last public employment—suggests a certain detachment towards the dominant Puritanism) now returned to help in putting the local militia in trim for the Restoration; so did Thomas Swift, who had represented the Propagation in Anglesey till the Protectorate, and—among those less deeply committed—the turncoat Thomas Ravens-croft in Flintshire.

Some of these old Roundheads who had fought against Charles I were now ready not only to organise but to lead into battle (if need be) the militia contingents raised in the cause of his son. The septuagenarian Sir Thomas Myddelton was past fighting, but his eldest son commanded the contingents for east Denbigh, Merioneth and Montgomery, and Sir John Carter those for west Denbigh, Flint, Anglesey and Caernarvon. Luke Lloyd and his son held commissions in Flintshire, and Gerald Barbour, who belonged to the Presbyterian wing of local Puritanism and died in that faith less than a year later, not only resumed his captaincy but served as treasurer for the whole North Wales force.[1] An ominous development is the exclusion of John Jones (who had always been reckoned with this group), along with his less eminent fellow-regicide from the south. Jones had been one of the most active members of the Rump on its first restoration, but now he lay under impeachment for opposing, as deputy commander in Ireland, the schemes of Monck, and not many weeks passed before he was paying a farewell visit to east Denbighshire as a prisoner on parole; with him there was no question either of accommodation to the turn of events or of seeking safety in flight.[2]

The budding Puritan communities of Gwynedd no longer counted in politics; it is chiefly among Cromwellian lawyers and placemen like Bodwrda, Foxwist and Twisleton that we find the neo-Royalists of this area. Bodwrda was soon to distinguish himself by turning informer on regicides and reaping his reward in lucrative jobs; it is possible, however, that to Twisleton's influence in the Clynnog neighbourhood (where he settled on his wife's estate) may be attributed the prevalence of Dissent there after the Restoration.[3] Glynne's younger brother Edmund of Plas newydd had no more scruple about this service than Thomas Glynne had had over Charles I's commission of array, and the same is true of Jones of Castellmarch; a few weeks later both were sitting as magistrates to hear evidence against Thomas Madryn, Jeffrey Parry and

---

[1] Llanfair and Brynodol MSS., bundle 94, 17 Apr., 1660; Palmer, *Parish Church of Wrexham*, pp. 131–2. Bussy Mansell commanded the Glamorgan militia—a much more sudden conversion (H.M.C., *Leyborne-Popham*, p. 170).

[2] *C.J.*, vii. 645–6; *C.S.P.D.*, 1659–60, p. 576.

[3] Williams, *P.H.*, p. 4; *T.C.H.S.*, vi. 32–6.

another old fellow-commissioner of the 1659 militia, who had
been seen galloping with armed attendants in the direction of
Traeth Mawr.[1] Whether it was conscience or mere mis-
calculation that decided this last move in the game of Box and
Cox between Madryn and Carter, so long the twin tyrants of
North Wales,[2] cannot now be determined. In Merioneth, too,
Owen of Dolserau, with some of his fellow-commissioners of
the last militia, was arrested by his successors as " dangerous
and in actual disturbance of the peace ", and lodged in Caernarvon gaol;[3] neither here nor in Anglesey was any Puritan
influence left (unless we count Thomas Swift) in the management of county affairs.

Having got rid of the chief trouble-making elements,
parliament proceeded to fill their places with moderate
Puritans who had previously been excluded (like the recently
returned victims of Pride's Purge in the House itself) for their
opposition to the King's trial, and with temporising Royalists
and " neuters " who had been got rid of when Booth was in
arms. Thus Sir William Lewis is back again, but this time on
the Brecknockshire committee; Annesley[4] and the Harleys,
in retirement since 1649, reappear on the Radnorshire list as
well as, for the former, that of Carmarthenshire, and for the
latter Monmouthshire; and Essex Meyrick, son of the Sir John
who had been Essex's right-hand man in the first Civil War
but had shared his patron's distaste for the use the army made
of its victory, was added to the Pembrokeshire committee, of
which his father had been a member in 1647–8. The Booth
suspects had been concentrated chiefly in Denbighshire, where
Wynne of Melai, Jeffreys of Acton, Eubule Thelwall and John
Edisbury were now brought back into office after their temporary exclusion; Rowland Bulkeley and Whyte of Friars are
parallel cases in Anglesey, but in Caernarvonshire a remarkable

---

[1] Llanfair and Brynodol MSS., bundle 94, depositions of 25 Apr., 1660.
[2] *C.W.P.*, 2156.
[3] Llanfair and Brynodol MSS., bundle 94, militia minutes, 25 Apr.,
and warrant of 28 Apr., 1660. Thomas Nicholl and (surprisingly) Vaughan
of Llwydiarth were among half-a-dozen Montgomeryshire men similarly
treated (H.M.C., *14th R.*, ii. 221).
[4] During this period when the Presbyterian Royalists were in power,
Annesley had a large share in the selection of South Wales magistrates
(Haverfordwest MS. 382).

feature is the absence, for the first time, of any member of the Gwydir family—not even Maurice the Receiver, who had hardly missed a committee since 1647; possibly the family had taken to heart what Glynne of Lleuar said to the heir on the eve of Booth's rising: " When a kingdom is tossed up in a blanket, happy are they who are out of it."[1] To balance this loss, the family of Williams of Penrhyn (the archbishop's heirs) is represented by both Sir Griffith and his son Sir Robert, who had been knight of the shire in Richard Cromwell's parliament, although his younger brother Edmund was believed to have been involved in plots against Richard's father a few years earlier.[2]

Sir Hugh Owen in Pembrokeshire, Sir Edward Mansell and Robert Thomas in Glamorgan, were the most notable South Wales personalities to return after their exclusion as suspected partisans of Booth; other families like that of Barlow of Slebech in the former county and Carne of Ewenny in the latter reappeared in county politics for the first time since the interregnum began. In West Wales the Golden Grove clan had trimmed its sails to each successive breeze of politics with a dexterity resembling that of its less powerful counterparts in the north, the Wynns of Gwydir; but whereas the Gwydir influence survived (with some difficulty) the Booth rising, only to be swept away when the Restoration was in sight, that of Golden Grove (with all its satellites) returned in full strength after the temporary eclipse of 1659, almost completely dominating the Carmarthenshire committee and spreading out into the neighbouring shires. Another West Wales family to return to politics after a prolonged absence was that of Williams of Rhydodyn (Edwinsford, Carmarthenshire), worth some £600 or £700 a year, which had been prominent in local affairs since early in the century and became increasingly so after the Restoration, distinguishing itself by combining staunch loyalty to the crown with a liberal attitude in both politics and religion;[3] and the same tendency is represented by those of Price

[1] C.W.P., 2188.
[2] Thurloe, iii. 166.
[3] Hist. Carm., ii. 30, 33, 45, 67, 147, 457–66; N.L.W., Edwinsford MSS.; H.L. MS. EL 7218.

of Pilleth and Lewis of Monachty (with a long parliamentary
record in Radnorshire), the border clans of Clive and Corbett,
and the Denbighshire family of Goodman, famed for its services
to the Welsh Bible.

This was the last of the parliamentary county committees,
for in little more than a couple of months the Restoration had
brought its answer to the prayer of the macaronic litany
circulating during what Price of Rhiwlas called the " dis-
tempered and bedlam times ":

> Rhag nerth y Committee hefyd
> *Libera nos domine.*

But the " roguish committee men and sequestrators " were not
forgotten.[1] Nearly a quarter of a century later the Recorder
of Carmarthen, Richard Vaughan of Derllys, in a speech of
welcome to the duke of Beaufort on his presidential progress
through the town, boasted that the whole county " never
gave birth to any such monstrous production, as a Sequestrator
or a *Committee man* ".[2] The claim will not, of course, bear
close scrutiny. We have seen that Carmarthenshire had its
committees like other counties; Vaughan's own father was a
member of one in 1657 and few were without some of his
kinsmen. But the italicising of " Committee man " must not
blind us to the fact that the real stress is on " Sequestrator ";
and here we are on firmer ground, for in Carmarthenshire the
work of sequestration was largely carried out by men from
other shires; of three who were chosen for the task in 1652
two refused the oaths, though one of them later relented.[3]
This tendency to equate " committeeman " with " sequestrator ", and the aura of expropriation which in consequence
continued to hang over the whole system, are apt to obscure
the extent of its success—especially in the heyday of the Protectorate—in harnessing to the new republican governments
the traditional forces of county society.

---

[1] *C.W.P.*, 2020, 2034; *Hen Gerddi Gymraeg* (*Cymdeithas Llên Cymru*, ii), vii.
(" From the power of the Committee too, Good Lord deliver us.")

[2] Dineley, *Duke of Beaufort's Progress*, 1888 facsimile, p. 234.

[3] *C.C.C.*, i. 557, 660, 691.

V

THE DAWN OF PARTY POLITICS[1]

AND as often as nede shall require to ellecte and choose any
knyghte or burges of the parliamente of and for the said countie
of fflint he shall and will geve his or their ellections withe the
said John Edwards & his heires or withe such personne or
personnes as hee or they shall nominate and withe none other.

IN these words, taken from an indenture between a landlord
and his tenant shortly before the Armada, we have a key
to the conception of a parliamentary election that prevailed
for half a century after Wales was enfranchised. To the Welsh
voter this new obligation (for the vote was an obligation before
it became a privilege) was interpreted in terms of what was
familiar and traditional; he looked on it as virtually an extension of the *cymorth*—the duty to rally round the *arglwydd* at
every time of stress. It is significant that the next clause in the
indenture quoted above places on the tenant the allied obligation to wear no livery but his lord's.[2] For the measurement
of a man's worth by the size of his *clientèle* had not yet been
superseded by the modern criterion of the size of his income,
a criterion which bardic conservatism was strenuously resisting; and until the benefits, whether personal or political,
accruing from attendance at Westminster had had time to make
themselves felt, election was coveted mainly as a matter of
prestige.[3] To lead to the polls a numerous posse wearing the
candidate's favours and supping on a princely scale at his
table—what was it but a legalised version of heading one of
those swarms of liveried retainers which the law now banned?
Even an uncontested election served the same purpose of

---

[1] The basic facts about elections are drawn from Williams, *P.H.* References to this source are not given except for the authentication of personal
details not easily procurable elsewhere.

[2] *E.H.R.*, lxv. 222.

[3] *Supra*, pp. 20-21; *T.C.S.*, 1942, pp. 8-10, 66-72.

parading the strength of the family connection; as late as
1675 Lord Bulkeley, returned unopposed at a Caernarvonshire
by-election, writes to Anglesey friends and neighbours to
accompany him from the country house outside Bangor where
he is staying, to the polling place at Caernarvon.[1]

The uncontested return, indeed, was long the normal
practice. We know of no contested elections before Elizabeth's
reign, and they are exceptional for a century after that. If
there was any doubt as to who should be returned, the gentry
preferred to decide the matter by an informal exchange of
views before polling day came round.[2] To a proud and well-
established county family, defeat at the polls was a disgrace
not to be tolerated; Sir Roger Mostyn would not let his sons
stand for Flintshire at James I's last general election because
opposition seemed likely, protesting that if the place could not
be had without a contest it was not worth the having; and
Sir John Trevor whisked off his son, the future Secretary of
State, to one of the pocket boroughs he had himself represented
during the Protectorate rather than " engage in a contest
with many great friends" for this same seat in the elections of
1660.[3] If a man of any weight did suffer defeat, he rarely
sat down under it; there would follow a Star Chamber suit or
(when the Commons took over the determination of disputed
elections) a petition to parliament, alleging irregular practices
on the part of his opponent or of the sheriff.[4] It can safely be
said that where contests occurred in Welsh constituencies in
the sixteenth century and until well on in the seventeenth,
the issue was not politics but precedence and prestige. The
pride and touchiness of the Welsh gentry were notorious; to
superior rank and breeding they were ready to pay all due
deference, but monopoly of power they would not abide.
And fortunately for the health of Welsh politics the structure
of society, until after the great concentration of property that
took place in the late seventeenth and early eighteenth centuries, was on their side, for in most counties there was a gentle

[1] N.L.W., Carreglwyd MS. ii. 208.
[2] E.g. *C.W.P.*, 915–33, 1172–1242, 1312–1329, 1674–89, 2108–75,
2219–94; Brogyntyn MSS. (unscheduled), 1 Feb., 1681.
[3] *C.W.P.*, 1186; N.L.W., Rhual MS. 98.
[4] E.g. *T.C.S.*, 1942, pp. 15–17, 41–2.

gradation from the most powerful magnate to the humblest freeholder, leaving no hard and fast line between those who were eligible as candidates and those who were not. It was the claim of a new family to a place in the political sun, or the threat of turning the county into a private preserve, that provoked conflicts comparable in their own microcosm to the wars and diplomatic manœuvres to maintain the balance of power in Europe.[1]

Very few families enjoyed such undisputed predominance in county affairs as (for example) the Bulkeleys in Anglesey. With a rent-roll of over £4,000 in an island that boasted only fifteen men of the grade of esquire (the lowest complement in Wales), they easily established their ascendancy over the next grade of gentry (none of them with fortunes over £800), and soon had the " corporation borough " of Beaumaris in their pockets. It is true that another family of comparable fortune acquired by marriage the neighbouring estate of Plas Newydd towards the middle of the sixteenth century, but the Bagenalls' fortune came mainly from land in Ireland and England, and although on three occasions when there did not happen to be a Bulkeley available they stepped into the vacant county seat, they never attempted to dispute the Bulkeley lead in the island.[2] Sir John Wynn of Gwydir nearly achieved a similar dictatorship in Caernarvonshire, until after drawing into his widespread network of alliances one after another of the neighbouring families, and treating each successive election as a game of chess in which he manipulated the pieces, he encountered in Lleyn the tough local patriotism that made the ancient *cymwd* (to its own bards) *trysor penn teirsir a'u porth*, and had to retire, discomfited but vowing vengeance, after the riotous election of 1620.[3] From then on, the family left the

---

[1] *Supra*, pp. 2-3.

[2] B.M., Harl. MS. 4164, fos. 29b–33; H.L. MS. EL. 7155; Pennant, *Tours*, ed. Rhys, iii. 388–94; *supra*, p. 131; *infra*, p. 212. The Woods of Rhosmor, the only family among the lesser squires to stand up to the Bulkeleys, were drawn by marriage into the family connection by the end of the seventeenth century. (Griffith, *Pedigrees*, p. 132).

[3] " Chief treasure and stay of three shires " (Morys Dwyfach in J. Jones (Myrddin Fardd), *Cynfeirdd Lleyn*, p. 180); see E. G. Jones, " The Caernarvonshire Squires, 1558–1625 " (unpub. thesis), chs. i and iv.

county representation severely alone, finding substitute seats in English boroughs or in neighbouring Welsh shires. It took twenty years to heal the breach; when Sir Richard Wynn, the loser in this historic fight, was canvassed in the elections to the Long Parliament on behalf of his victorious rival's son, he consented without enthusiasm, tartly observing that " for this twenty yeares I had reason to beleeve I was no freehoulder there for my voice (it seems) was not worth the desiring ".[1]

What Baron Hill was to Anglesey and Gwydir to Caernarvonshire, Golden Grove was to Carmarthenshire. Apart from the wealthy parent stock there were from the early seventeenth century four offshoots, each with substantial estates of the order of £700 a year, but they continued to act politically as an undivided Vaughan *bloc* until a judicious marriage policy had reunited them by mid-eighteenth century. On the other hand there were several county families like those of Williams of Edwinsford, Mansell of Muddlescombe and (at first) Jones of Abermarlais, with incomes reaching or approaching the £1,000 a year level, whose claims could not be passed over; even the ancient princely house of Dynevor, after suffering total eclipse in 1531, began to reassert itself in county politics (under the humbler style of Rice of Newton) towards the end of Elizabeth's reign; and there were important Pembrokeshire families with estates stretching across the border, who could by no means be always relied on to keep in step with Golden Grove.[2] Similarly with the Montgomeryshire Herberts. The Tudor settlement of mid-Wales was largely the work of the redoubtable Sir Richard Herbert (nephew of the first earl of Pembroke), and it left his family in an undisputed pre-eminence, appropriating as of right the representation of the shire at Westminster and the leadership in local government, drawing the other principal houses of the area into its orbit by politic marriages, and admitting each to its appropriate place in the county hierarchy. But the long tradition of headstrong independence died hard in this old marchland, even after it had been diverted into less turbulent channels by the " just and conscionable "

---

[1] *T.C.S.*, 1942, p. 42; *C.C.P.*, pp. 113, 115; H.M.C., *13th R.*, iv. 260; N.L.W. MS. 12404 E (letter of Sir R. Wynn, 23 Oct., 1640).

[2] *Hist. Carmarthenshire*, II. ch. i and pp. 472–7; H.L. MS. EL. 7128.

discipline imposed by old Sir Richard, and satellites did not always move in their appointed orbits. In 1588 Edward Herbert's own brother-in-law, whom he had previously put in for the borough seat (and his elder brother for the shire itself) actually set up against him at the polls, and the sheriff, who was Herbert's son-in-law, had to play fast and loose with arithmetic to maintain the natural order of things by giving Herbert the victory. Even after this the Herberts of Montgomery castle still had to share the seat with their kinsmen of Powis castle—an arrangement that worked amicably enough until the two branches took opposite sides in religion. Then came the intrusion of mercantile wealth from London through the purchase of the crown lordships of Kerry and Kedewain by the ex-Lord Mayor, Sir Thomas Myddelton, and so the way was prepared for the political divisions of the Civil War period.[1]

The pre-eminence of the earls of Worcester in Monmouthshire was such as to warrant a special guarantee of their interests there in the Act of Union itself; but the Act in creating the county recognised its superior wealth and population by giving it the English quota of two members. This left one seat at the unchallenged disposal of the house of Raglan till after the Restoration, while the other could be scrambled for by the gentry of the next grade below. It was this second seat that became the objective of one of the first known Welsh election contests in 1572, followed by the usual charges in Star Chamber from the defeated candidate of jerrymandering on the part of his rival's father the sheriff.[2] The Glamorgan gentry managed these things better. In a county boasting more than a dozen estates at or above the £1,000 level, an attempt to storm this solid phalanx from below was as unlikely of success as a threat of dictatorship, even from so fabulously wealthy a peer as the Earl of Pembroke, who was the principal landowner. It is true that the borough was at Pembroke's disposal when he wanted it, but his electoral influence was wide enough to provide

---

[1] Herbert of Cherbury, *Life*, ed. Lee, pp. 1–15; Lloyd, *Sheriffs of Montgomeryshire*, pp. 34–5, 89–116: Neale, *Elizabethan House of Commons*, ch. iv; *C.S.P.D.*, 1628–9, p. 220; *S.C.P.*, p. 125; *supra*, pp. 83–113.

[2] 27 Hen. 8, c. 26, s. 33; Neale, *op. cit.*, pp. 84–6.

elsewhere for his numerous connections without too exacting a demand on the Glamorgan electors,[1] so that for a century or more some half-dozen of the substantial gentry were able to maintain a rota in representation without landing the county in the expense of electoral contests. Glamorgan's galaxy of wealth in the upper stratum of county society was exceptional, but until the expenses of membership began to soar,[2] there was usually a fairly wide field of eligible candidates, and they were not always able to arrange things amicably among themselves; hence, for example, the contested elections of 1572 and 1597 in Radnorshire and of 1588 and 1601 in Denbighshire.

In Denbighshire, with its two ill-fitting halves deriving from two different Welsh principalities with widely differing backgrounds, a gentleman's agreement for rotation both of county office and of parliamentary representation between east and west was strictly observed for about half a century after the Act of Union; then the Salusburys of Llewenny, who held a commanding position in the west, showed signs of encroaching eastwards by marriage alliances comparable with those of the Wynns of Gwydir in the remoter west of Caernarvonshire, and the eastern squires revolted. In this case, however, the local " country party " was able to take advantage of a widespread religious and political *malaise*, at first within the county, and later on a national plane, and to superimpose on personal, family and regional quarrels some colour of common principle. The leader of the east Denbighshire malcontents of 1588 was John Edwards of Chirkland, whose family had actively upheld the ancient faith until the execution of the first local Catholic martyr four years earlier and returned to it after Gunpowder Plot; it was he who on succeeding to the estate introduced into some of his leases (not, however, in Denbighshire) the significant and exceptional clause quoted at the head of this essay. For the past ten years there had been a noticeable tendency for factions to form in the county on confessional lines, and matters had been brought to a head in 1586 by the execution of two Denbighshire squires, including the heir of Llewenny himself,

[1] *E.H.R.*, l. 242–56; *T.C.S.*, 1942, pp. 69–71.
[2] *Supra*, pp. 9-10.

on charges of complicity in Babington's conspiracy. The
successor at Llewenny was ostentatiously loyalist and Protestant, but the whole chain of events strengthened the hands of
those who opposed his east Denbighshire nominee in 1588.
They included some of Edwards's powerful Protestant relatives,
supporting him for family reasons, but also a considerable
body of small squires and freeholders—notably among Chirkland tenants and neighbours—who without open recusancy
were suspected of secret nostalgia for Rome. Much was made
of this aspect of the election in the Star Chamber proceedings
that followed Edwards's sensational victory, and we can be
reasonably sure that it had its bearing on the issue, despite the
victorious candidate's outward conformity.[1] It is barely
possible that these considerations apply also to the Montgomeryshire election of the same year, for Edward Herbert,
ancestor though he was of the strongly Protestant Herberts of
Cherbury, had been reckoned fourteen years earlier one of the
three leading Catholics of the shire.[2]

There can be no doubt about the Denbighshire election of
1601; the leaders of the faction which then disputed the seat
with Sir John Salusbury, many of them backers of Edwards in
1588 who had contrived to keep local government in their
hands for the past five years, were all more or less deeply
committed to the cause of the Earl of Essex, and came to the
poll with bands of armed men ready to put up a fight even
after their patron's attempt to raise London had ended in
barren tragedy. The sheriff, who was one of them, dared not
proceed to a poll for fear of bloodshed,[3] and when fresh writs
were issued the Essex faction faded away, leaving Salusbury
(in Siôn Tudor's phrase) *gŵr cynta, cnot y coron* after the *brad a
gad*.[4] This stormy episode was the culmination of a long period
of confusion in Welsh politics in which Sir Gely Meyrick, from
the time he succeeded Sir Roger Williams as Essex's Welsh

---

[1] *E.H.R.*, lix. 348–56; Neale, *op. cit.*, pp. 111–18. On Denbighshire
recusancy see E. G. Jones, *Cymru a'r Hen Ffydd*, 1951, pp. 22–6.
[2] *Cath. Rec. Soc.*, xiii. 110. His opponent's grandson was a Protestant
champion in the Long Parliament (*T.C.S.*, 1946–7, pp. 66, 72, 81, 83, 94).
[3] *E.H.R.*, *loc. cit.*; Neale, *op. cit.*, pp. 121–8.
[4] "Chief of men, mainstay of the crown" ... "treason and strife"
(*cywydd* on Salusbury's knighthood, 1601, *N.L.W.J.*, v. 261).

factotum, pursued a policy of infiltration on his master's behalf through the length and breadth of Wales, alike in local government and in parliamentary representation. The Radnorshire contest of 1597 was one of his failures, despite the strong territorial interests he held in the county through his wife; for his cousin and ally Roger Vaughan of Clyro failed to unseat James Price of Monachty, who had held the seat in the last parliament and was to keep it till 1620; yet Price was so unacceptable to Essex that in the Privy Council next year, during Pembroke's absence through illness, the president's nomination of him as deputy lieutenant was received by Essex with " scoffing laughter " because he wanted the place for Meyrick. In the ensuing Star Chamber suit the usual allegation was made of partiality on the part of the sheriff; strangely enough, when Vaughan carried the seat at an earlier election in 1572 against a relative by marriage of Price, the boot seems to have been on the other foot. Meyrick was more successful in the boroughs. In Carmarthen, which he himself represented in 1588, the electors allowed him to make his own nomination five years later (when the county was held by his " in-laws " of Golden Grove), and close associates of Essex were at the same time put in for Cardigan and Radnor.[1]

At this stage, however, the winning of a borough seat was hardly a major operation. It has been shown elsewhere[2] how the tiny Welsh boroughs, essentially rural in character and lacking a powerful trading community to fight their battles, were glad to accept the help of neighbouring landlords whether in protecting their corporate privileges and trading interests or in shouldering the burden of representation; while the gentry for their part found it convenient to have a substitute for the county seat when it did not happen to be available, and a means of obliging ambitious acquaintances from other parts of the country. So the boroughs tended to become appendages to the county seats, subject to the same bargaining between the gentry, which only occasionally gave rise to open conflict,

---

[1] *Supra*, pp. 56–7; Neale, *op. cit.*, pp. 80–1, 238; Mathew, *Celtic Peoples and Renaissance Europe*, pp. 352–3, 356–7; H.M.C., *Cecil*, viii. 233–4, xi. 43; *S.C.P.*, pp. 138, 140.

[2] *Supra*, pp. 31–2.

and like them varying between single and multiple control. Perhaps the nearest approach to a pocket borough was Beaumaris, where the Bulkeleys extended their hospitality to Caernarvonshire families crowded out of their own county; Montgomery and Cardiff were also generally regarded as preserves of the two great branches of the Herberts, until in the course of the seventeenth century the South Wales branch lost its electoral influence through indifference, the Powis branch because of its religion. It was the other way about with Monmouth, which showed a remarkable catholicity in its choice of members, few of whom had any roots in the district before the house of Raglan began to assert its claims in earnest after the Restoration. Sir John Wynn of Gwydir, with the best will in the world, completely failed to make another Beaumaris of Caernarvon.[1] Denbigh had powerful protectors in its absentee burgesses the London Myddeltons, and the elder branch that settled at Chirk continued to take an active interest in it; but the Salusburys of Llewenny were nearer neighbours, and between them the burgesses (with some three hundred votes, including those of non-residents) managed to keep a good deal of independence—witness their historic rebuff to Elizabeth's Earl of Leicester when he was lord of Denbighland.[2]

Haverfordwest, with its hundred voters, was fought for between two rival south Pembrokeshire camps, the one led by the Perrots of Haroldstone (to whom Henry VIII had transferred so much of the wealth and influence of the fallen house of Dynevor), with two branches of the Wogans as their allies, the other by the houses of Picton and Slebech, reinforced by the newly-settled Stepneys of Prendergast. When Sir John Perrot was away in Ireland in 1572, his rivals tried to snatch the seat for a Stepney, but they were foiled by the sheriff (a Perrot nominee). A Star Chamber verdict, however, went against the sheriff, and for the rest of Perrot's absence Stepney kept the seat (by no means without disturbance)—only to

C.W.P., 1043.
[2] See, e.g., N.L.W., Llewenny MS. 3.46, Chirk castle MSS. E. 1075, 1079, 1084; Pennant, *Tours*, ii. 163–5; Williams, *Ancient and Mod. Denbigh* chs. xiii, xix.

yield it up on his return. With some reshuffling of supporters the feud continued right up to the Civil War, and it may well have influenced the alignment of parties in the war itself.[1] The other principal boroughs of West Wales were from their geographical position less overshadowed by great estates, and for the first century of representation, until they became Naboth's vineyards to the more aspiring of the county magnates (as when Carmarthen fell to Golden Grove for a century from the end of James I's reign), they were generally represented by careerists at the bar, English carpet-baggers or unpretentious and ineffective borough officials. When elections were contested (as at Cardigan in 1601 and 1604), the defeated parties, not wealthy enough to fight the issue out in Star Chamber, were apt to find their petitions to parliament, without the backing of any powerful interest, treated with lofty indifference.[2] In these Welsh borough contests the out-boroughs which generally shared representation with the shire town were important pawns, a recurrent complaint of defeated candidates being the exclusion of this body of voters; not infrequently parliament had to adjudicate between two rival returns, one from the shire town, another from an out-borough.

The collapse of the Essex faction brought electoral politics back to normal. Contests again became exceptional; indeed the assumption that the dignity of knight of the shire was the prerogative of a limited group of families whenever they had a candidate to offer, though not quite unchallenged, grew in cogency as society became more stable and social grading more fixed. Denbighshire, as one of the storm centres of the Essex epoch, will serve as an example. Sir John Salusbury, whose interests were more literary than political, showed no desire to exploit his triumph of 1601—especially when he found that the line he had taken did not make him *persona grata* to the new King—while the tastes of his heir Sir Henry lay rather in the direction of overseas adventure. With the head of another western house fighting in Europe and the former candidate o

---

[1] Neale, *op. cit.*, pp. 255-60, cf. A. L. Leach, *Civil War in Pembrokeshire* ch. ii, J. Phillips, *Pembrokeshire*, 1909, p. 441.
[2] Glyn Roberts in *Hist. Carmarthenshire*, ii. 23; *T.C.S.*, 1942, p. 17.

the eastern group bent on retrieving fame and fortune in Ireland, there was elbow-room for aspirants to parliamentary honours even among the minor gentry. Meanwhile Sir Thomas Myddelton the city magnate had settled his heir and namesake at Chirk castle, as lord of Chirkland, in the east, aspirant to the lordship of Ruthin in the west, and the wealthiest landowner in the whole shire, and had married his daughter to the heir of Llewenny. The second Sir Thomas entered parliament at the end of James I's reign by succeeding one of his city uncles in the representation of an English pocket borough, which re-elected him to the next House; but his standing made him an obvious choice as knight of the shire for Denbigh, and when the county was summoned for the 1625 election, instead of contesting the seat with the last member (Sir Eubule Thelwall, a distinguished lawyer but not a major figure in county society), he persuaded Thelwall and his backers, with the goodwill of the sheriff, to change seats with him, and the electors readily concurred. For the next two elections Myddelton abandoned politics and Thelwall came back, but from 1640 onwards, excepting the interregnum and one memorable election of Charles II's day, the seat was at the disposal of any Myddelton who was of age as long as the male line remained unbroken.[1]

Such conflicts as arose seem to have been merely a continuation of the family feuds that had enlivened Elizabethan elections. The veteran Price of Monachty kept undisturbed possession of the Radnorshire seat till 1620, when he was once more unsuccessfully challenged by a Vaughan; this time the defeated candidate was reprimanded by the Commons for following the familiar but now outmoded procedure of carrying his complaints about the conduct of the election to the Star Chamber. Sir John Perrot's bastard son Sir James (an active left-wing parliamentarian) takes up the representation of Haverfordwest—apparently without reviving the old animosities—in the first three Stuart parliaments; but when he invades the county seat in 1624 his father's allies the Wogans turn against him, and after defeat at the next election he has

[1] *T.C.S.*, 1946–7, pp. 18–19, 1948, p. 16; Llewenny MS. 14.34; *supra*, p. 29.

to return to the county borough, where the interim member (a son-in-law of the mayor who had helped to keep the seat for the Perrot interest in 1571) holds out against him and makes the seat insecure for some time.[1] Clearly a re-grouping of family interests is in process; but there is nothing to suggest that Perrot's politics are the bone of contention.

The fact that several of the Pembrokeshire gentry held land in Carmarthenshire too is no doubt accountable for the continuing turbulence of borough elections there. In 1625, for example, the seat was snatched from the representative of Golden Grove (Carbery's younger brother Henry) who had held it in the last parliament and was to recover it for the next two, by Francis Annesley, whose only local tie was his marriage to a Philipps of Picton, a Pembrokeshire clan belonging to the Perrot circle. This election has some interest in the light of after-events; when the Civil War broke out and Carbery commanded for the King in West Wales, it was his more energetic brother Henry who deputised for him in the early Pembrokeshire campaigns, while among those who either opposed him from the start, or deserted him with the Perrots and Wogans when the tide began to turn, was a Philipps of Picton (formerly in the opposite faction), leaving the old anti-Perrot houses of Stepney and Barlow almost alone in south Pembrokeshire to sustain the royal cause. For Picton had now become a Puritan stronghold, and Annesley's son (the future Earl of Anglesey) followed his Picton mother's faith and served it in both Ireland and Wales under the Commonwealth. No such colouring can be given to the Flintshire election of the following year; from both contesting clans, Hanmer and Salusbury of Bachegraig, there emerged half-hearted Royalists, equally ready to compromise with the usurpers.[2]

In Caernarvonshire the triumph of the anti-Gwydir faction in 1620 proved the beginning of a lively period in county politics culminating in the Civil War. The dissidence of the victors in this fight (the Griffiths of Cefnamwlch) faded away

[1] *T.C.S.*, 1942, p. 65, 1945, p. 24; Williams, *P.H.*, pp. 155, 167, cf. Neale, *op. cit.*, p. 257.
[2] *T.C.S.*, 1946–7, pp. 18–19; Leach, *op. cit.*; *supra*, pp. 127–8, 135–6, 174 and *n.*

when the favour of the Lord High Admiral, Buckingham himself, was turned in their direction through the influence of their
Denbighshire " in-laws " the Trevors, who had long basked in
the sun of Admiralty patronage. Henceforth they were un-
swerving courtiers, and the leadership of the " baboons " (the
Bishop of Bangor's choice epithet for the dissatisfied backwoodsmen who would not bow the knee to Gwydir) passed to the
Glynnes of Glynllifon, who disputed the seat with Cefnamwlch,
with alternating success, for the next five elections. It was
Cefnamwlch and its allies that carried shire and boroughs in the
Long Parliament against the candidature of Glynllifon; and
although a parliamentary committee found both elections
irregularly conducted, the sitting members contrived to put off
any action until the issue was lost sight of in more pressing
concerns.

When war broke out Cefnamwlch, true to its recent courtly
traditions, identified itself with the preponderant loyalist
elements in the county; it had secured, in readiness for a by-
election if new writs were issued, the appointment of a friendly
sheriff, who made it one of his first concerns to see to the arrest
of the potential leaders of opposition: Thomas Glynne (the
defeated candidate), another of the Glynllifon faction who had
been " short-listed " for the shrievalty, and one of the Lleyn
backwoodsmen. The illness and death of the head of the house,
who sat for Beaumaris to make way for his worthless heir in
his own county, weakened the loyalist faction, which had little
effective support from the powerful but temporising house of
Gwydir; on the other hand Glynne and his associates were not
strong enough to do more than slow down the county's war
effort for the King, in which they outwardly co-operated until
the defection of Archbishop Williams gave the signal for a
general retreat from the royal cause; and then these original
dissidents were reinforced from Lleyn and from among malcontent families further east. Caernarvonshire thus provides
another example of how family feud could melt into political
faction.[1]

There were also two contested Welsh borough elections to
the Long Parliament, both resulting in double returns which

[1] *B.B.C.S.*, xii. 44–8, xiv. 42–5; *supra*, p. 130.

came before the House for settlement. No conclusions can be drawn from the Monmouth election, since neither candidate had any local connections and both remained in public life after the interregnum; but the Brecon contest does gain some significance from the fact that Herbert Price, who held the seat pending investigations that never matured, was an intemperate partisan of the court while most of his colleagues were still in active opposition, whereas his opponent's family sat in Cromwell's parliaments and worked with the Country Party after the Restoration.[1] This must not be taken to imply that elections to the Long Parliament found Wales divided into Royalists and Roundheads; on the contrary, all the evidence points to a remarkable unanimity against the grievances of the day and a strong desire to avoid hampering divisions. The return of Sir Thomas Myddelton for Denbighshire was technically invalid because the poll was held too late, but his nephew Sir Thomas Salusbury was strongly advised not to provoke a feud by contesting the seat in the event of a by-election; yet less than two years were to pass before Salusbury mobilised the military forces of the shire to prevent his uncle from putting into force the parliament's Militia Ordinance. Myddelton's efforts in the House to preserve a united front against the popish menace abroad proved equally utopian.[2] Within twenty months the Welsh united front at Westminster had been reduced to seven members, the rest having " deserted " their seats to join the King at Oxford, and it was not long before the seven came down to five, including a recent by-election recruit. The remaining four represented Denbighshire and Pembrokeshire constituencies—where faction had so long been rampant—and the Earl of Pembroke's connection in Glamorgan.[3]

The end of the war saw a spate of by-elections—twenty in all—to fill the vacancies. Little is known of these elections, but in the presence of a victorious Roundhead army (with many of its officers among the candidates) it is unlikely that any of

[1] *N.L.W.J.*, vi. 252; *T.C.S.*, 1946-7, pp. 77-8, 1948, p. 54; *supra*, pp. 122-3, 133, 150.
[2] Llewenny MSS. 3.30, 3.40, 3.54, 3.72, 3.98. Actually, of course, Myddelton kept his seat; so generous a contributor to the loan for paying off the Scots was not a man parliament could afford to lose on a technicality.
[3] *T.C.S.*, 1948, pp. 51-2.

them were contested. Many of the principal gentry who usually arranged these matters between them were either standing aloof or under proscription, and their mantle fell on some of the smaller squires who had hitherto been passive electors; for example, in the Merioneth by-election of September, 1647 (fateful because it introduced to the House the future regicide John Jones), the chief canvasser on his behalf was Howel Vaughan of Glan y llyn, a *parvenu* in county politics, though fate made him an ancestor of one of Wales's great political dynasties, the Wynns of Wynnstay.[1] John Jones himself formed with Harrison and Vavasour Powell the triumvirate which nominated the six Welsh " saints ". to Barebone's Parliament.[2] Here no question arose of electors or even of local constituencies, but the idea of a member of parliament as a partisan rather than the spokesman of a community made its first fleeting appearance.

Elections to Cromwell's parliaments, though marked by an increasing return to traditional procedure, tended in the same direction. By now many of the county gentry who had been out of politics since the war had come to terms with the new government and were allowed to participate in elections, and there was clearly some measure of freedom of choice. Contests occurred in the counties of Merioneth and Brecknock for Cromwell's first parliament, and in each the defeated party (a Roundhead of proven loyalty) alleged undue pressure, on the part of the sheriff in one case and the powerful Vaughan of Llwydiarth in the other, in the interests of untrustworthy ex-delinquents. Protests were sent to Cromwell himself against the return for Montgomeryshire of Sir John Price, the Long Parliament member—not, as with his great-uncle in the 1588 election, on family grounds, but because of his kaleidoscopic political record.[3] That such considerations should enter into a candidate's credentials was indeed a novelty, and one that took long to establish itself.

Correspondence about the next elections in Denbighshire and Caernarvonshire, very much on the traditional lines of

[1] *Supra*, p. 131.
[2] *T.H.S.L.C.*, n.s. i. 226.
[3] *C.S.P.D.*, 1654, pp. 271–2, 299–300.

electioneering correspondence, reveals a general readiness to accept John Jones in the former, and in the latter John Glynne, as one of the two members for what had now become (with the other shires) a two-member constituency. If Jones's fortune was recent and his patrimony small, he came of old and honourable stock, and Archbishop Williams's reference to him as " the most universally hated man in these parts " seems to lack confirmation; Glynne for his part was the younger and more eminent brother of the defeated candidate of 1640. Caernarvonshire was even willing, now that it had a second seat to fill locally, to accept with surprising docility Glynne's suggestion, when he chose to serve for Flintshire instead, of a complete outsider (Henry Lawrence, president of the Protector's council) as his substitute. But there was strong opposition to the re-election of the English fortune-hunter John Carter, who had made himself generally detested since his election to the last parliament, and Caernarvonshire flatly refused to re-elect his fellow-harpy and tyrant from Lleyn, Thomas Madryn, either in this or in Richard Cromwell's parliament, when swords were drawn at the polling in Caernarvon town hall.[1] In this last Protectorate parliament Cromwell's attorney general Edmund Jones, the successful but unpopular ex-Royalist candidate for Brecknockshire at the last election, was victorious again in the county, but against opposition which provoked a long and acrimonious debate when parliament met. A third contested seat in 1659 was Carmarthen borough, where a prominent Cromwellian official was returned over the head of a Puritan malcontent (with a clear majority of votes) through the partiality of the sheriff, who was summoned to the House to apologise for his misconduct.[2] The double return in Pembroke borough appears to have had no political bearing; it arose out of a familiar quarrel between borough officials as to the delimitation of their offices.

Welsh political life was evidently not stifled under the Protectorate, and from the frequency of borough contests it appears that the measures so often taken to secure a pliable

---

[1] *C.W.P.*, 1834, 2108–31; *supra*, pp. 120, 173–4.
[2] Burton, *Diary*, iii. 233–49, 502, iv. 275. The Carmarthenshire sheriff is wrongly identified in my article in *T.C.S.*, 1948, p. 68.

corporation[1] (comparable to the steps taken towards the same end by the crown after the Restoration) were not always successful. Yet in the background, rarely brought into play at election time but ever present to the minds of the electors, was what no previous government had had at its disposal—an efficient standing army. There is an ominous ring about John Jones's preference for Wrexham as the venue of the Denbighshire election of 1656 (against the general wish for Denbigh or Ruthin) because the troop of horse stationed there would be handy in case of disturbances.[2] Still more of a departure from precedent is the conception of their function held by those elected; for in the House, while not neglecting matters affecting their constituents, they behaved and spoke primarily as party men.[3] The initial *raison d'être* of the Commons before their irruption into high politics had been " to communicate to the House such business as they brought from their countries", and in this spirit the Welsh members had early developed into a national *bloc*; but the " Welsh interest ", already disintegrating in the heat of faction during the Long Parliament, showed little sign of animation under the Protectorate, and it was one of the things the Restoration failed to restore.

Elections to the " free parliament " that recalled the Stuarts were conducted in a spirit of " safety first ", the bulk of those returned being repentant Roundheads who had not compromised themselves too far for reconciliation, or unrepentant Cavaliers who had returned to public life in despair of a restoration (or, latterly, in hopes of turning to account the confusion of their foes)—or else just plain trimmers with no hampering loyalties. Of unbending Royalists not more than four can be counted. Brecon rejected Sir Herbert Price, with his long record as a courtier, while Cardiff returned in Bussy Mansell an active Cromwellian who had sat in Barebone's Parliament. In Haverfordwest the return of a moderate from the Picton Castle clan (with a policy of " let bygones be bygones ") was challenged by his defeated rival, that " subtle

---

[1] *T.R.H.S.*, III. vi. 129–62; *Hist. Carmarthenshire*, ii. 17, 29; Williams, *Anc. and Mod. Denbigh*, ch. xiii; N.L.W. MS. 1546 E (iii), fo. 94.

[2] *C.W.P.*, 2123.

[3] *T.C.S.*, 1948, p. 70.

ambo-dexter " Roger Lort, whose political gymnastics during
the Civil War and Commonwealth had brought him into such
general opprobrium that a group of prominent burgesses sub-
mitted to the parliamentary committee a list of cogent " reasons
why Mr. Lort is unfitt to serve for this place, or indeed any
place else, considering his former actings "; and when on the
issue of new writs Lort changed his tactics yet again and recommended to the electors an outsider with a distinguished post
and strong backing at court, they would have none of him
either—not even that staunch Royalist Sir John Stepney.[1]
Full collaborators were equally at a discount; three others
besides Mansel might be put into this category, and they were
men with booty to safeguard (like Glynne and Carter), or
essentially non-party men with a taste for public life (like
James Phillips in Cardigan). Montgomery borough turned
down its Cromwellian member, preferring Sir Thomas Myddelton, who had just been declared a traitor for holding Chirk
Castle against the forces of the Commonwealth in a premature
bid for the King's return.[2] In Flintshire a contest was avoided
only by the fact that John Trevor, who had represented the
county continuously (and actively) in every parliament since
1646, gracefully retired to an English borough and left the
field clear for an uncompromising Royalist.[3] The total number
of contested seats seems to have been under half-a-dozen.

It was after the Restoration became a *fait accompli* that
elections to Charles II's first and longest parliament revealed
the most startling changes of temperature. Only four Welsh
members of the Convention came back, with close relatives of
two others. The pre-war parliamentary families provided at
least two-thirds of the membership, and fully half-a-dozen
uncompromising loyalists were elected. Even Sir Thomas
Myddelton's son, with a baronetcy newly conferred in recogni-
tion of his services in promoting the Restoration, met some
opposition in west Denbighshire (though it was not pressed),
presumably because of his association with his father in the

[1] N.L.W., Haverfordwest MSS. 375–89; cf. *supra.*, pp. 118, 141, 144, 153.
[2] *Supra*, p. 162; *C.S.P.D.*, 1659–60, p. 170.
[3] N.L.W., Rhual MS. 98; cf. Taylor, *Hist. Notices of Flint*, pp. 144–5.

Civil War.[1] Brecknockshire is the only county seat known to have actually been contested, and there three successive polls had to be held before it finally went in 1662 to Edward Progers of Gwernvale, a Catholic courtier, high in the favour of Charles II, who no doubt owed his election to influence from that quarter; Sir Herbert Price had to fight once more for the borough, but this time parliament confirmed his election after a double return. James Phillips lost his seat for Cardigan boroughs after a contested election which was quashed as irregular, but the electors adopted his suggestion that they should take in his place an English friend who shared his literary tastes and held a profitable post at court.[2] The Haverfordwest election was also declared invalid, and it was not till 1663 that the borough at last found a member in a judge of Great Sessions. Robert Thomas, whose election for Cardiff was confirmed by the Commons after investigation, had been a somewhat unsteady Royalist, but at least he could claim, as his opponent could not, to have been twice in the black books of the Puritan republic, and to have put the restored monarchy on its guard against some of the more factious spirits in South Wales.[3]

This universal sentiment of loyalty was not maintained, and faction began to show its head again as grievances accumulated. Discontent first came to a head in 1667, when on top of the Plague and the Fire the Dutch fleet sailed up the Medway and King and parliament quarrelled over finance. A by-election for one of the Monmouthshire seats in that year brought into the House Sir Trevor Williams of Llangibby, one of those hereditary clients of the Earl of Pembroke who " under pretences of dislike of Popery " had led the defection of south-east Wales from the royal cause (which they at first supported) after Naseby—and then saved his estates after yet another *volte-face* in the second Civil War by conciliating the Protectorate. It was a contested election, and Sir Trevor's backers were drawn from the same family and political set; one of them

[1] *C.W.P.*, 2294; H.M.C., *Portland*, i. 684; *C.J.*, vii. 769, 791, 834; *C.S.P.D.*, 1644, p. 505, 1659–60, p. 170; *supra*, p. 173.

[2] N.L.W., Wynnstay MS. 1204. For Flintshire see N.L.W. MS. 1593 E, fo. 157.

[3] *Supra*, pp. 144, 153–4, 157–8, 175; Williams, *P.H.*, p. 17.

had lent his house as Roundhead headquarters when Raglan castle was besieged, another had helped to inventory its contents when it surrendered. The by-election was due to the death of the Earl of Glamorgan and the consequent removal of the new head of the house of Raglan (one of the county's members) to the Lords as Marquis of Worcester; its issue shows the growing strength of the forces opposed to Raglan, which had always been loyal to the court and had kept the county loyal through the Long Parliament and the Civil War until after Naseby. But even if the losing candidate's petition had succeeded, the court would have fared little better, for he was the son of an old Roundhead who had sat on the Propagation Commission and the Commonwealth Council of State.[1]

The Monmouthshire by-election was one of sixteen caused by casualties among Welsh members during the seventeen years' life of this parliament, but few of them present any points of interest. In most constituencies the seat was kept in the family or passed on to the ex-member's natural successor among his neighbours; at Haverfordwest Clarendon's own cousin happened to be a judge on the local circuit and could conveniently be slipped into the vacancy, till he too died and was replaced by a Perrot. But two later elections, after Clarendon's fall and in the growing exacerbation of feeling that followed the revelation of the King's intrigues with France and the papacy, suggest a more definitely political aspect. On the death of the pre-eminently loyal judge Sir Richard Lloyd in 1677, his place as member for Radnorshire was filled by Richard Williams of Caebalfa, whose father had represented the county in Cromwell's parliaments and co-operated actively with the Puritan *régime* in local government;[2] and the vacancy caused in Brecon the following year by the death of the life-long courtier Sir Herbert Price was filled by a son of Bussy Mansell. But the resurgence of party strife is best illustrated in the Shrewsbury by-election of 1677, which was watched with interest by non-resident voters in Montgomeryshire. Lord Herbert of Cherbury directed his agent to win as many

[1] *N.L.W.J.*, vi. 250, 255-6; Clark, *Limbus Patrum*, p. 293.
[2] *Supra*, p. 133.

as possible of these for Sir Richard Corbett, the "opposition" candidate, but he found some already engaged for his opponent Edward Kynaston, a member of a widespread border clan which had been active for popery in Elizabeth's day and deeply involved in a plot to raise Shropshire and Montgomeryshire for the Stuarts at the heyday of the Protectorate,[1] and he failed to persuade Kynaston's backers to stay at home.

" There was the greatest Labouring for voyces [he writes] . . . that ever I heard of, and report is that 5*li* is given for a single vote on Kinastons account if this be true heele be sure of the Rabble party that wants money and in all probability will prevaile unlesse Sir Richard who has the Mayor and officers on his side can out with the Drinking party and prevaile with the Mayor to make a returne."

A man who would have given his ears to help the " rabble party " in its efforts on behalf of his distant connection the court candidate (and in the disposal of his cash and liquor), if only he could have established his claim to a vote in the borough, was the chronically impecunious border squire Edward Lloyd of Llanvorda (father of Edward Lhuyd the antiquary). Lord Herbert's agent, however, proved a false prophet; whether it was the mayor's machinations or the tide of popular feeling that prevailed against such open-handed liberality, the court was discomfited once more.[2]

It was these repeated rebuffs that steeled the King against the rising clamour for a general election. His announcement at the end of November, 1675, of a prorogation for fifteen months was generally hailed as the prelude to a dissolution, and young Sir Thomas Myddelton, who had not been of age to fill the vacancy in Denbighshire when his father died in 1664 (so that one of the other county families had to provide a stop-gap), began sounding his neighbours on the prospect of an unopposed return to the family seat. He found even some of those who had jibbed at his father's election now ready to support him;[3] but the crisis passed, and the House lived through another two stormy sessions before the King appealed to the country in

[1] Griffith, *Pedigrees*, p. 216: *E.H.R.*, lix. 353; Thurloe, iii. 207, 225, 245, 253, 317; *supra*, p. 156 and *n*.

[2] N.L.W., Powis castle MSS., 17th cent. correspondence 88, Sweeney Hall MS. 3 (25 Feb., 18 March, 1677). Wrongly described as Montgomery election in *N.L.W.J.*, iii. 141.

[3] N.L.W., Chirk castle MSS. E. 6090, 6145; *C.W.P.*, 2730, 2731.

1678. That he was able to stave off the evil day so long was due, partly of course to French gold, but partly also to the skill of Danby and his lieutenants in avoiding further repulses in the House by marshalling the Cavalier vote into something like a trusty instrument of royal policy. For the first time lists began to appear, some drawn up by the King's ministers, some by opposition pamphleteers, of the court party in the House, soon to be known as Tories. The lists do not always agree with each other, and they owe too much to wishful thinking or personal likes and dislikes to be always a reliable guide; for example Secretary Williamson includes in one of his lists Sir Trevor Williams, who was a personal friend but far from a reliable supporter of the court. But for what they are worth they indicate that nineteen of the Welsh members who sat in the House during the seven years from Danby's rise to power till the end of the session were reckoned among the courtiers.[1]

The principal means of enforcing party discipline was inevitably the power of the purse, and this parliament has earned in history (somewhat unfairly in view of its frequent displays of independence) the name of the Pensioned Parliament. In part these conditions were a legacy of the Civil War; for without some sort of compensation, Cavaliers who had impoverished themselves in the royal service could be of little further help to the crown, and Wales had more than its share both of loyal Cavaliers and of needy squires. It is unlikely that much heed was paid to the flamboyant claim of Edward Lloyd of Llanvorda to compensation out of the " fund for loyal officers " for losses in the King's service which he contrived to add up to £8,000, for he was always pestering someone for money.[2] It was different with supplicants like Rowland Pugh, whose house of Mathafarn (Merioneth) had been burnt down by Myddelton's men,[3] or with Sir John Owen, the *gŵr purffydd* who had fought so strenuously to keep the Roundheads out of Snowdonia, and his brother William,

---

[1] *Bull. Inst. of Hist. Res.*, xi. 1–23.

[2] Sweeney Hall MSS. 4 and 5.

[3] N.L.W. MS. 12403 E (6 June, 1663); Lloyd, *Powys Fadog*, vi. 39; *supra*, p. 146.

hero of a new saga of the Men of Harlech; for their loyalty had cost them dear in cash as well as in comfort.[1] And Welsh claimants had literally a friend at court in Maurice Wynn, nephew of the great Sir John and Groom of the Privy Chamber, who could see to it that petitions from his brother Welshmen were kept near the top of the mounting pile.[2] Yet there was obviously not enough money to go round even the legitimate claimants, so what more natural than that the plums should be reserved for men likely to give some sort of political *quid pro quo?*

Pugh and the Owens were not in parliament, so they could help only in local affairs. In the House itself a secret service pension of £400 a year was held by John Robinson (of Gwersyllt in Denbighshire and Monachdy in Anglesey), M.P. for Beaumaris, whose lands had been seized by parliament when he fled abroad to the exiled court after fighting for it in Cheshire and Anglesey, and had to be repurchased at a cost that permanently crippled the estate.[3] The £400 conferred (together with the stewardship of Denbighland) on John Wynne of Melai, who kept the Denbighshire seat warm during the Myddelton minority, may have been by way of compensation for his father's death in the King's cause; it is harder to find grounds for the £500 of Sir Thomas Hanmer, an old courtier and Cavalier who had shown considerable shrewdness in saving his estate by keeping on terms with the other side.[4] Roger Whitley, who sat for Flint borough but belonged primarily to Cheshire, had a better war record, but hardly eminent enough to justify the " vast estate " out of the farm of the post office with which he was credited; nor was there much valid reason for " compensating " to the tune of £500

---

[1] *Supra*, p. 37; Phillips, *C.W.*, ii. 332–4; *C.S.P.D.*, 1660–1, pp. 70, 112, 442, 1661–2, pp. 169, 180, 1663–4, pp. 35, 95; *T.S.A.S.*, II. iv. 57.

[2] N.L.W. MSS. 12403–5 E.

[3] Phillips, *C.W.*, ii. 99, 294–7, 311–3; A. N. Palmer, *Gresford*, pp. 59–65; Pennant, *Tours*, 1889, i. 392–3, iii. 35, 67–8, 286; H.M.C., *Ormonde*, n.s. iv. 517.

[4] H.M.C., *5th R.*, pp. 141–2, *6th R.*, p. 88, *12th R.*, ix. 40; *Declaration of Sir T. Middleton*, 1644; *C.C.C.*, ii. 943; Thurloe, iv. 277, 294, 319; Hanmer, *Parish and Family of Hanmer*, pp. 80–88, 100–10, 141–3; Phillips, *C.W.*, i. 143 *n*.

a year the services rendered by Edward Progers (M.P. for Brecknockshire) from the snug corner at court in which his family had basked since the days of James I. And if Sir Herbert Price had fought valiantly, he certainly was not underpaid if it be true that his office of master of the household brought him £10,000 a year.[1] The preponderance of the court interest in North Wales has perhaps an economic explanation: with few exceptions her squires simply could not afford to display the independence of their brethren in the south, and especially the south-east.

A contemporary pamphlet put out by the opposition gives a list of nine Welsh members in receipt of government money in some shape or form, from plutocrats like Price or Progers, through staider civil servants like Lord Vaughan (of Golden Grove) with his £1,000 a year as governor of Jamaica, down to the humble £400 a year pensioners.[2] It is fair to add that two of the nine were not Welsh at all, but had been thrust into Welsh constituencies just because of their positions at court. Nor were they all courtiers in the more opprobious sense of the term. The machinery of government was expanding and creating a succession of new offices without adjusting either their duties or their emoluments to those of existing posts, or evolving a specialised body of non-political experts. A recent investigation of the subject rebuts the suggestions

" that all payments to members of Parliament were of the nature of bribes, that all pensions were without justification, that all place-holders voted automatically at the bidding of the Government, or that large numbers supported the king who really sympathised with his opponents."[3]

To take a single example: Roger Whitley's " vast fortune " from public sources did not prevent him from making himself extremely awkward to the government in the two ensuing parliaments.[4] What was significant for the Welsh members in these new political developments was the new type of bond they created. With the slackening of the tie which had held them together as guardians of the interests and traditions of

[1] *N.L.W.J.*, vi. 254.
[2] *A Seasonable Argument for a New Parliament*, Amsterdam, 1677, printed Cobbett, *Parl. Hist.*, IV. xxxii ff. (cf. H.M.C., *Ormonde*, n.s. iv. 517).
[3] A. Browning in *T.R.H.S.*, IV. xxx. 26.
[4] *N.L.W.J.*, vi. 254.

Wales, they found a new one as members of a group cutting across geographical or cultural boundaries, united in the pursuit (whether disinterested or otherwise) of common political aims, and dividing them from the minority of their compatriots who opposed the court. With few exceptions their family connections were not such as to give them weight in the House; it was only as adherents of English party groups that they could be effective. And this association tended to draw them away from their own constituents and towards their English colleagues, preparing the way for the tone of Welsh society in the next century. An offering to Williamson, the " boss " of the court party, of " the Irish liquor of Usquibagh "[1] was more in keeping with the spirit of the age than the gifts of venison or game with which the Welsh gentry used to greet their President at his Christmas courts at Ludlow.

Those who opposed the court—the nascent Whig party— had no such means of rallying their followers into an organised group. They had to rely on the exploitation of grievances; and this was the basis of Shaftesbury's striking victory over the court when at last the election came early in 1679. Never before had Wales known so many contested seats; never had so many of her tried loyalists had to give way to men of much more dubious antecedents. Most of the elections, it is true, went on normal lines, the retiring member being re-elected or replaced by a relative or one of his " set "; but there are some significant features even about these routine replacements. It was natural that Sir Thomas Myddelton should now step into the family seat he had coveted four years earlier;[2] but his election meant the substitution of an independent gentleman for a pensioner. Edward Vaughan of Llwydiarth as premier landowner of his county was just as inevitable a choice for Montgomeryshire (in fact he kept the seat for nearly forty years); but if he was (despite his Roundhead antecedents) a rabid courtier, he was not a pensioner and a stranger like the Shropshire knight he succeeded.[3] Matthew Price, his opponent

---

[1] N.L.W. MS. 3575 D (12 March, 1671).
[2] Chirk Castle MS. E. 1206.
[3] N.L.W., Brogyntyn MSS. letter 1001; *supra*, p. 131; *infra*, p. 229.

at the polls, was likewise the son of an old Roundhead, and one who had supported the governments of the interregnum right up to Monck's *coup d'état*.[1] In the borough election Price carried the day against a local captain of militia.

Far more striking is what happened in Brecknockshire. The King was particularly anxious to have his favoured courtier Progers re-elected, and he went so far as to instruct Williamson to write enlisting Ormond's help with a view to " inclining " John Jeffreys of Abercynrig, who had been out of the House since Progers deprived him of the county seat on petition in 1662 (and was then visiting Dublin), to back up his former rival's candidature in return for Progers's support in the borough. The only part of the plan that succeeded was Jeffreys's victory over Bussy Mansell's son in the borough (one of the few cases where a zealous loyalist won the day in contest with a man of opposite background); but in the shire neither William Morgan of Tredegar (who had appeared on almost every government list as one of its firm supporters) nor even the courtly Marquis of Worcester—lord of the manor of Crickhowel and now President of Wales—would back so arrant a courtier and a papist to boot; and Williams of Caebalfa, who had carried Radnorshire in the 1677 by-election, now went in for Brecknockshire in flat defiance of the court. Williams's successor in Radnorshire was Rowland Gwynne, Macaulay's " honest country gentleman ", who was already a political enemy of Worcester and became a prominent Whig of William III's reign.[2] But if the electorate would not take dictation from the court, neither would it abdicate to the territorial magnates. Worcester wanted one of the two Monmouthshire seats for his son and the nomination to the borough as well. The gentry were quite willing for him to share the county with Morgan of Tredegar (no friend of his), displacing Sir Trevor Williams, but he could not prevent the borough from giving Sir Trevor a seat.[3]

Two other notable setbacks for the court were in Glamorgan, where Bussy Mansell returned to the House for the first time

[1] *N.L.W.J.*, vi. 256; *supra*, pp. 128, 168.
[2] *Infra*, p. 228.
[3] *C.S.P.D.*, 1679–80, pp. 64, 74, 90.

since his election of 1661 was invalidated, replacing his kinsman and namesake Sir Edward, whom Danby and Williamson always reckoned one of their " safe " men; and in Cardiff, which Sir Robert Thomas (who had succeeded to the family baronetcy) held against the opposition of a member of the loyal clan of Stradling of St. Donats. Cardigan borough, vacated by a civil servant of tried loyalty but a stranger to the country, went to James Phillips's brother Hector, who had been associated with him as an active supporter of the Commonwealth and Protectorate.[1] Altogether as many as seven Welsh elections came up for review by the Committee for Privileges on account of a double return or the petition of the defeated candidate.[2] Four have already been mentioned; the only other of any significance is that at Haverfordwest, which resulted in the victory (over a colourless local lawyer) of William Wogan, a future judge and a spokesman of the opposition in the ensuing parliament.[3]

If the court lost ground in Wales by this election, the House as a whole was even less amenable. Its attack on Danby and its attempt to exclude the King's brother from the succession on account of his faith brought it to an untimely end before the summer was out, and new elections followed in the autumn. The heated atmosphere in which they were carried out breathes through the correspondence of the time, and the interest they excited appears in the fact that nearly a fortnight before the session ended, the member for Caernarvon boroughs, while professing (unconvincingly) his assurance of " a good correspondency between the King and the present Parliament ", was already canvassing the out-boroughs of Lleyn and Eifionydd to secure his re-election when the dissolution came—and even so he was turned out.[4] Yet there was little change in the Welsh membership, except for some minor interchanges between borough and county seats. A reshuffle of this kind in Monmouthshire, however, has a deeper import, for here two local crises had brought feelings to boiling point. One was the

---

[1] *Supra.*, p. 150.
[2] *C.J.*, ix. 569–72, 576, 579–80.
[3] *N.L.W.J.*, vi. 257.
[4] N.L.W. MSS. 9346 B (22 Oct.), 12405 E (12 July), 12406 C (13 July, 1 Aug.), Brogyntyn MSS. (unsched.), 16 May, 1679.

execution at Usk of the devoted Jesuit David Baker, long affectionately remembered as *tad y tlodion*, who after years of impunity had been denounced (with his fellow-priests) in a letter to the speaker of the House of Commons—then in a state of hysteria over the supposed Popish Plot—by John Arnold of Llanthony.[1] Arnold had recently been dismissed the Monmouthshire bench, in company with eight of his neighbours whom Worcester considered politically dangerous; and at such a time a contrast was bound to be drawn between Raglan's hostility towards this Protestant zealot and its reluctance to invoke the law against its own former co-religionists. Arnold also supported the agitation of Sir Trevor Williams, Morgan of Tredegar and others of the local gentry, against Worcester's attempt to override traditional rights of common of timber in Wentwood forest in the interest of his ironworks.[2] All this gave point to Sir Trevor's wresting of the county representation from Worcester's son, who was left to fight Arnold for the borough seat—successfully at the poll, but only to be set aside in favour of Arnold on the latter's appeal to a friendly House of Commons. Preparations seem to have been made for contesting Thomas's seat at Cardiff;[3] if so, nothing came of them. The only other noteworthy contest was in Flintshire, where the " courtier " Sir John Hanmer failed to capture the seat that had been his father's from the loyal but independent Davies of Gwysaney.

The court had certainly not retrieved its position, and it is not surprising that Charles put off meeting the new parliament for fifteen months, and then dismissed it after a week spent mainly in attacks on the heir to the throne and his fellow-Romanists, in which Sir Trevor Williams, Rowland Gwynne and John Arnold all took part, with Worcester as their immediate target.[4] In Monmouthshire the atmosphere was ominously suggestive of that of forty years back; when Arnold's heyday had passed, witnesses were found to depose how at this

[1] " Father of the poor " (*St. Peter's Mag.*, Cardiff, 1923, pp. 159–68, 189–97, 219–61); H.M.C., *12th R.*, ix. 68; *C.J.*, ix. 463, 466–9.
[2] *C.S.P.D.*, 1678, pp. 25–6; H.M.C., *9th R.*, iii. 116–17; *St. Peter's Mag.*, 1924, p. 43; *supra*, pp. 19, 26.
[3] Penrice and Margam MS. L. 153.
[4] H.M.C., *12th R.*, ix. 101–6, 114–15.

time he was consorting with Samuel Jones of Brynllywarch—once an itinerant preacher under the Propagation and still an unrepentant Dissenter—raising mysterious funds and even corrupting the loyal principles of the Monmouth school-children. Worcester did not scruple to call his county " as ill-affected as any in England ", adding a strong plea for better defences against a rising.[1] In his whole province the President instituted a general purge of county government such as might ensure the return of better-affected members to the next parliament; twenty-five Welsh magistrates were struck off the rolls,[2] and the usual change of sheriffs followed.

Whether or not as a result of these precautions, the elections that came early in 1681 brought some resounding triumphs for the court. Most dramatic was the Denbighshire contest held, like its famous predecessor of eighty years back, at Wrexham, and like it nearly ending in bloodshed. The aggressor, Sir John Trevor, had hitherto sat for English boroughs, and contrived to combine a noisy Protestantism with fulsome adulation of the court (where his services, as a rising barrister, to one of the King's mistresses made him *persona grata*) and championship of his cousin and patron Jeffreys, the future judge and already a bugbear of the opposition. Having recently inherited the small family estate of Brynkynallt, Trevor now made bold to challenge the Myddeltons, his hereditary enemies, in their own domain;[3] and backed by the Jeffreys influence (which was strong round Wrexham) he gained considerable support in the east as well as winning over a few families like the Thelwalls in the west. Whether this would have been enough in itself to gain him the seat cannot now be determined—his opponents conceded him eight hundred votes, whereas they are known to have mustered at least a thousand—for the matter was decided (as an observer put it) " not by Poleing but by a point at law ", the sheriff disqualifying Myddelton by a pettifogging appeal to an obsolete statute prescribing that candidates must be resident in the constituency at the time

[1] *C.S.P.D.*, 1682, pp. 221–2, 275–6, 288–9, 538–9, 575–6; Roxburgh Club, *Memoirs of Earl of Ailesbury*, 1890, i. 30, 46.

[2] *N.L.W.J.*, vi. 249–59.

[3] *T.C.S.*, 1938, pp. 184–93; *S.C.P.*, p. 68; W. M. Myddleton, *Chirk Castle Accts.*, *1605–66*, p. 14 and *n.*; *C.J.*, ii. 783.

the writs are issued.[1] As Trevor (who rarely visited the county) had made sure of being on the spot himself, the suggestion of a prearranged plot is irresistible. We have vivid eye-witness accounts depicting one band of Myddelton's voters flocking to the poll " 5 or 6 in abreast " in " such a company that for the number seldom came togeather to an eleccion ", and of another passing through Denbigh to the accompaniment of " shouting hooting and cryeing of Trevor and withall some tymes flinging of hatts at the horses and Cudgelling of them that all went thorow", while Myddeltonians had their windows broken, their candidate's town house was attacked, and some who had " got a lap of good ale . . . were disposed to fight it out " but for the intervention of peace-makers. The fight had its aftermath in prosecutions for riot and a challenge to Trevor from Myddelton's brother to give satisfaction for calling their grandfather, the Roundhead general, a traitor.[2] Trevor seems to have planned a similar *coup* in the borough against Salusbury of Llewenny, Myddelton's chief backer in the shire (now that the temporary estrangement of Civil War days was healed); his agent was the accommodating Lloyd of Llanvorda, but the petition presented on behalf of their candidate (who had previously had his eye on the county) met with no success.[3]

Contests in the neighbouring shires may have been less colourful, but they showed no lack of interest. " Wee are as buissie in these partes ", wrote a sardonic Flintshire lawyer more than five weeks before polling began, " rideing about to secure votes for a New Eleccion, as if the next Parliament were assured of all the Prosperous successe Imaginable." In this county the retiring member decided, after some hesitation, not to stand for re-election—wisely, his friends told him, for he would have stood no chance against the court influences arrayed behind Hanmer, who now recovered the seat.[4] Actually the Gwysaney record of war service for the crown

[1] Cf. *C.W.P.*, 925.
[2] Chirk castle MSS. C. 1–3, E. 53, 558, 6313; N.L.W. MS. 12406 (18 Feb., 1681).
[3] *C.W.P.*, 1711; Sweeney Hall MS. 7 (5 Feb., 7, 8, 11 and 14 March, 1681).
[4] N.L.W. MS. 12,406 C (28 Jan., 18 Feb., 1681).

would stand closer scrutiny than that of Hanmer, but the King's election manager must have deemed Hanmer the safer man in the present crisis; the hollowness of the judgment appeared in the next reign, when Sir John, whom James allowed to keep his army commission when Davies's son was dismissed from office, used it to betray Hull to William III, apparently for £5,000.[1] " They tug hard in Merionythshire ", writes our Flintshire observer; the " tug " was between the friends and foes of young Sir Robert Owen, now a landowner in Caernarvonshire and Merioneth by inheritance from his grand-father Sir John, the Royalist colonel, and a Caernarvonshire magistrate by filling a vacancy arising from the late " purge "; what more natural than he should aspire to represent Merioneth in parliament ? He was high in the President's favour, and through him stood well at court, but was opposed by some of the " young and ignorant " for his opposition to the Exclusion Bill—to the intense indignation of old-fashioned neighbours who looked on this novel sort of political opposition as that of " senselesse people " wantonly " unkind . . . to an honest worthy Gent ". Even the sheriff was reported " not so cordiall for Sr. Robert as he Ought ". But the retiring member was ill and stood down, and after much manœuvring (and liberal " gratuities " by Owen's opponents, according to his friends) the field was left clear for Sir Robert.[2]

The court did less well in South Wales. Arnold got in again for Monmouth in defiance of Worcester, and Sir Edward Mansell, who had been turned off the Glamorgan bench (presumably for his opposition to Worcester's earlier high-handed action in dismissing Arnold) recovered the county seat, leaving his kinsman Bussy to find one in Cardiff.[3] Wogan on the other hand lost Haverfordwest but won Pembrokeshire instead—a form of being " kicked upstairs "; and Radnor

[1] *Infra*, p. 226; H.M.C., *11th R.*, vii. 27, *14th R.*, ix. 449–50.
[2] N.L.W. MS. 12406 C (18 Feb.): Brogyntyn MSS. letters 1635–7, 1607, 999, 1600, 1649 (3 Jan.–8 Feb.), and unscheduled letter of 1 Feb., 1681. The statement in Brogyntyn 1607 that Owen " voted for ye D:Y: [Duke of York] in ye last Pa: " is puzzling because he is not known to have sat before, but there seems no doubt about the dating.
[3] There is good evidence that on this occasion Sir Edward was definitely elected as an anti-court candidate (H.M.C., *Ormonde*, n.s. vi. 148, *C.S.P.D.*, 1682, p. 77).

borough fell (on a second poll following a double return) to Sir John Morgan of Kynnersley, son of the Roundhead colonel and Cromwellian knight who had redeemed himself by helping Monck to prepare the way for the Restoration.

The opposition was still unquelled, and its violence ensured for the new parliament as abrupt a termination as its predecessor's. Lloyd of Llanvorda was not exaggerating when a month after this dramatic turn of events he referred to it as " the late revolution ";[1] but it was a revolution of which the end was not yet in sight, for party strife grew more furious than ever. In the summer an anonymous " Cambro-Briton " denounced to his fellow-countryman Secretary Jenkins the " unlawful parliamentary stirs " that Sir Trevor Williams was fomenting over " barrels of ale " in Monmouthshire, with Arnold as his chief of staff, " most of the youth of the country at his command ", and " numerous " sectaries joining in the clamour for the release of their hero Shaftesbury (now in the Tower)—all indications that " rebellion may begin " here unless prompt measures are taken to silence the ringleaders.[2] More than two years passed before the government felt ready to pounce. In the July of 1683, after the revulsion of feeling caused by Shaftesbury's flight abroad and the discrediting of the other Whig leaders by the Rye House Plot, Worcester had the satisfaction of conveying to the deputy lieutenants of all the shires in his presidency instructions to disarm at their discretion all " dangerous " persons; and in November he obtained in King's Bench verdicts of *scandalum magnatum* against his two arch-enemies Williams and Arnold, with fines heavy enough to keep them out of mischief for some time to come.[3] His elevation to the dukedom of Beaufort followed almost immediately, and his regal progress through Wales consolidated his triumph.

Six months later the reign came to an end, and it was in this milder climate that the elections to James II's only

[1] Sweeney Hall MS. 7 (24 Apr., 1681).

[2] *C.S.P.D.*, 1680–1, p. 38, cf. 1683 (2), pp. 269, 285–6, 325. On the other side cf. the printed pamphlet *Advise to the Men of Monmouth Concerning the Present Times*, 1681.

[3] Brogyntyn MS. 24; Luttrell, *Brief Relation*, 1857, i. 291; H.M.C., *12th R.*, ix. 88.

parliament took place in the spring of 1685. Court influences prevailed almost everywhere, even in South Wales. Beaufort's son, now his successor in the marquisate of Worcester, was elected to no fewer than four Welsh constituencies as well as one in England; he chose Monmouthshire, which he shared with an ardent loyalist, relegating both the borough and Brecknock county to sons of Cromwellian officials who had presumably seen the error of their parents' ways, and Brecon to John Jeffreys, the candidate whom Raglan had supported in 1679 against the court nominee.[1] In Pembrokeshire the county seat went to William Barlow of Slebech, and Wogan had to content himself again with Haverfordwest. The Barlows were a family reputed faithful to Catholicism as late as Charles I's day, and certainly faithful to Charles himself (but for the vagaries of some junior members) after most of the other Pembrokeshire gentry deserted him; William was to uphold the family tradition by going into exile with James II and returning after his death to join the Jacobite coterie at home.[2] Cardiff turned its back on Bussy Mansell and elected a local man who as a prominent official at court had up to now represented English constituencies—and this, it seems, without his even having to bribe the corporation![3] Radnor borough elected a son of one of the North Wales pensioners of the "Pensioned Parliament", and Sir Rowland Gwynne (as he now was) lost his seat for the county.

North Wales had already toed the line pretty completely in the last elections, so there was less call for change here. The court itself was alarmed at the explosion of partisanship in Denbighshire, and the new King directed Beaufort to bring the candidates and their chief supporters together to arrange a compromise; under this Myddelton was given a "walk-over" in the county on condition of supporting Trevor in the boroughs.[4] In Flintshire, Caernarvonshire and Merioneth the

---

[1] Jeffreys was now very much *persona grata* at court (H.M.C., *Ormonde*, n.s. vi. 89, vii. 340).

[2] *C.S.P.D.*, 1627–8, p. 487; *Camb. Reg.*, i. 164; R. Fenton, *Tour in Pembrokeshire*, 1903 ed., pp. 157–64, 255; *W.W.H.R.*, iii. 117–52; *T.C.S.*, 1946–7, p. 219.

[3] Penrice and Margam MS. L. 181.

[4] Chirk castle MSS. C. 2–3, E. 51.

familiar game of "general post" was resumed, apparently without contest and with no outstanding result save that (somewhat surprisingly) so good a King's man as Sir Robert Owen was momentarily left out in the cold. In Caernarvon boroughs Thomas Mostyn of Gloddaeth, who had been in mild opposition to court Catholicism since the Exclusion struggle, was replaced by a Griffith of Cefnamwlch whose father had actively promoted the Restoration in Caernarvonshire and whose grandfather had spent his last months trying to rally the county behind Charles I.[1] The only Welsh contest to come before the Commons was provoked by the candidature for Montgomery boroughs of William Williams, whose intemperate partisanship against the court in the last House had just lost him the recordership of Chester (which he had represented in parliament since 1681). His career was that of a highly successful lawyer, but twenty years earlier he had acquired by marriage the small Denbighshire estate of Glascoed, to which more recently he had added another on the border by his purchase of the heavily mortgaged lands of Edward Lloyd of Llanvorda, long in his legal clutches. Opposition was provoked not so much by his political record as by his temerity in invading a Herbert preserve. He won the election, but his opponent Charles Herbert appealed successfully on the familiar ground of failure to consult the out-boroughs, and he was unseated.[2]

The lowering of the political temperature since Charles II's successful *coup* is manifest everywhere; it will be shown in the next study how his brother threw away these advantages and whipped up party strife afresh in several of the arenas where it had died down since 1681. Thus Sir Trevor Williams and John Arnold both re-emerged from political quarantine in the elections to the Convention Parliament of 1688, regaining the Monmouthshire county and borough seats. Worcester (who, as will appear later,[3] had shown himself less compliant than his father towards the schemes of James II) had the other

---

[1] *N.L.W.J.*, vi. 253; *T.C.S.*, 1948, p. 61; *T.C.H.S.*, xi. 36–9.

[2] Wynnstay MSS. L. 533, 413–14, 1233; Sweeney Hall MSS. 3 and 5; *N.L.W.J.*, ii. 142; *M.C.*, xxi. 267–72; *C.J.*, ix. 715–16.

[3] *Infra*, pp. 219–20, 229.

county seat; but Jeffreys, the family's old client, was defeated in Brecon by Morgan of Tredegar, now drifting into the camp of its foes. Sir Rowland Gwynne recovered Radnorshire; Pembrokeshire returned to its traditional allegiance to the Owens of Orielton (friends of the Revolution) when Barlow fled to the exiled court in France; and Bussy Mansell displaced the elder and more conservative branch of his house in the representation of Glamorgan. In West Wales and North Wales politics are less obtrusive. The replacement of the Golden Grove interest in Carmarthenshire (after a tenure of the seat rarely interrupted, save during the interregnum, since Elizabeth's day), by a son of one of the Civil War turncoats, was due simply to the lack of a male heir ready to take over. On the other hand the cadet branch did not relax the grip it had kept on the borough since the Restoration; indeed the member of it who had made his *début* in James II's parliament, remembered for the undiluted loyalty of his speech of welcome to Beaufort the year before, stayed pat for another forty years, although his colleague the mayor (a Williams of Edwinsford) lost his office for too favourable a response to the King's Indulgence policy.[1]

It is not likely that politics entered into the re-election for Cardigan, by 385 votes to 363 over John Vaughan of Trawscoed, of John Lewis of Coedmawr, son of a Roundhead colonel and Cromwellian M.P. Lewis had displaced Vaughan's father in the last parliament after a clear run since the Restoration, and the rivalry went on till the end of the century; but the Lewises were an older parliamentary family than the Vaughans, who had only swum into the political horizon with the great judge and lawyer Sir John, and the whole episode is probably no more than a normal exhibition of family rivalry.[2] The Montgomery election dispute settled itself by the transfer of Sir William Williams (now dignified with a baronetcy) to Beaumaris, in spite of the efforts of the bishop of Bangor to keep him out as an enemy of the Church who in his days of opposition had shown too much countenance to Dissenters, and

---

[1] *Hist. Carmarthenshire*, ii. 31, 33; *supra*, pp. 175-6.
[2] S. R. Meyrick, *Cardiganshire*, 1808, pp. 125, 322; **Wynnstay MSS.** 1206–10; *supra*, p. 132.

latterly as solicitor general had thrown himself with too obvious a relish into the prosecution of the Seven Bishops.[1] This left the field clear for the Herbert claimant, who had been in the King's black books. Politics may possibly account for Sir Robert Owen's failure to wrest the nomination for Caernarvonshire from another Sir William Williams (of Vaynol), the grandson of a Cromwellian sheriff, but they did not prevent his election for the boroughs.[2] Sir John Trevor abandoned Denbigh boroughs for an English constituency; the fact that his successor had been one of the anti-Myddelton faction of 1681 is relevant to local history rather than to national politics.

All this points to a slackening of the tensions of the past twenty years and a movement towards something like stability in Welsh politics. The explanation must probably be sought in economic rather than in purely political factors; for we are now on the threshold of the great age of family settlements and agrarian consolidation, when in one county after another a single family rose to undisputed pre-eminence in wealth and prestige, and could treat the county seat (and sometimes the borough one too) as its private freehold. This lasted from various dates between Restoration and Revolution until, about the second decade of the eighteenth century, a series of unconnected chances brought the parliamentary dominance of many of these great houses to a sudden stop, whether it was failure of heirs in the main line (as with the Myddeltons in Denbighshire or the Vaughans in Carmarthenshire and in Merioneth), or political indiscretions (as with the Harleys in Radnorshire), or the rivalry of a family of wealthy intruders (as with the Owens of Orielton in Pembrokeshire). The parliamentary sway of the Bulkeleys in Anglesey had started much sooner, and after a temporary usurpation of the seat during much of the eighteenth century by the successors to the Bagenalls at Plas Newydd (now much enriched by discoveries of copper on the island as well as by wealthy alliances), it emerged again in the nineteenth to cross swords with the new democracy. The union of the interests of Vaughan of

[1] N.L.W., Plasgwyn MS. 84.
[2] *Supra*, p. 160; Brogyntyn MSS., letter 1549.

Llwydiarth, Wynn of Wynnstay, Williams of Glascoed and Lloyd of Llanvorda produced the still more imposing political force of the Williams Wynns, who with negligible intervals dominated Denbighshire from the end of the Myddeltons' reign, and Montgomeryshire too from a generation later. When it too fell before the onslaught of democracy Welsh politics lost a veritable dynasty of king-makers. There is a revealing passage in a letter from a lady whom Sir Watkin was canvassing on behalf of his nephew in Merioneth in 1772 in which she assures him

" she would not be so ungrateful as to give what little interest she has here against the nephew of Sir Watkin, who had done Mr. Owen [her husband] the honour to offer him a seat in Parliament for that county before Mr. Kinaston."[1]

But the Williams Wynn dynasty was rooted in its native soil, whereas in West Wales a similar fusion of the interests of Vaughan of Golden Grove, Lort of Stackpool and Pryce of Gogerddan (all old parliamentary families) in the same period led to the enthronement of a branch of the Scottish clan of Campbell.

This process was still in its initial phases in the later seventeenth century, when the new agrarian code of the Restoration was beginning to tell, and the mounting scale of expenditure both in public service and in the households of the gentry was forcing the small squire and the yeoman into the ditch.[2] The yeoman indeed—if we accept Vaughan of Llangyndeyrn's definition of this elusive personage as " he that tilleth the ground, getteth his living by selling of corn in Markets, and can dispend yeerly fortie shillings sterling "[3]—had never been more than a passenger in politics, but the squire of £100 a year had been a factor to reckon with. Now he emerged from political obscurity only in times of acute crisis, such as the election of 1741, when Walpole was fighting in the last ditch and the new House was left with as many as nine Welsh elections petitions on its hands.[4] Even the middling sort of gentry

---

[1] *Id.*, unscheduled letter of 13 May [1772].
[2] *T.C.S.*, 1948, pp. 72–4.
[3] *Golden Grove*, 1608, III. xxiii.
[4] *Gent. Mag.*, 1741, p. 52, 1742, p. 44.

had little political initiative except in a few counties like Caernarvon or Flint, or Glamorgan after the short period when the two branches of the Mansells united their interests and ran the county between them, or Monmouth, with its two seats to ring the changes upon. From soon after the Restoration it became a normal practice, in counties where the devolution of the seat was not yet automatic, to hold a meeting of the principal landowners soon after the dissolution with a view to deciding on a common course of action and avoiding the expense of a contest.[1] Flintshire will provide an example of the way this principle of rotation worked—or broke down. There four families shared representation between them for fifty years from Charles II's last parliament, and contests arose only if one of the four declined to stand down " when " (in the indignant words of his opponent on one such occasion) " other gentlemen require to have their turn of serving ".[2]

It is against the background of this long-term process that the ebullition of party strife under the later Stuarts falls into proper perspective. Family remained, as it had always been, the dominant *motif* in elections, party being at first no more than a borrowed battle-cry to give cohesion to the various family groups that were trying to storm their way into the governing oligarchy. The significance of the post-Restoration electoral struggles lies in the fact that in them we have the first timid hint of partisan preferences cutting across tribal loyalties. " That mere political partisanship should override local and personal obligations ", it has been well observed of English elections of the same period,[3] " seemed monstrous to those who thought themselves entitled to the support of their humbler neighbours." And in Wales, with its strong blood attachments, this was even truer than in England. The political veneer must not blind us to the survival of the under-lying element of family feud. The antagonisms aroused in Elizabethan Pembrokeshire by the towering personality of Sir John Perrot were not extinct a hundred years later. There

[1] E.g. Mostyn MS., ii. 50; Brogyntyn MSS., unscheduled letter of 1 Feb., 1681; Chirk castle MSS. E. 1076, 1084; L. A. Cust, *Chronicles of Erthig*, i. 68.

[2] H.M.C., *Kenyon*, p. 428 (Sir T. Hanmer, 1702).

[3] Mrs. Eric George in *E.H.R.*, xlv. 554.

had been re-grouping, of course; in Elizabeth's day the court interest (which meant, broadly, the ruling set) was also the Protestant interest, and when later the court was suspected of dallying with Rome, its hereditary champions had to make their choice between Protestantism and prerogative. But it is a striking fact that over a century after the great Haverford-west election of 1571, a descendant of the Barlow of Slebech who had then been a leader of the anti-Perrot faction should be disputing the seat with a descendant of the Wogans of Wiston, who had been Perrot's champions.

A still more pronounced continuity can be traced between the Denbighshire elections of 1601 and 1681. The two pro-tagonists in the later election, it is true, belonged to families that had not yet risen to the top of county society in 1601; but Myddelton's chief backer in the county election of 1681, and the successful candidate in the borough contest, was a great-grandson of the Salusbury who had fought in the court interest in 1601. Against him was ranged a descendant of the Elizabethan Brereton of Borras whose second marriage had transferred him and his progeny from the Llewenny connection to that of its foes, while the sheriff who lent such timely aid to Trevor in 1681 sprang from the Hollands of Kinmel who had been among the more turbulent adherents of the anti-Salusbury and anti-court faction of a century earlier.[1] Here, to the Welsh elector of the seventeenth century—and to his children and children's children for many a generation afterwards—lay the unchanging realities of politics. That is why 1868, which saw the wholesale dethronement of these great parliamentary dynasties, is such an *annus mirabilis* in Welsh history.[2]

[1] *E.H.R.*, lix. 349–52, 356, 361; Griffith, *Pedigrees*, pp. 102, 259; Palmer, *Old Parish of Wrexham*, opp. p. 162.

[2] Much information about post-Restoration Welsh politics will be found in the MS. thesis, " The activities of Welsh Members of Parliament, 1660–1688," by D. M. Elis-Williams (Bangor, 1952). This was not available till after the above study was already in proof, but I am indebted to it for a few references added in footnotes.

VI

THE GLORIOUS REVOLUTION

THE devotion of the Welsh towards the British monarchy, a devotion born when Harry Tudor ascended the throne in fulfilment of bardic prophecy, survived many rude shocks in the two centuries that followed. First came the shock of the Reformation, which foreign observers expected to provoke a Welsh revolt; the disappointment of these expectations was due largely to the fact that Rome came to be identified in Welsh minds with the menace to their long and ill-defended coasts from Spain and Ireland. Then came the substitution of a Scottish for a Welsh dynasty—yet Wales showed the same loyalty towards the first two Stuarts as she had shown towards Elizabeth and the Henrys. The shifty and unimaginative policy of Charles I towards his Welsh subjects threatened at times to snap the bond, but gentry and peasants rallied to the crown in the Civil War with almost complete unanimity, and the thought that buoyed them up during the years when monarchy was in abeyance was *Fe ddaw'r brenin etto*.[1] The success of Puritan rule in ridding the Welsh coast of the long-standing threat from Ireland and Catholic Europe was over-shadowed by its deep offence of allowing low-born fanatics to " insult over the Gentry " and to batten on their estates.[2] And so, when fanaticism reared its head again under Charles II in an attempt to exclude the Duke of York from the succession because he was a Catholic, the Welsh gentry would have none of it, save only a few personal enemies of Beaufort, the Lord President, who was on cordial terms with the Duke, and dubbed one of his " twelve disciples " in company with Danby,

---

[1] " The King will come again " (William Phylip in *Eos Ceiriog*, 1823, I. x–xi); *T.C.S.*, 1948, pp. 29–63.

[2] *Supra*, pp. 120–1, 176.

Lauderdale and some of the high Tory bishops.[1]

The triumphant accession of the object of these attacks accordingly caused no fluttering in the Welsh dovecotes. When Beaufort accepted a renewal of his term of office from James II, the cheering which had greeted his great presidential tour of the Principality had barely died away, and his influence was still pervasive enough to ensure for the second James, as Cecil had for the first James when he first entered England, that " not a dog should bark " at his accession. The Duke of Monmouth's revolt in the first summer of the reign evoked no Welsh support—not even from old admirers or fellow-campaigners like Lord Herbert of Cherbury and Roger Whitley of Hawarden, who had espoused his claims five years earlier, in the days of the Exclusion struggle.[2] Beaufort for his part was commissioned to raise a regiment of ten companies (some five hundred in all) for the defence of Bristol and the south-west against the rebels—too late, however, for them to help in Monmouth's defeat at Sedgemoor.[3]

Welsh lawyers were equally assiduous in the new King's service; Judge Jeffreys, who had been James's solicitor when he was Duke of York and had risen from that post to become head of the Welsh judicial system and then of the King's Bench itself, gave such satisfaction by the ferocity of his sentences on the rebels that he was raised soon afterwards to the woolsack—to the great satisfaction of neighbours and kinsmen in north-eastern Wales.[4] It is true that his old *protégé* and admirer William Lloyd, bishop of St. Asaph, lamented how he had now " become a stranger " to the judge; but this was before the Bloody Assize and long before Lloyd himself became estranged from the King, so it had nothing to do with politics.[5] Jeffreys' goodwill towards the popish monarch was matched by that of his cousin Sir John Trevor of Brynkynallt, who at the height of the Popish Plot scare of the last reign had presided over the Commons' committee that

---

[1] H.M.C., *14th R.*, ix. 370, *Ormonde*, n.s. v. 459, vi. 262, *Leyborne-Popham*, p. 258; *N.L.W.J.*, vi. 249–51; *C.S.P.D.*, 1679–80, p. 68.
[2] N.L.W., Milborne MS. 978 (28 Mar., 1685); *N.L.W.J.*, vi. 254, 256.
[3] H.M.C., *11th R.*, v. 127, *H. of Lords*, n.s. ii. 281.
[4] *Home Counties Mag.*, xii. 3–18, 81–91.
[5] N.L.W., Brogyntyn MSS., letter 13; cf. *T.C.S.*, 1948, p. 76.

listened (none too critically) to the charges laid by John Arnold of Llanthony against his Catholic neighbours in south-eastern Wales, and so helped to provoke the last great outburst of religious persecution there. The skill with which, as Speaker, Trevor piloted James's only parliament through its first session won him at its close the post of Master of the Rolls, while his earlier repute as a militant but loyal Protestant gained him a seat on the Privy Council during those closing months of the reign when the King was trying desperately to win back Anglican support.[1]

Some years ago Archbishop Mathew pointed out (in a lecture which has never been published in full),[2] how strong was the Welsh and border element among James's legal advisers. They included not only *arrivistes* like Jeffreys but men who had reached the top by the more humdrum process of slow and steady promotion from the Welsh circuits; yet none of them smelled danger either to the common law or to the Anglican establishment in the early policy of the new King, and all, with the exception of Sir John Powell (of whom more later) showed a complaisance in sharp contrast with the demeanour of Charles I's Welsh lawyers.[3] The only lawyer of note who might have made trouble—William Williams of Llanvorda, one of the most vociferous of the Exclusionists of the last reign —was momentarily silenced by his successful rival Jeffreys through the imposition of a crippling fine arising out of his conduct as Speaker in the last parliament; and although he was elected for Montgomery borough at the opening of the reign and promptly included in the Committee for Privileges, he was unseated on petition on the ground that the " out-boroughs " of Llanfyllin, Llanidloes and Welshpool had not been included in the poll—whereupon the seat was given to his opponent, Charles Herbert of Aston, son of Charles I's

---

[1] On the other hand, Lodge's assertion (*Pol. Hist.*, viii. 283) that he was put on the Council to conciliate Dissenting opinion appears to be based solely on the fact that the two admitted with him were old Dissenters; possibly too there is a confusion with the other Sir John Trevor (of Trevalun), the former secretary of state, of whom the statement, *mutatis mutandis*, would be true.

[2] *T.C.S.*, 1938, pp. 119–23.

[3] *B.B.C.S.*, xii. 106–7; *T.C.S.*, 1948, pp. 22–3, 28, 47–8.

attorney general and brother of the admiral who later carried the Whig lords' invitation to William of Orange.[1]

It was not until the second year of the reign that the potential dangers from a popish monarchy began to reveal themselves, and another two years passed before the Welsh Tory and Anglican squires were seriously shaken by them. In July, 1686, the Earl of Powis, Beaufort's Catholic brother-in-law (whom he had defended from the attacks of Williams and the Country Party under Charles II) was admitted to the Privy Council, made a marquis, and included in the inner circle of James's advisers. Early in 1687 the royal policy of thrusting co-religionists into key posts in civil and military administration hitherto held by uncompromising Protestants, and of buying off Dissenters by including them with Catholics in a general Indulgence for their own worship, began to appear more openly. In February, when the King was due to meet his parliament for a second session, he wrote to Beaufort enjoining him to use his influence to secure compliance among the Welsh M.P.'s and to ensure that any pending by-elections went the right way; in particular he was to warn Sir John Morgan of Kynnersley, member for Herefordshire and ex-member for Radnor, that " if he will not comply . . . he shall no longer be in my pay ". For Sir John, like his father Sir Thomas, the Roundhead soldier of fortune, followed the profession of arms, and had been gazetted to the Ninth Foot at the time of Monmouth's rising. He had won the good opinion of the court in Charles II's day, but there was evidently some doubt whether the son of a man who had fought in the Protestant cause all his life might not stick at the admission of Roman Catholics as fellow-officers. The threat was carried out, but Morgan remained loyal till the final crisis of the reign.[2] By a queer irony of fate one of the first victims of James's new policy of Catholicising the army was Beaufort's own son the Marquis of Worcester. Soon after the first Declaration of Indulgence was issued in the April of 1687 Worcester, a less pliant Protestant than his father, was deprived of the commission he had held in the

[1] *Supra,* p. 210.
[2] H.M.C., *12th R.,* ix. 89–90, *Downshire,* i. 242; N.L.W., Penrice and Margam MS. L. 151; Williams, *P.H.,* p. 180.

Duke of York's regiment since the last reign, to make way for
Powis's son.[1] The reason is not far to seek: Worcester had
been one of the two Welsh members of the committee which
drew up the address from the Commons in November, 1685,
requesting James to withdraw the commissions granted in
defiance of the law to popish officers at the crisis of Monmouth's
rebellion—a challenge that drove the outraged King to put an
end to the session when it had lasted barely a fortnight, and
deterred him from ever calling the members together again.[2]
A later victim was Charles Herbert of Aston, Williams's
supplanter in Montgomery borough, who lost his " Captain-
shipp " after cross-questioning in Council; he was destined to
perish in the service of William III in Ireland.[3] On the other
hand, William Barlow of Slebech, M.P. for Pembrokeshire,
whom Charles II had made a captain of horse and James had
promoted to a colonelcy, stuck to the loyal traditions of his
house and followed the King into exile, returning only after
James's death to join the coterie of Jacobites in West Wales.[4]

After many prorogations the King made up his mind that the
best hope of parliamentary sanction for his religious policy lay
in the election, under proper safeguards, of a new parliament.
Accordingly the old one was finally dissolved in July, 1687,
and James began his preparations for ensuring himself against
a similar rebuff from its successor. The first step was to direct
the lords lieutenant to find out which of the principal gentry in
their respective counties were prepared to support the abolition
of religious tests and penalties and which were not. It was on
Beaufort, as universal lord lieutenant, that the task devolved
in Wales. In the autumn of 1687 he summoned the magistrates
and deputy lieutenants to Ludlow, but he got little satisfaction
from them. More than half excused themselves on various
pretexts, and of those who came only the merest handful gave
the right answer.[5] A start was therefore made at purging

[1] Luttrell, *Brief Relation*, 1857 ed., i. 403; H.M.C., *7th R.*, p. 504, *Portland*,
iii. 398; *C.S.P.D.*, 1679–80, pp. 165–6, 232, 379.
[2] *C.J.*, ix. 757, 759, 761.
[3] N.L.W., Powis Castle MSS., 17th cent. corr., 137; Williams, *P.H.*, p. 149.
[4] Williams, *P.H.*, p. 156; *supra*, p. 209.
[5] H.M.C., *12th R.*, ix. 91. See also the valuable analysis of the replies
by Dr. T. Richards in *Cymdeithas Hanes Bedwyddwyr Cymru, Trafodion* 1924,
pp. 27–37.

county government of the more obdurate Anglicans, and substituting men of more pliable cast. For this purpose James looked to Dissenters, whose gratitude for favours shared with their Romanist fellow-subjects had been expressed in several addresses to the crown, including three from Wales. Dr. Richards has shown how far these petitions were from reflecting the sentiments of the more influential and thoughtful of the Welsh Dissenters, and James himself lived to regret having " lost his credit with the Church party for having gathered those vipers from the dunghill where the laws had laid them ".[1]

In any case, the number of the Welsh Dissenters, especially of those of sufficient estate to qualify them as magistrates, was too small to make any substantial difference at election time; there was more hope in the few influential friends they had among the conforming gentry. John Arnold of Llanthony, who had hobnobbed with Samuel Jones of Brynllywarch and other Welsh sectaries of the south-east in the days of the Popish Plot, was of too little weight, and too bitter a personal foe of Beaufort, to be used for the purpose, so he was left to serve out the prison sentence he had incurred through non-payment of the fine imposed for his " scandalous " attacks on the Lord President.[2] But William Williams was just the man for the purpose. A lawyer whose abilities matched his ambitions, he was also a churchman (bred in an Anglesey vicarage) whose marriage had brought him into close association with the Dissenters of north-eastern Wales; for his wife was a daughter of Watkin Kyffin, steward to Sir Thomas Myddelton the Roundhead and brother-in-law to Jones the Regicide. His " dear cousin " John Jones junior, the regicide's son, later sold him the paternal house at Wrexham where young John had been brought up under the tuition of Morgan Llwyd while his widowed father was serving in Ireland, and Williams let it be used as a manse for John Evans, Llwyd's successor in the pastorate of the Wrexham Independents, and possibly for a

[1] Richards, *loc. cit.*, pp. 15–18.
[2] *C.S.P.D.*, 1680–81, p. 381, 1682, pp. 221–3, 275–6, 288–9, 538–9; H.M.C., *12th R.*, ix. 88.

time as a place of worship for his flock.[1] Naturally, Williams
was ready to listen to any overtures that would help him to
repair the depleted fortune to which Jeffreys's vindictiveness
had reduced him, while from the King's standpoint his credit
with the Dissenting interest was an asset to be played off
against the Chancellor's intractable Anglicanism, which had
already caused James to draw back on the threshold of adding
to his honours a Welsh earldom.[2]

In October, 1687, Williams was restored to his old recorder-
ship of Chester; in December he was knighted and raised to
the office of solicitor general; and in the following March
Chancellor Jeffreys had the distasteful task of writing to ask
the rival he thought he had finally silenced for names of
Dissenters suitable to put on commissions of the peace.[3]
Beaufort had already produced a list of ten such names for
Wales—five each from north and south.[4] Most striking of all
is the nomination in early January of Williams's " cousin "
John Jones as sheriff of Merioneth, where he had inherited
lands from his father. Jones, excommunicated for nonconformity in 1663, had since conformed, but without abandoning
hereditary sympathies, still less living down his father's name.
Before the appointment became effective, however, someone
(we do not know who) must have put a spoke in the wheel,
for a week later another name was substituted—that of Sir
Robert Owen of Brogyntyn and Clenennau, grandson of the
gallant cavalier Sir John, and himself a doughty champion of
the Church against Dissent in the disputations of Charles II's
day.[5] There is no evidence that the suggestions of Beaufort

[1] *N.L.W.J.*, vi. 256; N.L.W., Plas Yolyn MSS., 2, 52, 106, 136, 190, 196,
N.L.W. MS. 114401D, fos. 43, 103. Williams did not buy the house till
1692, and Jones was still paying rent to him for part of it in 1699 (Plas
Yolyn 160, 189), while another part was in the hands of Lady Eyton of
Eyton Isaf, a member of Evans's congregation (Palmer, *Older Nonconformity
of Wrexham*, p. 189). It is Calamy who states (without date) that Evans
and his wife " kept a conventicle at Brynyffon [sic], a house they rented
from Sir Wm. Williams " (A. G. Matthews, *Calamy Revised*, 1934, p. 185).
[2] H. M. Hyde, *Judge Jeffreys*, p. 274.
[3] N.L.W., Wynnstay MSS., C. 24.
[4] Richards, *loc. cit.*, pp. 38–42.
[5] P.R.O. *List of Sheriffs*, p. 261; Palmer, *op. cit.*, p. 43; N.L.W., Plas
Yolyn MS. 198, Brogyntyn MSS., letter 1859.

and Williams ever bore fruit; even if they had, so slight a leavening could have had little total effect.

Equally slow in operation was the method of influencing the electorate by remodelling municipal corporations after the pattern set by Charles II. Lord Powis was made chairman of a committee to carry out this work in 1687, but even in his own county he met with stiff opposition in his attempts to bring Montgomery borough to heel, especially from Anglican members of his own clan like his old political foe Lord Herbert of Cherbury, the castellan, and Charles Herbert of Aston, the borough member, with the " underhand " backing of the unseated member, Sir William Williams himself. As late as the June of 1688 proceedings here had only just reached the stage of the impanelling of a mixed jury of Catholics and Protestants to hear evidence, and Powis's son was urging " what a fatal blow it would be to the King's concerns in all the neighbouring counties if the Quo Warranto took no effect ", since " though it be but a small place few Corporations have more gentry of their body than they have, and perchance few places in this subject are of greater consequence to the King ".[1] Matters had advanced no further in Conway, and in the Glamorgan boroughs preliminary enquiries had barely begun in October.[2]

By this time the march of events was making the prospect of a compliant parliament remoter than ever. It was in June that Sir William Williams as solicitor general failed (to the undisguised joy of Jeffreys) to procure a verdict against the Seven Bishops for their " false, malicious and seditious " petition against the second Declaration of Indulgence issued two months earlier. If the prosecuting counsel was Welsh so too was one of the bench of judges that acquitted them—Sir John Powell, a Carmarthenshire man who had been called to the bench in Cromwellian times and subsequently became recorder of Brecon and a judge of Great Sessions;[3] and the rejoicings that greeted their acquittal in London could not

[1] Powis Castle MSS., *loc. cit.*, nos. 125, 137, 419; *N.L.W.J.*, iii. 142; H.M.C. *Ormonde*, n.s. iv. 574.
[2] N.L.W., Mostyn MS. 238, fo. 47, Penrice and Margam MS. L. 202.
[3] W. R. Williams, *Welsh Judges*, p. 141.

but find some echo in Wales, for the acquitted included Lloyd of St. Asaph, described by the historian of his diocese as " one of the most learned, laborious and successful bishops that ever occupied the see ", and the subject of laudatory verses by Huw Morus, the veteran *bardd teulu* of Sir Robert Owen, and by the Denbighshire drover poet Edward Morris. For although born in England Lloyd came of old Anglesey stock and remained fluent in the language, which from the outset of his episcopate he resolved to use for " confirmation and addresses " —without waiting for Edward Morris's reminder that

> Pum gair mewn eglwys lwys lân
> sydd well, os hwy ddeallan,
> na myrddiwn mewn mawrddawn maith
> a doe athro dieithriaeth.[1]

He was on excellent terms with the neighbouring gentry, and although he was a stern upholder of Anglican principles against Dissenters, his main efforts were directed towards winning them over by persuasion, even to the point of public disputations with Presbyterians and Quakers.[2] At this crisis he used his widespread influence against the court and in favour of the Whig lords whose eyes were turning towards the King's Protestant son-in-law at The Hague. John Stevens the antiquary, a captain in the royal army who later fought for James II in Ireland, was at this time stationed at Welshpool (with frequent visits to the neighbouring counties of Merioneth, Cardigan and Radnor), and he tells us in an unpublished autobiographical fragment how Bishop Lloyd's release from the Tower was followed by a " Progress through the Country " in which he " preach'd at almost every Church, and din'd or supp'd at the Houses of most Gentlemen of any note, where all the rest met, to incense the People against the King, and dispose them to what follow'd "; and we learn elsewhere that he even used his Presbyterian contacts towards the same end.[3]

---

[1] " In the church, holy and undefiled, better five words, so they be understood, than a myriad in long-winded rhetoric from a preacher in a strange tongue."

[2] D. R. Thomas, *St. Asaph*, 1908 ed., i. 124–35, 230–231; O. M. Edwards (ed.) *Gwaith Edw. Morris*, 1904, pp. 21–4; *Eos Ceiriog*, ii. 389.

[3] B.M., Lansdowne MS. 828, fo. 10; *D.N.B.*, liv. 231; D. R. Thomas, *op. cit.*, i. 127.

Edward Morris wrote (but of course did not publish) an ode
on the release of the Seven Bishops, in which he held up to the
King all the warnings he could muster from sacred and profane
history against the deadly sin of presumption.[1]

As yet, however, there was no thought among the Welsh
gentry of deserting their King; the most they sought was the
calling of a free parliament which could set up adequate safeguards for the Church, such as the more moderate opponents of
Exclusion (like Thomas Mostyn) had advocated in 1679.[2]
As for the King, like his father before him he looked to Wales
to rally to the crown in this new crisis of its fortunes. The birth
of the Pretender, coming as it did two days after the committal
of the Seven Bishops to the Tower, might be the last straw
for the English opposition; in Wales it had another aspect.
There had been no Prince of Wales for nearly forty years, and
the title still had a subtle magic in it. A copy of the *Gazette*
with news of the Prince's birth was promptly sent to Sir
Robert Owen of Brogyntyn by that tireless purveyor of court
news to the Welsh gentry, Owen Wynne, the Anglesey-born
lawyer who had first been introduced into the bureau of the
Secretary of State by Sir Leoline Jenkins, remained as under-
secretary to his successors, and was soon to serve as clerk to
the commissioners sent by James II to treat with William of
Orange. Wynne was obviously perturbed about the bishops'
trial (" how it will goe with them," he sighs, " god knowes ");
but he found in the birth of a prince " the Occasion of Our
present Joy, god Continue and preserve it ".

" Its Luvly Boy [he adds], well-guifted, and like to Live. Your Bard Hu.
Morris may Exercise his Muse upon his Own prince. Not an honest Man
went to bed sober these two nights, and Bells and Bonfires never ceased.
Nothing but this happy incident could have united all of Our thoughts."[3]

Wynne's views were no doubt coloured by his official position,
for his chief, Secretary Godolphin, was one of the staunchest
of James's servants. Other Welshmen were more restrained in
their " present joy " over a Prince of Wales only too likely to

[1] *Gwaith*, pp. 109–10.
[2] *H.M.C., 12th R.*, ix. 110.
[3] Brogyntyn MSS., letter 1695; Williams, *Welsh Judges*, p. 140; Griffith,
Pedigrees, p. 111.

be confirmed in his father's faith by the influence of his gover-
ness, Lady Powis; and so far from effecting that happy union
of thoughts foreseen in the rosier visions of the under-secretary,
this new development only intensified the conflict of loyalties.
Huw Morus never wrote his birthday ode, and at Oxford,
where James's gross infringements on College liberties remained
unforgiven, Anthony Wood observed that not even the loyal
Welshmen of Jesus broke the sullen silence with which the
birth of the Prince was greeted.[1]

James concluded that the time was ripe for a personal appeal
to his subjects. In August he was received in state by Beaufort
at Badminton, much as his father had taken refuge with the
Duke's grandfather at Raglan on the morrow of Naseby;
thence he proceeded with great pomp through Gloucester,
Worcester, Ludlow, Shrewsbury and Whitchurch to Chester,
receiving on the way every mark of loyalty, including a letter
of thanks sent on behalf of a group of Monmouthshire Dissenters.[2] The royal progress bore an ominous resemblance to
Charles I's recruiting tour on the outbreak of Civil War, but
with the difference that on this occasion the Prince of Wales
was too young to go with his father to draw the cheers of the
multitude; moreover James did not, as Charles had done,
cross the Welsh border to receive the plaudits of the Prince's
own people.[3] He did, however, attempt some measures of
conciliation there; for example, during the next two months
some at least of the displaced magistrates were restored to the
commission of the peace. One was Robert Davies of Gwysan-
ney (Flintshire), naturalist and antiquary, and grandson of a
loyal soldier of Charles I; another was John Griffith of
Carreglwyd (Anglesey), son of a chancellor of St. Asaph and
Bangor.[4] More significant still is the fresh commission to
Beaufort, a week before William of Orange made his first
false start for the English shore in October, to raise ten thousand
men in Wales, including a special regiment styled the Prince

[1] *Life and Times*, ii. 268.
[2] Macaulay, *Hist.*, ch. viii; Richards, *loc. cit.*, pp. 19–22.
[3] Cf. supra, p. 68.
[4] H.M.C., *3rd R.*, p. 259, *5th R.*, p. 414; N.L.W. MS. 1593 E, fos. 191,
209–11; Lloyd, *Powys Fadog*, v. 201 ff.; Griffith, *Pedigrees*, pp. 26–7.

of Wales's regiment, to be recruited in the south by Colonel Thomas Carne of Ewenny.[1]

At this juncture Captain Stevens was called away from Welshpool to London; he tells us that although " the Fame of the Intended Invasion from *Holland*, was spread all over the Nation, and most men were preparing for the General Insurrection which ensu'd ", he left mid-Wales quiet enough, if " ill-inclin'd ". At the same time the militia in Glamorgan was putting itself in readiness to resist the invader, and local officials were at pains to see that news of the King's latest concessions was conveyed to remoter towns off the post-roads.[2] James had apparently left North Wales out of his defensive schemes, since it did not lie on the direct path of invasion from Holland; but several local squires volunteered to fill in the gap by raising forces in their own districts. Among these were Sir Robert Owen, Thomas Mostyn and Robert Pugh of Penrhyn Creuddyn. Of the last, a zealous Roman Catholic who later fell fighting for his faith in Ireland, no less could have been expected; but Owen was an equally zealous Anglican, and had suffered rebuff after rebuff from the court: he had been disappointed of the constableship of Harlech, which his great-uncle had defended to the bitter end for Charles I, he had only just seen his grandfather's office of vice-admiral for North Wales granted over his head to (of all people!) Sir William Williams, and he had all but been passed over for the shrievalty of Merioneth in favour of the regicide's son. Mostyn, too, although married to a recusant, had taken part with the moderate Protestant opposition under Charles II, and had lost his place as deputy lieutenant in consequence. But the King, wavering between fight and flight on hearing of his son-in-law's landing at Torbay, turned down all three offers and even instructed Carne to stop recruiting for the Prince of Wales's regiment.[3] On the other hand, he ordered that strict watch should be kept on the activities in Pembrokeshire of Sir Hugh Owen of Orielton, son and namesake of the

[1] H.M.C., *12th R.*, vii. 214.
[2] Lansdowne MSS., *loc. cit.*; Penrice and Margam MSS. L. 203-4.
[3] H.M.C., *5th R.*, pp. 347-8; Brogyntyn MSS., letter 13; Griffith, *Pedigrees*, p. 372; *N.L.W.J.*, vi. 253.

irresolute Roundhead of Civil War days, and still more on Sir Rowland Gwynne of Llanelwedd, ex-member for Radnorshire, who was busy undermining the loyalty of the south with the zeal which was to bring him to the front rank of Whig politicians after the Revolution.[1]

The most the King could now hope for from Wales was that it should be " kept quiet ". Beaufort's reports on the eve of the Prince of Orange's landing were not too encouraging, and James, while expressing complete confidence in his Welsh deputy and a desire to have him near his person should he decide to take the field, could not yet risk removing him from the area. Captain Stevens, arriving back at his post at Welshpool a week after the news from Torbay, was shocked at " so great an alteration " in the climate of opinion " in so short a time ". " The Generality of the People ", he writes, " began to be more open-hearted, than they had been when I left them, discovering their Inclination to the Prince of Orange, and an Aversion to the King ". Meanwhile James's fatal irresolution, preventing him from either putting himself at the head of his troops while they still outnumbered the enemy, or cutting the ground from under the opposition by calling the long-promised free parliament, produced an effect reminiscent of the defection of South Wales from Charles I, for similar reasons, in 1645–6, and gave time for the propaganda of Bishop Lloyd in the north and Sir Rowland Gwynne in the south to bear fruit. During the next week or so news came in of desertions, in rapid succession, of those nearest the King, " whom it is no Buziness of this Place ", Stevens protested, " to take Notice of ".

" This [he continues] encourag'd others to rise, . . . follow'd, at first, by only a few of their own Tenants and Servants . . . [but] soon reinforc'd from all Parts of the Country, Fathers leading their sons and masters their servants, with their best Horses, and Arms, and for fear of any Turn of affairs, giving out that they ran away; thus making a sure Interest on both sides, by staying themselves, if the King had prosper'd, and by sending those under their Command, if the Prince of *Orange* succeeded; a Practice well known in the Days of King *Charles* the first . . .

The King's Revenue was every where seiz'd by those who were up in Arms, and no serviceable Horse was safe, for either those same People took them violently from such as refus'd to follow their example, or else

[1] H.M.C., *5th R.*, p. 348; Penrice and Margam MS. L. 205; Williams, *P.H.*, p. 174; *supra*, pp. 156, 202, 204, 209, 211.

they were in that Time of confusion, safely stolen by such as improv'd that Opportunity to rob, and plunder whom they pleas'd."

Stevens himself saved his horses by having them conveyed to Edward Vaughan of Llwydiarth, who remained faithful to James II, in spite of the Roundhead traditions of his family[1]

When at last the King joined his army in mid-November, the moment for action was already past. Some ten days later Beaufort had to report that he could no longer hold Bristol against the growing strength of the Orange faction,[2] and Lord Herbert of Cherbury was able to occupy Ludlow from Montgomeryshire without opposition.[3] Just at the time when Bristol was lost, William was joined near Oxford by Beaufort's own son (that Marquis of Worcester whose services had been spurned by James), along with Sir John Morgan (a deserter from Carne's regiment) and two or three hundred horsemen.[4] It was at this point that the King took the step now being urged on him even by high Tories like Beaufort[5]—the issue of writs for a parliament to meet in January; but once more he had missed the boat. " I . . . cannot Conceive ", wrote Sir Robert Cotton from Cheshire to a Denbighshire " cozen ", " how a free Parliament can in this Juncture bee either chosen or sett with ffreedom ". As a safeguard Cotton urged his Denbighshire neighbours to " reserve their votes " till the local gentry should have met and decided on a common line of action. This was done, and in a matter of days there was general agreement (including even Vaughan of Llwydiarth, who was a voter here too) to re-elect Sir Richard Myddelton for the county; there was still some hesitation about the borough, where Sir William Williams was trying to thrust his son in, and some made their support of Myddelton conditional on his opposing this manœuvre.[6]

These discussions, however, were by now purely academic, for while they were still afoot James was busy with preparations

---

[1] H.M.C., *loc. cit.*; Lansdowne MSS., *loc. cit.*; *supra*, p. 131.
[2] H.M.C., *11th R.*, v. 222, *12th R.*, vii. 224.
[3] Skeel, *Council in the Marches*, p. 187; Lansdowne MSS., *loc. cit.*
[4] Penrice and Margam MS. L. 206; H.M.C., *11th R.*, v. 222.
[5] H.M.C., *5th R.*, p. 350.
[6] Cust, *Chronicles of Erthig*, i. 68; N.L.W., Chirk Castle MSS., E. 1075–6, 1079, 1084.

for flying abroad to evade meeting a parliament whose opposition to his whole policy was a foregone conclusion. His flight
on December 12 gave the *coup de grâce* to loyalist hopes in
Wales. Only the day before, Sir Edward Mansell of Margam
had been telling Sir Rowland Gwynne of Carne's continued
efforts for the King in his own despite, while assuring him that
the rest of the local gentry were solidly for the Prince of
Orange.[1] It needed but a spark to set the country ablaze by
spreading to the rank and file the agitation so far confined to
the gentry and their immediate circle. This was provided
when the delayed action of the King's follies raised afresh the
spectre, which Cromwell had seemed to lay for good, of an
Irish descent on Wales. James's dealings with Tyrconnell in
Ireland bore an unhappy resemblance to his father's with
Strafford; the Irish regiment he had brought over to London
in June was only too suggestive of the Glamorgan negotiations
of 1645.[2] No sooner had the King fled his capital for an unknown destination than panic spread through London; houses
of prominent Romanists were attacked and the air was thick
with tales of the outrages committed by this handful of Irish
soldiers.[3] It did not take long for the alarm to reach Wales.
A week later Dolgelley was agog with rumours that an Irish
army was on its way, killing all before it—whereupon the
panic-stricken mob seized what arms they could lay hold of,
and thirty of them forced open the gaol and freed the prisoners,
assaulting the gaoler (David Owen) with clubs and swords and
declaring that neither he nor the sheriff (Sir Robert Owen)
had any authority now that the throne was vacant. When a
group of strangers was espied descending the mountain towards the village next day, they were fired on under the impression that the Irish had arrived, and one was killed before
it was discovered that they were only the excise commissioners
on their lawful occasions![4]

Welshpool had been a-simmer ever since Lord Powis began
his proceedings against the corporation, but boiling-point was

[1] Penrice and Margam MS. **1. 207**.
[2] Cf. *supra*, pp. 203, 207 and *n*.
[3] Lodge, *Pol. Hist.*, vii. 296; H.M.C., *5th R.*, p. 324.
[4] Brogyntyn MSS., letter 2983.

reached with a duel between the borough member, Charles Herbert, and Owen Vaughan (probably an unidentified member of the Llwydiarth clan), which in turn provoked street fighting between Protestants and Papists. Powis castle, whose owner clung to the King to the point of following him into exile, was naturally an object of attack. Park and ponds were " destroy'd in a maner ", and the house (according to the same eye-witness account) " reduc'd to such a Condition as some of ye Lewd Houses at London ". Intruding zealots from Shropshire joined the *mêlée*, and another of the Earl's houses, near Buttington, was plundered by a local mob breathing threatenings and slaughter against all who would not declare for the Prince of Orange.[1] Inevitably the infection spread to the Creuddyn peninsula, with its ancient body of Catholic gentry and its relatively fresh memories of similar scares in the 'forties.[2] Shortly before Christmas the local magistrates, Thomas Mostyn of Gloddaeth and Robert Wynne of Berthddu (son of a Royalist colonel) sent out scouts to ascertain the truth about the supposed Irish visitation, and resolved to await their return before calling out the militia or taking any further steps beyond the precaution of disarming local recusants. A search of Penrhyn for this purpose produced only the arms of a single foot soldier (for which Pugh was liable) and one other sword, but the constable and his assistants took occasion to deface the private chapel which Pugh had recently repaired for Catholic worship.[3]

The panic was now subsiding, but it flared up afresh in Anglesey as late as the following March, with the news that James had landed in Ireland, bent on making it a base for the recovery of his throne on his own terms. Here a rumour went round (suggested, obviously, by the memory of Civil War experiences)[4] that Tyrconnell was demanding grain from the island and threatening to swoop down on it if he were refused. There were minor affrays at Holyhead, precautions against a surprise landing, and the usual tales of Irish atrocities, but that

[1] *Id.*, 1174; Cust, *op. cit.*, i. 69; Lansdowne MSS., *loc. cit.*
[2] E.g., *C.W.P.*, 1695.
[3] Mostyn MS. 238, fo. 48.
[4] E.g., N.L.W. MS. 1546 E (iii), fo. 99.

was all.[1] For by now the Convention had met and proclaimed
William and Mary joint sovereigns; the country had a settled
government once more. Elections to the Convention had gone
quietly enough in Wales, with a great preponderance of
unopposed returns. Edward Vaughan's hostility to the
Revolution, whatever it may have amounted to, did not
prevent him from accepting the *fait accompli* and retaining to
the end of his life his Montgomeryshire seat. In the south,
however, Welsh membership of the Convention included a high
proportion of men whose attitude towards the Revolution was
something more positive than passive submission to *force
majeure*. Sir Rowland Gwynne (soon to be the new King's
Treasurer of the Chamber), Sir Trevor Williams, Sir Hugh
Owen of Orielton, John Arnold of Llanthony, Bussy Mansell
of Britton Ferry, and Charles Herbert of Aston all recovered
seats they had lost in the election of 1685; Worcester retained
the representation of Monmouthshire. William Wogan, who
had joined him in drafting the offending address to urge on
James the removal of popish officers, was re-elected for Haverfordwest and rose to high legal office under William III.[2] The
turn of events did not interrupt the legal advancement of
either Sir William Williams or Sir John Trevor, nor (so far
as is known) of any other Welsh lawyer except on one side
Sir John Powell, who was relieved of his post till William III
reinstated him, and on the other Robert Price of Giler, whose
opposition cost him his attorney generalship of Glamorgan and
town clerkship of Gloucester, which he avenged by successfully
stirring up his fellow-countrymen against the alienation by a
Dutch king to a "Dutch Prince of Wales" of crown lordships
in North Wales.[3] Beaufort himself was by now outwardly
reconciled to the new court, and overt opposition in Wales was
confined to less than a score of clerical non-jurors and the few
laymen who (like the burgesses of Abergavenny) refused the
Association Oath of 1696.[4]

Perhaps the only title of the Revolution of 1688 to the epithet

[1] Brogyntyn MSS., letter 1860.
[2] *Supra*, pp. 203, 207, 209.
[3] E.C [urll], *Life of . . . Robert Price*, 1734.
[4] Richards, *Piwritaniaeth a Pholitics*, 1927, Sections i and ii.

" glorious ", so far as its effects in Wales are concerned, lies in the fact that it was accomplished without the battle, murder and sudden death that once seemed imminent. The martial ardour that found expression here in the recruitment of rival forces was now concentrated in a standing regiment for common defence, soon to be known as the Royal Welsh Fusiliers, with Lord Herbert of Cherbury as its first colonel, followed by his cousin Charles Herbert of Aston and (on the latter's death in Ireland) by Sir John Morgan of Kynnersley.[1] Yet although the immediate effects of the Revolution on Welsh life were far less striking than those of the Civil War and Commonwealth, its long-term consequences are not without significance. For two hundred years the crown had been the focus of Welsh political life and the main centre of a unity rarely achieved under the native princes. It had dealt with the country as a distinctive unit through Ludlow; but the Welsh Council was now no more,[2] and the crown had lost much of its glamour and some of its effective authority. Towards parliament Wales stood in no such special relationship; her members, whose cohesion as a group had been breaking down ever since the Long Parliament, were merged in a wider body, her interests overlaid by national policies of diminishing moment to Wales herself.[3] Her representatives carried weight only in so far as they were able to hang on to the skirts of the ruling oligarchy. Few were wealthy or important enough for this, and to a growing extent Welsh politics became centred in the struggle of these few for a place in the political sun, leaving to others whose means were unequal to the strain the task of creating a new centre of unity from within.

NOTE: WELSH RECUSANTS AND THE REVOLUTION

Among the old recusant houses of Wales there is little sign of the critical detachment which Burnet (*Own Times*, 1724, i. pp. 733–4) found in the " Lay-Papists " of England towards

[1] H. A. Tipping, *Hist. of the Royal Welsh Fusiliers*, n.d., ch. i and pp. 20, 26, 36, 40, 262.
[2] *Supra*, pp. 74–5.
[3] *T.C.S.*, 1948, pp. 83–5, 88.

the more wholesale plans foisted on James II by " ambitious
Priests, and hungry Courtiers," nor of the qualms attributed by
Halifax in his *Character of a Trimmer* (*Life and Letters*, ed. Fox-
croft, ii. 319–20) to such of them as held abbey lands, at
the prospect of a papal restoration complete enough to put
these spoils in jeopardy. The Earl of Powis stuck to James
through thick and thin, and even the Duke of Beaufort did not
(like his Protestant-bred son) let his desertion of the King's
faith alienate him from the King's policy. His neighbours and
connections the Morgans of Llantarnam had followed him into
the Protestant camp, but the main line died out in 1681, to be
succeeded by a branch which clung to the ancestral faith and
rejected the Revolution (G.E.C., *Baronetage*, 11. 171; Mathew,
Celtic Peoples and Renaissance Europe, 492–3; Foley, *Records*, iv.
334–5; Williams, *P.H.*, pp. 121, 127; *C.C.C.*, iii. 2310–2). Two
other South Wales families whose Protestantism went back
only a generation or two—the Barlows of Slebech and the
Carnes of Ewenny—remained staunch to the King, to say
nothing of the Pughs of Penryn in the north, whose loyalty to
Rome had never wavered. Of these six families two provided
companions to James in exile, three were ready to oppose the
Prince of Orange in arms, and the sixth swelled the ranks of
of the non-jurors. All of them held important monastic proper-
ties; it would seem that the rôle of these lands as a buttress of
the Reformation in Wales has been considerably exaggerated.

INDEX

A

Abbey Cwmhir, 133
Abenbury, *see* Lloyd, Daniel
Aber, 10
Abercynrig, *see* Jeffreys
Abergavenny, 232
Aberglasney, *see* Rudd
Aberhafesp, *see* Morgan, Matthew
Abermarlais, *see* Jones
Abernant Bychan, *see* Lewis
Aberystwyth, 26, 32
Acton, *see* Jeffreys
Acts of Union, 20, 35, 36, 46, 49, 74, 181, 182
Algiers, 35
America, 77 (*see* also Cambriol, Maryland, Massachusetts, Virginia)
Amwythig, *see* Shrewsbury
Anglesey, 14, 15, 17, 21, 23, 27, 38, 57, 79, 86, 103, 109, IV *passim*, 178, 180, 199, 212, 221, 224, 225, 226, 231
Anglesey, Earl of, *see* Annesley
Annesley, Arthur, 135, 142, 145, 174 and *n.*, 188
Annesley, Francis, 188 (*see* also Mountnorris)
Antrim, 90
Anterliwt, 13–14
Anwyl (Penmachno), Richard, 130, 145
Anwyl (Parke, Merioneth), Robert, 130, 131, 140, 146 and *n.*
Archangel, 25
Ardudwy, 5, 6, 104, 106, 113
Armagh, 83 *n.*
Arnold, John, 204, 207, 208, 210, 218, 221, 232
Arwystli, 16
Association Oath, 232
Astley, Sir Jacob, 96

B

Aston, *see* Herbert
Azores, 81

Babington Plot, 183
Bachegraig, *see* Salusbury
Badminton, 73, 226
Bagenall (Plas Newydd, etc.), 179, 212
Bagenall (Plas Newydd, etc.), Sir Henry, 80
Baker, 125
Baker, Fr. David, 204
Ball, Thomas (Capt.), 144, 147, 154, 163, 167
Baltimore, Lord, 34
Bangor (Caernarvonshire), 42, 85, 178, 189, 226
Bangor Iscoed, *see* Ellis
Baptists, 48, 125, 151
Barbican, 63, 65
Barbour, Gerald, 144, 162–3, 167, 173
Bards, 2, 3, 6–8, 12–14, 19, 62–3, 224–5
Barebone's Parliament, *see* Parliaments
Barlow (Slebech), 123, 175, 185, 188, 209, 211, 215, 220, 234
Baron Hill, *see* Bulkeley
Bartlett, Capt., 90
Bassett (Broviskin), 124, 138, 149, 172
Baxter, Richard, 51, 72
Beachy Head, 83
Beaufort, Duke of, 73–4, 99, 176, 209, 216, 219, 220–2, 226, 228–9, 232, 234 (*see* also Raglan, Worcester)
Beaumaris, 32, 42, 75, 89–90, 98, 100, 103, 163, 168, 179, 185, 199
Beddgelert, 47

Berry, James (Major Gen.), 2, 14, 71, 157, 158, 160, 164, 169
Berthddu, see Wynne
Berw, see Holland
Bible (Welsh), 41, 46, 47, 62, 129, 176
Bishop's Castle, see Broughton
Bishops' Wars, 86, 89, 91, 114
Blackwater, 80
Blayney, (Gregynog), 82
Blayney, Edward, 81
Blayney, Henry, 83
Blayney, Lord, 83
Blethin, William, 125
Bloody Assize, 217
Bodeon, see Owen
Bodidris, see Lloyd
Bodorgan, see Meyrick
Bodwrda, 140
Bodwrda, Griffith (1), 89 n.
Bodwrda, Griffith (2), 108, 130, 159, 163, 167, 173
Bodwrda, John, 114, 130, 140
Bold (Tre'rddol), 15n., 131, 147, 159
Booth, Sir George, 153n., 162, 164, 166, 167, 172, 174, 175
Borras, see Brereton
Bosworth, 9
Boulton (Beaumaris), 142, 146
Boulton (Beaumaris), Richard, 152
Boverton, see Seys
Bowls, 13
Bradshaw, John, 164
Brampton Bryan, see Harley
Brecknockshire, 17, 26, 38, 94, IV passim, 191, 192, 195, 200, 202, 209
Breckonia, 33
Brecon, 71, 134, 150, 171, 190, 193, 196, 202, 209, 211, 223
Brereton (Borras), 215
Brereton (Borras), Owen, 127, 140, 215
Bridgewater, Earl of, 61-8, 72
Bristol, 22, 29, 32, 35, 43, 48, 60, 70, 81, 112, 217, 229
Bristol Channel, 24, 35
Britton Ferry, see Mansell
Brogyntyn, see Owen
Bromfield and Yale, 104, 149, 154
Bronclydwr, see Owen
Broughton (Bishop's Castle), Richard, 56

Broughton (Kington), Edward, 134
Broviskin, see Bassett
Brownists, 44n. (see also Independents)
Brussels, 45
Brymbo, 152, 164, 167
Bryn (Flintshire), see Lloyd
Brynddu, see Bulkeley
Brynkynallt, see Trevor
Brynllywarch, see Jones, Samuel
Bryn y ffynnon, 222n.
Buckingham, Duke of, 33, 61, 85, 188
Buckland, see Games
Bulkeley (Baron Hill), 114, 131, 179, 185, 212
Bulkeley (Baron Hill), Thomas, Visct. (1), 135
Bulkeley (Baron Hill), Robert, Visct. (2), 159
Bulkeley (Baron Hill), Richard, Visct. (3), 178
Bulkeley (Brynddu), 109
Bulkeley (Porthamel), Rowland, 159, 174
Bushell, Thomas, 26, 28
Buttington, 231
Butter trade, 24, 30, 46
Button, Sir Thos., 35
Byron, Lord, 69, 98-9
Bunet, Bp., 233

C

Cadiz, 81
Cadwgan, Capt., 90
Caebalfa, see Williams
Caerau, see Lloyd
Caer Gai, see Vaughan
Caernarvon, 32, 100, 101, 131, 159, 164, 168, 174, 178, 185, 203
Caernarvonshire, 26, 28, 37, 45, 57, 75, 100, IV passim, 179, 180, 185, 188-9, 191-2, 209, 210, 212, 214
Cambridge, 4
Cambriol, 33-5, 47
Campbell, 213
Cannon, 151
Capel, Arthur (Lord), 69
Carbery, Earl of (2), 69, 72, 75, 88, 93, 132, 141, 150, 188
(3), 200 (see also Vaughan (Golden Grove))

Cardiff, 30, 32, 54, 68, 124, 136, 158, 185, 193, 195, 203, 204, 207, 209

Cardigan, 30, 32, 33, 184, 186, 194, 195, 203, 211

Cardigan Bay, 32

Cardigan Priory, *see* Phillips

Cardiganshire, 5, 26, 85, IV *passim*, 224

Carew Castle, 118

Carmarthen, 31, 41, 68, 148, 151, 176, 184, 186, 192, 211

Carmarthenshire, 31, 33, 72, 94, IV *passim*, 180, 188, 192n, 211, 223

Carne (Ewenny), 175, 234

Carne (Ewenny), Richard, 10

Carne (Ewenny), Thomas, 227, 229, 230

Carreglwyd, *see* Griffith

Carter (Sir), John (Col.), 120, 139, 147, 154, 163, 164, 172, 173, 174, 192, 194

Castellmarch, *see* Jones

Castle Island, 78

Catchmay, 157

Catholic Recusants, *see* Recusants

Cattle trade, 23-4, 77

Cavalier Parliament, *see* Parliaments, Charles II

Cefnamwlch, *see* Griffith

Cefnheyley, *see* Williams

Cemlyn, *see* Lewis

Cemmes (Montgomeryshire), 31

Charles I, 51, 60-1, 64-5, 67-70, 84, 91, 94-8, 124, 170, 216, 226, 228

Charles II, 38, 67-70, 162, 170, 195, 202, 210, 220, 223

Cheadle, 114, 131

Chepstow, 32, 95, 144, 145

Cheshire, 144, 155, 164, 165, 199, 229

Chester, 27, 30, 39, 43, 68, 73, 81, 85, 87, 90, 97-8, 149, 165, 210, 222, 226

Chirk, 15, 19, 27, 29, 126, 162, 185, 187, 194

Chirkland, 29, 44, 47, 113, 126, 182-3, 187

Churchyard, Thos., 50, 51, 75

Cilfriw, 125

Cilhendre, 152

Clarendon, Earl of, 71, 92, 108, 196

Clarendon, Code, 48, 126, 157

Clive, 176

Clenennau, *see* Owen

Clergy, 39-45

Clwyd, Vale of, 40

Clynnog, 173

Clyro, *see* Vaughan

Coal, 26-8, 32, 85

Cock fighting, 12

Coedmawr, *see* Lewis

Coetmor, *see* Coytmor

Cogan, *see* Herbert

Colby Moor, 96

Coldbrook, *see* Herbert

Commission for the Propagation of the Gospel in Wales, *see* Propagation

Commissioners of Array, 110, 113, 114, 127, 130, 131

Committees (county), Welsh:
  Assessment, Monmouthshire, 1643, 114
  Assessment, Monmouthshire, 1645, 114-15
  West Wales Association, 1644, 111-12
  Standing Committees, 115
  Committees of Accounts, 115-16, 129, 156
  Sequestration, 117-23, 126, 133, 134, 146, 147, 150, 151, 153n., 156, 159, 162, 176
  Assessment, 1647, 123-36
  Assessment, 1648, 137
  Militia, S. Wales, 1648, 138
  N. Wales Association, 1648, 139
  Militia, Dec. 1648, 141-3
  S. Wales Sequestration, 1649, 118-19, 143-4
  N. Wales Composition, 1649, 118-19, 144-5
  Assessment, 1649 (Apr.), 145-7
  Assessment, 1649 (Dec.), 147-8
  Assessment, 1650, 149
  Assessment, 1652, 149-51
  Poor Prisoners, 1653, 150n., 151-2, 156
  Scandalous Ministers, 1654, 150n., 152-3
  Propagation finance, 1654, 153-4, 156, 157, 169, 172

Assessment, 1657, 150n., 154–61
Militia, 1659, 162–6
Assessment, 1660, 150n., 166–70
Militia, 1660, 170–6
Common land, 18
Compton, Spenser (Earl of North-ampton), 58–60
Comus, 61
Confederate Catholics, 92–100
Connaught, 107
Convention, see Parliament
Conway, 32, 89, 139, 160, 168, 223
Conway, River, 27
Cooper, Thomas, 164
Corbett, 176
Corbett, Sir Richard, 197
Corn trade, 16, 30, 32, 85
Cornish Hall, see Peck
Cornwall, Cornish, 137, 143, 144
Cors y gedol, see Vaughan
Corvisors, 30
Cotton, Sir R., 229
Council of Wales, 18, 30, 71, II passim, 201, 233
Country Party, 108, 124, 153, 190 (see also Whigs)
Court Party, 198–201 (see also Tories)
Courtney, Hugh, 103, 144, 149, 155, 163
Cowbridge, 144
Coytmor, Richard, 146 and n., 163
Coytmor, Robert, 135, 146, 160, 163
Coyty, 146
Cradock, Walter, 40
Creuddyn, 231
Crickhowel, 202
Critchley, Thos., 154, 172
Critchley, Ralph, 172
Croes Newydd (Gwasnewydd), 37
Cromwell, Henry, 103 and n., 104
Cromwell, Oliver, 14, 77, 102n., 107, 138, 145, 154, 155, 160, 162, 169, 191, 230
Cromwell, Richard, 36, 103n., 145, 154, 162
Cuney, 141
Cuney, Walter, 144
Curtler, Robt., 156, 168
Cymortha, 20 and n.
Cynfal, 5
Cwm (Herefordshire), 44

D

Dafydd Benwyn, 55n.
Danby, Earl of, 198, 203, 217
Darby, Abraham, 27
Darowen, 40
Dauntsey, John, 147, 155, 157, 166, 168
Davies, Edward (Llangollen), 120
Davies, Humphrey (Darowen), 40
Davies, John (Mallwyd), 7, 40
Davies (Gwysaney), 206
Davies (Gwysaney), Thomas (Col.), 12, 164n.
Davies (Gwysaney), Mutton, 204
Davies (Gwysaney), Robert, 207, 226
Dawkins, Jenkin, 161n.
Dawkins, Rowland (Major Gen.), 125, 146, 147, 154, 166, 171
Declaration of Indulgence, 211, 219, 223
Dee, River, 27
Denbigh, 17, 19, 30, 47, 127, 139, 168, 185, 193, 206, 209, 212
Denbigh, Earl of, 143, 145
Denbighland, 185, 199
Denbighshire, 2, 4, 12, 22, 24, 27, 28, 35, 37, 39, 61, 68, 69, 74, 80, 84, 89, 103, IV passim, 182–3, 186, 187, 189, 190, 191, 193, 194, 197, 199, 205–6, 209, 210, 213, 215, 229
Derby, Earl of, 160
Derllys, see Vaughan
Devereux, 36, 142
Devereux, Geo., 139, 156, 168
Devereux, Geo., 139, 156, 168 (see also Essex and Hereford)
Devonshire, 33
Digby, Lord, 89
Diodati, Chas., 61
Dissenters, 167n., 205, 211, 218, 219, 221, 222, 224, 226 (see also Baptists, Brownists, Independents, Presbyterians, Puritans, Quakers)
Doctors, 38–9
Dolarddyn, see Wynn
Dolben, Sir Wm., 38
Dolgelley, 113, 152, 230
Dolobran, see Lloyd

Dolserau, *see* Owen, Robert
Douay, 43
Drovers, *see* Cattle trade
Duckenfield, Robt., 149, 154, 155, 165
Dublin, 83, 85, 87, 103, 105, 107, 108, 109, 202
Dungannon, *see* Trevor (Brynkynallt)
Dunraven, *see* Windham
Dutch, 136, 195, 232 (*see also* Holland, Netherlands)
Dymock (Willington), Thos., 128
Dynevor, 180, 185
Dyserth, *see* Hughes, Ralph

E

Edgehill, 124
Edisbury, John, 127, 140, 143, 174
Education, 4–6, 15
Edward ap Raff, 4n., 8n., 81
Edwards (Chirkland), 29, 44
Edwards (Chirkland), John, 29, 126, 177, 182–3
Edwards (Nanhoron), Richard, 159, 163, 167
Edwards (Cilhendre), Thomas, 152, 154
Edwinsford, *see* Williams
Eifionydd, 159, 203
Eisteddfod, 13
Elections (Parliamentary), 8, 15–16, 74, 113, 127, 132, 134, V *passim*, 218–19, 229, 232 (*see also* Parliaments)
Ellice (Croes Newydd), Robert (Col.), 37, 159
Ellis, Andrew, 152, 162, 172
Elizabeth I, 56, 58, 82, 107
Emral, *see* Puleston
Enclosure, *see* Common lands
Esclus, 68 (*see also* Lloyd, Richard)
Essex, 113, 135
Essex, Earl of (2), 34, 56–7, 81–2, **142, 156,** 183–4, 186
Essex, Earl of (3), 88, 142
Evangeliographa, 165
Evans, John, 221, 222n.
Ewenny, *see* Carne
Exclusion Bill, Exclusionists, 72, 207, 210, 217, 218, 225

Eyton (Eyton Isaf), Mary, Lady, 222n.
Eyton (Eyton Isaf), Philip, 149

F

Fairs, 31
Falkland, Lord, 33
Field, Theophilus (Bp.), 42
Fisher, Rev. Chancellor J., 43
Fisheries, 32, 85
Flint, 199
Flintshire, 20, 21, 22, 27, 28, 44, 69, 80, 85, IV *passim*, 178, 188, 192, 194, 195n., 204, 206, 209, 214, 226
Fonmon, 122 (*see also* Jones)
Football, 13
Fowler (Abbey Cwmhir), Richard, 133, 145
Fox, George, 168 (*see also* Quakers)
Foxwist, Wm., 130, 159, 163, 173
Franklyn, Jenkin, 151
France, French, 30, 32, 35, 37, 46, 96, 101, 196, 198, 211
Freeman, Edw., 169
Friars (Ang.), *see* Whyte

G

Gamage, Edmund, 146, 157, 161, 166, 171
Games (Buckland), 134, 150
Games (Buckland), Edward, 146
Games (Buckland), Roger, 166
Games (Buckland), Thos., 116
Garth (Moel y garth, Montgom.), *see* Lloyd
Gelligoch, *see* Vaughan, Rice
Gellihir, *see* Price, John
Gerard, Charles (Sir, Lord), 70, 74, 93, 96 (*see also* Macclesfield)
Giler, *see* Price
Gladherbert, 79
Glamorgan, 2, 8, 14, 18, 22, 24, 25, 30, 33, 35, 94, 97, IV *passim*, 181–2, 190, 202, 211, 214, 223, 227, 232
Glamorgan, Earl of, 64, 72, 92–9, 107, 108, 124, 196, 230 (*see also* Herbert (Lord), Worcester (Earl of), Somerset, Raglan)

Glanbran, *see* Gwynne, Howell
Glan y llyn, *see* Vaughan, Howel
Glascoed, 210
Glascwm, *see* Dauntsey
Glasgrug, *see* Lewis, John
Gloddaeth, *see* Mostyn
Gloucester, 42, 226, 232
Gloucestershire, 25, 26, 115, 125, 138
Glovers, 30
Glyn (Cywarch) (Mer.), *see* Wynn
Glynllifon, *see* Glynne
Glynne (Glynllifon and Plas Newydd), 140, 189
    Edmund, 130, 173
    John (Sir), 23, 135, 137, 140, 143, 145, 160, 164, 192, 194
    Thos. (Col.), 114, 130, 135, 140, 173, 189, 192
Glynne (Lleuar), 161, 175
Godolphin, Sidney, 225
Gogerddan, *see* Pryse
Golden Grove, *see* Vaughan
Goldsmith, Oliver, 84
Goodman (Ruthin), 176
Gower, 145
Great Sessions, 49, 52–4, 66, 195, 218
Gredington, *see* Hanmer, Roger
Gregynog, *see* Blayney
Gresford, *see* Ball, Thomas
Griffith (Carreglwyd), 15, 131
Griffith (Carreglwyd), John, 226
Griffith (Cefnamwlch), John (2), 188. John (4) 210. William, 161
Griffith (Llanfair Isgaer), Richard, 100–1
Griffith (Penrhyn), 80
Griffith, John (Montgomeryshire), 156, 163
Griffith, Morris (Caernarvonshire), 159
Griffith Hiraethog, 62
Grouse shooting, 12
Guilsfield, *see* Pierce, Lloyd
Guinea coast, 25
Gunley, *see* Price, Richard
Gunpowder Plot, 44, 45*n*, 126, 182
Gunter (Tredomen), John, 169
Gustavus Adolphus, 37
Guto'r Glyn, 27, 31
Gweddi Gyffredin, see Prayer Book
Gwent, 26, 125

Gwern y go, *see* Price
Gwernvale, *see* Progers
Gwersyllt, *see* Robinson
Gwydir, *see* Wynn
Gwynedd, 10, 90, 97, 98, 130, 148, 158, 164 (*see also* Snowdonia)
Gwynne (Glanbran), Howell, 118, 133, 134, 146, 150, 158, 165, 171
Gwynne (Glanbran), Rowland, 133*n*.
Gwynne (Taliaris), Rowland, 133 and *n.*, 165
Gwynne (Llanelwedd), George, 156, 166, 171
Gwynne (Llanelwedd) (Sir), Rowland, 156, 202, 204, 209, 211, 228, 230, 232
Gwysaney, *see* Davies

H

Hafren, *see* Severn
Hagget, John, 169
Halifax, Earl of, 75, 234
Hamburg, 24, 46
Hanbury, 25, 28
Hanbury, John, 125
Hanmer (Hanmer and Bettisfield), 207
Hanmer, Sir Thos., 70, 188, 199
Hanmer, Sir John (2), 204, 206–7
Hanmer (Gredington), Roger, 128, 143, 145
Harbours, *see* Ports
Harlech, 199, 227
Harley (Brampton Bryan), 174, 212
Harley (Bampton Bryan), Sir Robert, 134, 137, 145
Harley (Brampton Bryan), Sir Edward, 137
Haroldston, *see* Perrot
Harrison, Thos. (Maj. Gen.), 71, 147, 154, 191
Haverfordwest, 32, 112, 127, 185, 187, 193–4, 195, 196, 203, 207, 215, 232
Hawarden, 152 (*see also* Ravenscroft, Whitley)
Henry VII, 54, 216
Henry VIII, 185
Hengwrt, *see* Vaughan

Herbert, 54, 55 and *n.*, 125, 180-1, 185, 210 (*see also* Earls of Pembroke and Powis)

Herbert (Aston), Charles (1), 78

Herbert (Aston), Charles (2), 210, 212, 218, 220, 223, 231, 232, 233

Herbert (Aston), Arthur, Earl of Torrington, 83

Herbert, Lord, of Cherbury, 183

Herbert, Lord, of Cherbury (1), 46, 79

Herbert, Lord, of Cherbury (2), 86, 157

Herbert, Lord, of Cherbury (3), 26, 28, 156, 164, 168, 196, 217

Herbert, Lord, of Cherbury (4), 74, 83, 223, 229, 233

Herbert (Cogan), William (1), 124 and *n.*, 136

Herbert (Cogan), William (2), 124 and *n.*, 136, 149

Herbert (Coldbrook), William, 124, 125

Herbert (Coldbrook), Henry, 112, 124, 125, 157

Herbert (Friars, Cardiff), William, 124*n.*

Herbert (Montgomery), 82, 108, 180-1

Herbert (Montgomery), Sir Richard 180-1

Herbert (Montgomery), Edward, 181, 183

Herbert (St. Julians), Sir Wm., 78-80, 106

Herbert (Swansea), Sir John (Sec. of State), 46

Herbert, Lord, of Raglan, 65, 69, 91 (*see also* Earls of Glamorgan and Worcester, Raglan, Somerset)

Hereford, 43, 71

Hereford, Visct., 142, 145, 156 (*see also* Devereux)

Herfordshire, 64, 68, 115, 134, 147, 219

Heriot, 20

Hertford, Mqs. of, 68

Heylyn, Rowland, 47, 62, 129

Heylyn, Peter, 47

Holland, 37, 95, 136, 227 (*see also* Dutch, Netherlands)

Holland (Berw), 131

Holland (Kinmel), 215

Holt, 39

Holyhead, 89, 101, 109, 155, 231

Holywell, 44

Homilies, Book of, 41

Hookes (Conway), 160

Hopton, Ralph, 101

Horse racing, 12

Housing, 22

Howell, Jas., 43, 76

Hughes (Dyserth), Ralph, 128, 140, 164, 167

Hughes, Richard, 45*n.*

Hughes, Stephen, 121

Hull, 207

Humphreys, Humphrey (Bp.), 42

Hunt (Salop), 130

Hunt (Salop), Rowland, 129-30, 156, 164, 168

Hunting and hawking, 11-12

Huw, Machno, 5, 37*n.*

Hyde, Sir Edw., 71 (*see also* Clarendon)

I

Independents, 164, 221 (*see also* Brownists)

Indulgence, *see* Declaration

Inns of Court, 4, 9, 85, 101

Ireland, Irish, 17, 20, 24, 30, 32, 35, 43, 46, 47, 52, 58, III *passim*, 112, 124, 127, 137, 165, 170, 173, 179, 185, 187, 188, 216, 220, 221, 224, 230, 231

Irish Sea, 35, 108, 109

Iron industry, 25-7, 32

J

Jacobites, 209, 220, 232, 233-4 (*see also* Non-jurors)

Jamaica, 169, 200

James I, 53, 58, 76, 82, 83, 107, 178, 217

James II, 10, 70, 73, 83, 108, 207, 209-10, VI *passim*

Jeffrey, Evan Lloyd, 80-1

Jeffreys (Abercynrig), John, 202, 209 and *n.*, 211

Jeffreys (Acton), 205

Jeffreys (Acton), George, Lord (judge), 161, 205, 217, 218, 222, 223
Jeffreys (Acton), John, 161, 174
Jenkins, David (judge), 138
Jenkins, Sir Leoline, 46, 208, 225
Jersey, 36
Jesuits, 44
John Wynn ap John, 84
Jones (Abermarlais), 180
Jones (Castellmarch), Sir Wm., 83
Jones (Castellmarch), Griffith, 130, 159, 173
Jones (Fonmon), Philip (Col.) 121–2, 125, 147, 149–51, 153–8, 161 and n., 165, 166, 169–71
Jones (Maes y garnedd, Taltreuddyn, etc.), John (Col.), 6, 20, 47, 101–2, 113, 126, 131, 139, 149, 152, 163, 165, 167, 173, 191–3, 221
Jones (Maes y garnedd, Taltreuddyn, etc.), John (2), 221, 222 and n.
Jones (Maes y garnedd, Taltreuddyn, etc.), Henry, 106
Jones (Nantoes), John (Col.), 104 n., 118
Jones, Edmund, 150, 166, 169, 192
Jones, Henry (Bp.), 84–5, 103
Jones, John (Dean), 42
Jones, Lewis (Bp.), 84
Jones, Michael (Maj. Gen.), 85, 87, 100–1
Jones, Samuel (Brynllywarch), 205, 221
Jones, Sir Theophilus, 85
Jonson, Ben, 7, 51
Juckes, 157

K

Kedewain, 181
Kerry (Co.), 78–9
Kerry (lordship), 181
Kilkenny, 92
Killaloe, 84
King, Richard, 147, 168
Kington, 134
Kinmel, 215
Knappan, 13
Kyffin, Moris, 6, 7
Kyffin, Watkin, 126–7, 162, 172, 221

Kynaston, Edw., 197
Kynaston, John, 156 and n., 163
Kynaston, Capt., 100
Kynnersley, *see* Morgan
Kynwal, Richard, 3n., 20n.

L

Lancashire, 70, 142
Langdale, Sir M., 97
Lasynys, 18
Laud, Wm. (Abp.), 40
Lauderdale, 217
Laugharne, 141, 158
Laugharne, Rowland, 36, 115, 138 and n.
Lawyers, 4
Lawrence, Henry, 160, 164, 192
Lawes, Henry, 61
Lead mining, 26–8, 46
Leicester, Earls of:
    Robt. Dudley, 185
    Robt. Sidney, 57, 136
Leighton, *see* Lloyd
Lewis (Abernant Bychan and Coedmawr), 211
Lewis (Abernant Bychan and Coedmawr), James, 132, 146
Lewis (Abernant Bychan and Coedmawr), John 211
Lewis (Cemlyn), 159
Lewis (Glasgrug), John, 5, 112, 148, 165
Lewis (Llangorse), Sir Wm., 134, 137, 150, 156, 157, 166
Lewis (Monachty), 176
Lewis (Van), 171
Lewis, Evan, 150n., 171n.
Lewis, John (Carmarthenshire), 116, 151
Lhuyd, Edward, 32, 197
Llancaiach, *see* Pritchard
Llandaff, 42, 118
Llanelly, 31, 32
Llanelwedd, *see* Gwynne
Llanfaches, 48, 112
Llanfaethlu, *see* Owen
Llanfair Isgaer, *see* Griffith, Richard
Llanfihangel Ysceifiog, *see* Williams
Llanfyllin, 218
Llangattock, *see* Morgan
Llangibby, *see* Williams

Llangoed, 159

Llangorse, *see* Lewis

Llangyndeyrn, *see* Vaughan

Llanidloes, 139, 218

Llanigon, *see* Watkins

Llanover, *see* Rumsey

Llanrhaeadr ym Mochnant, 39

Llanrwst, 38

Llantarnam, *see* Morgan

Llanthony, *see* Arnold

Llannwchllyn, 11

Llanvihangel (Cowbridge), *see* Thomas, Robt.

Llanvorda, *see* Lloyd and Williams

Llanwnog, *see* Lloyd

Llanymawddwy, 39

Lleuar, *see* Glynne

Llewenny, 19, 21, 39 (*see also* Salusbury)

Lleyn, 108, 159, 179, 189, 192, 203

Lligwy, *see* Lloyd

Lloyd (Abenbury), Daniel, 144, 145, 167

Lloyd (Bodidris), 114

Lloyd (Bodidris), Sir J., 81

Lloyd (Bryn, Flints.), Luke, 128, 173

Lloyd (Caerau), 146

Lloyd (Dolobran), Charles (1), 36, 129, 139, 168

Lloyd (Dolobran), Charles (2), 27, 168

Lloyd (Esclus) (Sir), R., 49, 65–8, 71, 196

Lloyd (Moel y garth), 146

Lloyd (Halghton), 143 and *n.*

Lloyd (Leighton), 46

Lloyd (Leighton), Brochwel, 36

Lloyd (Leighton), Sir C., 36, 86

Lloyd (Leighton), Sir Godfrey, 37

Lloyd (Llanvorda), 213

Lloyd (Llanvorda), Edw., 197, 198, 206, 208, 210

Lloyd (Llanwnog), Evan, 129, 168

Lloyd (Lligwy), 131, 147, 159

Lloyd (Trawscoed), Thos, 151, 152

Lloyd (Vaerdref), John, 148

Lloyd, Ellis, 101

Lloyd, Wm. (Bp.), 40, 217, 224, 228

Lloyd, Wm. (Caernarvonshire), 114, 140

Llwyd, **Hump**hrey, 1, 5

Llwyd, Morgan, 5, 106, 107, 113, 114, 126, 144, 154, 155, 157, 167, 172, 221

Llwydiarth, 113 (*see also* Vaughan)

Llyfr Plygain, 41

London, 8–10, 15, 24–5, 26, 29, 32, 38, 43, 46–7, 62, 63, 66, 75, 101, 104, 121, 126, 129, 134, 135, 181, 183, 185, 223, 227, 230, 231

Long Parliament, *see* Parliaments

Lort (Stackpool), 123, 138, 141, 165, 213

Lort (Stackpool), Roger, 118, 123, 144, 153, 154, 158, 194

Lort (Stackpool), Sampson, 144, 148, 153, 168

Ludlow, 8, II *passim*, 226, 229, 233 (*see also* Council of Wales)

Ludlow, Edmund, 101, 103, 170

Lynn, 93

M

Macclesfield, Earl of, *see* Gerard

Machen, 26, 28 (*see also* Morgan)

Machynlleth, 129

Madryn, Thos (Col.), 120, 147, 160, 163, 164, 167, 173, 174, 192

Maesmawr, *see* Pierce

Maes y garnedd, *see* Jones

Mallwyd, 7

Manley, John, 157, 167

Mansell (Britton Ferry), 214

Mansell (Britton Ferry), Bussy, 124, 153*n.*, 165, 166, 171, 173*n.*, 193–4, 196, 202, 207, 209, 211, 232

Mansell (Britton Ferry), Thos., 202

Mansell (Margam), 26, 158, 211, 214. Sir E., 10, 158, 161, 171, 175, 203, 207 and *n.*, 230

Mansell (Margam), Sir R., 35

Mansell (Muddlescombe), 180

Marchwiel, *see* Edisbury

Margam, *see* Mansell

Markets, 31

Massachusetts, 48

Martin, Robt., 137

Maryland, 34, 38, 89

Mary, Queen of Scots, 76, 78

Mason, Thos. (Col.), 139, 155

Mathafarn, *see* Pugh

Mathrafal, 36

Maurice, Prince, 70
Maurice, Sir Wm., 9, 37, 76
Mennes, Sir J., 90, 97
Meredith, Sir Wm., 167
Methodism, 63
Meillionydd, see Williams, J.
Melai, see Wynne
Merioneth, 2, 20, 24, 31, 40, 84, 103, 104, 108, IV passim, 191, 207, 209, 212, 213, 224, 227
Meyrick (Bodorgan), 131
Meyrick (Pembrokeshire), Sir Gely, 34, 56–8, 81, 86, 183–4
Meyrick (Pembrokeshire), Sir John, 36, 86, 174
Meyrick (Pembrokeshire), Essex, 174
Meyrick (Ucheldre), Edmund, 131, 140, 146
Michael, Thos., 142, 159
Miles, John, 48
Milford, Milford Haven, 32, 81, 93, 94, 97
Militia Ordinance, 142, 143, 190
Milton, John, 61
Minera, 27
Monachdy (Ang.), see Robinson
Monachty (Rad.), see Lewis
Monck, Geo., 100, 103, 166, 170, 173, 208
Monmouth, 71, 93, 95, 97, 114, 137, 143, 185, 190, 204, 206; 207, 210
Monmouth, Duke of, 217, 219, 220
Monmouthshire, 2, 8, 17, 18, 25, 32, 36, 49, 78, 79, 86, 94, 95, 97, IV passim, 180, 181, 191, 195–6, 197, 202, 208, 209, 210, 214, 226, 232
Montgomery, 93, 185, 194, 197n., 202, 210, 211, 218, 220, 223
Montgomeryshire, 2, 22, 24, 26, 31, 36, 39, 46, 81–2, 86, 108, IV passim, 183, 196, 203–4, 213, 229, 232
Montrose, Duke of, 96
Morgan, 36, 125
Morgan (Aberhafesp), Matthew, 128, 139, 168
Morgan (Llangattock and Kynnersley), Sir Thos., 36, 169–70, 219

Morgan (Llangattock and Kynnersley), Sir John, 208, 219, 233
Morgan (Pencarn), Sir Thos., 36
Morgan (Pencarn), Sir Chas, 36, 136
Morgan (Llantarnam), 234
Morgan (Pencrug), Wm., 144
Morgan (Machen), Thos., 169
Morgan (Tredegar), 26. Wm., 202, 204, 211
Morgan, David, 148
Morgan, Wm. (Bp.), 41
Morgannwg, 125 (see also Glamorgan)
Morris (Perthi Llwydion), Edw., 23, 224, 225
Morus, Huw, 14, 224, 226
Morys Dwyfach, 179n.
Mostyn (Mostyn and Gloddaeth), 27, 30.
Mostyn (Mostyn and Gloddaeth), Sir Roger (1), 8, 178
Mostyn (Mostyn and Gloddaeth), Sir Roger (2), 12, 90
Mostyn (Mostyn and Gloddaeth) (Sir), Thos., 9, 210, 225, 227, 231
Mostyn, Ambrose, 139
Mountnorris, Visct., 136 (see also Annesley)
Muddlescombe, see Mansell
Munster, 107
Myddleton (Denbigh, Ruthin and London), 104, 132, 185
Myddleton (Denbigh, Ruthin and London), Sir Hugh, 26, 28, 47, 126
Myddleton (Denbigh, Ruthin and London), Sir Thos. (Ald.), 3, 36, 46–7, 62, 129, 181, 187
Myddleton (Denbigh, Ruthin and London), Sir Wm., 126
Myddleton (Chirk), 9, 19, 27, 29, 47, 113, 185, 199, 205, 212, 213
Myddleton (Chirk), Sir Thos. (1), 12, 28, 47, 69, 101, 113, 115, 117, 120, 125–7, 128, 133, 139, 143, 152, 162, 166, 172, 173, 187, 190 and n., 194, 221
Myddleton (Chirk), Sir Thos. (2), 126, 194

Myddleton (Chirk), Sir Thos. (3), 198, 201, 205
Myddleton (Chirk), Sir Richard, 206, 209, 215, 229
Mytton (Halston), Thos., 126, 135, 139, 154
Mytton (Pontyscawryd), 151

N

Nanhoron, see Edwards
Naseby, 48, 95-6, 124, 169, 195, 196, 226
Nannau, Nanney, 7, 140
Nanney, Griffith, 145, 161
Neath, 32
Needham (Pool Park), Sir Robt., 127, 140
Netherlands, 37 (see also Holland)
New England, 47 (see also Massachu-setts)
Newfoundland, 33-5
New Moat, 153
New Radnor, see Radnor
Newport (Mon.), 32
Newry, 81, 84
Newton (Carmarthenshire), 180
Nicholl, Thos., 129-30, 168, 174n.
Non-jurors, 232, 234
Northampton, Earl of, see Crompton
Northumberland, Earl of, 142, 145
Nottingham, 68

O

Oates, Roger, 158 and n.
O'Neill, Sir Phelim, 106
Orielton, see Owen
"Orinda", 141
Ormond, Mquis. of, 88-90, 93-102, 108, 202
Oswestry, 31, 32, 47
Owen (Broclydwr), Hugh, 160
Owen (Bodeon, etc.), 131, 147, 159
Owen (Clenennau and Brogyntyn), Sir John (Col.), 12, 37, 97, 100, 131, 198-9, 222
Owen (Clenennau and Brogyntyn), Wm. (Col.), 198-9
Owen (Clenennau and Brogyntyn), Sir Robt., 6, 75, 207 and n., 209, 212, 222, 224, 225, 227, 230

Owen (Dolserau), Robt., 113, 152, 160, 163, 174
Owen (Llanfaethlu), 159
Owen (Orielton and New Moat), 211, 212
Owen (Orielton and New Moat), Sir Hugh (1), 31, 123, 144, 149, 153, 158, 162, 165, 175, 227
Owen (Orielton and New Moat), Sir Hugh (2), 227 232
Owen (Orielton and New Moat), Arthur, 141, 153, 158, 165
Owen (Plas Du), 46
Owen (Plas Du), Hugh, 45, 46
Owen (Plas Du), John, 76
Owen, David, 230
Owen, Edw., 129, 139, 156, 168
Owen, John (Bp.), 41
Oxford, 4, 7, 68, 84, 92, 93, 168, 190, 226, 229

P

Padua, 38, 45
Pantglas, 3n.
Park (Mer.), see Anwyl
Parke (Mont.), see Price
Parliament, 9-10, 34, 46, V passim
  Elizabeth I, 31, 136
  Jas. I, 17, 24, 60-1, 85
  Chas. I, 65, 136
  Chas. I, Long, 24, 49, 65-6, 86, 104, 113, 114, 122, 136, 143, 160, 161, 166-76, 233
  Rump, 110-51, 162-6, 173, 229, 232
  Barebone's, 114, 124, 129, 134, 144, 151-2, 155.
  Protectorate, 129, 133, 152-61, 175
  Protectorate, "Other House", 158, 165
  Convention, 1660, 136
  Chas. II, 73, 74, 123, 178, 1717-18
  Jas. II, 218-20, 225, 229
  Convention, 1689, 232
  Wm. and Mary, 74-5
Parliament Explained to Wales, 112, 148
Parry (Rhydolion), Jeffrey, 159, 163, 168, 173

Parry, Sir Thos., 46

Peck, John, 126–7, 162, 167, 172

Pembroke, 30, 31, 33, 140, 192

Pembroke, Earls of, 112, 124, 181, 190, 195 (*see also* Herbert)

Pembroke, Earls of (1st creation), 78, 180

Pembroke, Earls of (2nd creation) (2), 51, 54–9, 63, 64

Pembroke, Earls of (2nd creation) (3), 68, 97

Pembroke, Earls of (2nd creation), (4 and 5), 124

Pembrokeshire, 2, 10, 17, 21, 22, 30, 31, 32, 36, 56, 64, 85, 86, 94, 96, IV *passim*, 180, 185, 188, 190, 207, 209, 211, 212, 214, 220, 227

Pencarn, *see* Morgan

Pencrug, *see* Morgan

Penhesgin, *see* Wynn

Penllyn, 11

Penmachno, *see* Anwyl

Penmaenmawr, 109

Penmynydd, 16, 131 (*see also* Theodore)

Pennsylvania, 48

Penrhyn (Bangor), 80, 175

Penrhyn, Creuddyn, 231 (*see also* Pugh)

Penry, John, 112

Pentreheylyn, 47

Pen y benglog, 7

Perrot (Haroldston, etc.), 82, 138, 185, 188, 196, 215

Perrot (Haroldston, etc.), Sir John, 77–8, 83, 185, 187, 214

Perrot (Haroldston, etc.), Sir James, 10, 83, 85, 187

Perrot (Haroldston, etc.), Herbert, 165

Perthi Llwydion, 23

Philipps (Picton), 123, 136, 185, 188, 193

Philipps (Picton), Sir Erasmus, 144, 165, 172

Phillips (Tregibby and Cardigan Priory), James, 141, 146, 150, 158, 165, 166, 172, 194, 195, 203

Phillips (Tregibby and Cardigan Priory), Hector, 150, 203

Phylip, Griffith, 44n.

Phylip, William, 44n., 216n.

Picton, *see* Philipps

Pierce (Maesmawr, Guilsfield), Lloyd, 116, 122, 139, 151, 156

Pilleth, *see* Price

Plas Berw, *see* Berw

Plas Du, *see* Owen

Plas Gogerddan, *see* Goderddan

Plas Kynaston, 156

Plas Newydd (Ang.), *see* Bagenall

Plas Newydd (Chirk), *see* Edwards

Plas Newydd (Caernarvonshire), *see* Glynne

Plas y Ward, *see* Thelwall

Plymouth (Mass.), 48

Pontypool, 25

Pool Park, *see* Needham

Poor Law, 17–18

Popish Plot, 48, 83, 204, 217, 221

"Popish Army", 86

Porkington, *see* Brogyntyn

Porthamel, *see* Bulkeley

Ports, harbours and shipping, 30, 32–3, 43, 77, 86, 89–90, 94–5, 97, 100, 109, 231–2

Powell, Daniel, 51

Powell, Sir John, 218, 223, 232

Powell, Rice (Col.), 141

Powell, Vavasour, 105, 112, 129, 133n., 134, 139, 147, 155, 156, 159, 163, 166, 168, 172, 191

Powis Castle, 15, 20, 27, 139, 168, 231

Powis, Lord, 82, 181, 231 (*see also* Herbert)

Powis, Lord, 1st Mquis., 219, 220, 223, 234

Powis, Lord, 2nd Mquis., 220, 223, 230

Powis, Lady, 226

Powys, 36, 172

Poyer, John, 118, 138, 146, 149, 153

Prayer Book, 6, 43

Prendergast, *see* Stepney

Presbyterians, 130, 134, 136, 137, 142, 156, 168, 173, 174n., 224

Preston, 138

Pretender, *see* Prince of Wales

Price (Brecon), (Sir) Herbert, 190, 193, 195, 196, 200

Price (Gellihir), John, 125, 171

Price (Giler), 157, 164

Price (Giler), Robert, 232

Price (Gunley), Richard (Capt.),
129, 147, 154, 163, 168
Price (Gwern y go), Hugh, 139,
152, 168
Price (Monachty), James, 184, 187
Price (Newtown), Sir John, 113,
128, 156, 164, 168, 191
Price (Newtown), Sir Matthew,
168 and n.
Price (Parke), John, 128, 150n., 164,
168. Matthew, 201–2
Price (Pilleth), 176. Charles, 37, 82,
86, 136
Price (Rhiwlas), 176
Price, Lewis, 120, 139, 151–2, 157,
163, 168
Price, Peter, 148, 156, 168
Prichard, Rhys, 6
Pride, Col., 141, 174
Prince of Wales, 26, 225–6, 232
Prince of Wales, Arthur, 50
Prince of Wales, Charles (I), 51
Prince of Wales, Charles (II), 67–9
Prince of Wales, James Edw. ("Old
Pretender"), 225–6
Prince of Wales's Regiment, 226–7
Pritchard (Brymbo), Hugh, 152,
155, 162, 167, 172
Pritchard (Llancaiach), Edw., 124
Progers (Gwernvale), Edw., 195,
200, 202
Propagation of the Gospel in Wales,
Act and Commission for, 48, 71,
102, IV passim, 196, 205
Prys, Edmwnd, 40, 43
Pryse (Gogerddan), Sir Richard (1),
132, 141
Pryse (Gogerddan), Sir Richard (2),
132, 158, 165
Pugh (Mathafarn), John, 146
Pugh (Mathafarn), Rowland, 198–9
Pugh (Penrhyn), 44, 234
Pugh (Penrhyn), Robt., 227, 231
Puleston (Emral), John (Judge),
137, 162
Purcell (Nant y cribba), 157, 168
Puritans, Puritanism, 13, 43–4, 56,
63, 83, 107, 108, IV passim, 188,
192 (see also Baptists, Brownists,
Dissenters, Independents, Presby-
terians, Quakers)

Pury, Thos., 125
Pwllheli, 32

Q

Quakers, 27, 48, 114, 129, 148, 224

R

Radnor (New), 134, 184, 207, 209,
219
Radnorshire, 2, 8, 22, 37, 56, 68,
IV passim, 182, 184, 187, 196,
202, 211, 212, 224, 228
Raglan, Castle and Lordship, 2, 68,
91, 96, 150, 196, 226
Raglan, House of (Somerset family),
44, 48, 54, 59, 61, 64, 69, 112,
181, 185, 196, 204, 209 (see also
Beaufort, Herbert, Glamorgan,.
Worcester)
Rathmines, 101
Ravenscroft (Bretton), Thos., 128,
162, 172
Recusants, 44, 48, 113, 126, 156n.,
157, 183, 195, 197, 202, 204, 209,
218, 219, 227, 230, 231
Rhiwlas, see Price
Rhosmor, see Wood
Rhydodyn, see Edwinsford
Rhydolion, see Parry
Rice (Newton), see Dynevor
Rhys ap Gruffydd, 81
Rhys, Siôn Dafydd, 38
Richard ap Howel, 9
Robert, Gruffydd, 7, 8
Roberts, Lewes, 46
Robinson (Gwersyllt and Monach-
dy), John, 199
Roath, see Stradling
Rome, 45 (see also Recusants)
Rouen, 81
Rowton Heath, 98
Round, J. H., 92n.
Rowlands, Henry, 17
Royal Welsh Fusiliers, 109, 233
Ruabon, see Wynn, William
Rudd (Aberglasney), Sir Rice, 133,
142, 144
Rûg, see Salusbury
Rumsey (Crickhowel), 170
Rumsey (Crickhowel), Edw., 134,
146, 157

Rumsey (Llanover), Walter (Judge), 170

Rupert, Prince, 37, 69-71, 88-9, 92-102

Ruthin, 47, 127, 139, 187, 193

Ruthin, Lordship, 187

Rump, see Parliaments

Rye House Plot, 208

S

St. Asaph, 41, 42, 217, 224, 226

St. Augustine, 43

St. Davids, 39, 42

St. Donats, see Stradling

St. Fagans, 138

St. Julians, see Herbert

St. Winefride's Well, 44

Saints' Parliament, see Parliament, Barebones

Salesbury, Wm., 7

Saltonstall, Sir Richard, 164

Salusbury (Bachegraig), 188

Salusbury (Bachegraig), Owen, 128, 140, 143, 145, 162, 164

Salusbury (Llewenny), 10, 127n., 185, 215

Salusbury (Llewenny), Sir John (1), 183, 186, 215

Salusbury (Llewenny), Sir Henry, 6, 33, 34, 84, 186

Salusbury (Llewenny), Thos., 182

Salusbury (Llewenny), Sir Thos., 190

Salusbury (Llewenny), Sir John (2), 206

Salusbury (Rûg), William, 127

Salusbury (Rûg), Owen, 127, 131

Saye and Seele, Lord, 152

Scotland, Scots, 16, 39, 76, 92, 96, 97, 99, 106, 166, 170, 190n., 213, 216 (see also Bishops' Wars)

Sedgemoor, 217

Sequestration, see Committees

Sermons, 40-1

Seven Bishops, 212, 223, 225

Severn, 8, 62, 155, 168

Seys (Boverton), 138

Seys (Boverton), Evan, 125, 166, 171, 172

Shakespeare, 14

Shaftesbury, Earl of, 201, 208

Sheriffs, 53, 63, 75, IV passim, 178, 181, 183, 184, 189, 191, 192 and n. 205, 207, 215, 222, 227

Ship money, 64, 128, 143

Shipping, see Ports

Shrewsbury, 8, 9, 14, 24-5, 29, 30, 32, 43, 50, 68, 70, 71, 73, 155, 157, 167, 196, 226

Shropshire, 68, 127, 129, 135, 152, 156, 164, 168, 197, 201, 231

Sidney (Penshurst and Coyty), Sir Henry, 25, 51, 77, 136

Sidney (Penshurst and Coyty), Sir Philip, 52

Sidney (Penshurst and Coyty), Robt. (Earl of Leicester), 57, 136

Sidney (Penshurst and Coyty), Algernon, 136, 172

Slates, 30

Slebech, see Barlow

Snowdonia, 37, 99, 111, 117, 198 (see also Gwynedd)

Somerset (county), 169

Somerset (dukedom), 92

Somerset (family), see Raglan

Sontley (Sonlli), Robert, 126-7, 157

Sontley (Bron Deg), Roger, 157, 160, 167

Spain, Spaniards, 34, 43, 79, 81, 216

S.P.C.K., 42, 47

Stackpool, see Lort

Staffordshire, 133

Stansty, 167

Star Chamber, 21, 66, 116, 178, 181, 183-7

Stephenson, Geo., 109

Stepney (Prendergast), 185, 188

Stepney (Predergast), Sir John, 194

Stevens, John (Capt.), 224, 227-9

Stewards, 15-16

Stradling, 138

Stradling (Roath), 171

Stradling (St. Donats), 203

Strafford, Earl of, 78, 91, 108, 135, 136, 230 (see also Wentworth)

Strickland, Walter, 136

Suffolk, Earl of, 31

Swansea, 30, 121

Swift, Thos. (Major), 155, 163, 172, 174

Sychnant Pass, 109

T

Tailor, 6, 15
Talerddig, 135
Talbeddwyn, 142
Taliaris, *see* Gwynne
Taylor, Edw. (Capt.), 166 and *n.*
Taylor, Silvanus, 142, 145, 155, 166, 168
Thelwall, 164
Thelwall (Bathafarn), Sir Eubule, 187
Thelwall (Bathafarn), Eubule, 174
Thelwall (Bathafarn), Simon, 113, 126, 143, 164
Thelwall (Plas y Ward), 127*n.*, 205
Thelwall (Plas y Ward), Owen, 127, 164
Theodore (Penmynydd), 131, 159 (*see also* Tudor)
Thomas (Aber), William, 10
Thomas (Brecon), William, 171
Thomas (Llanvihangel), (Sir) Robt., 144, 153, 158, 161, 171*n.*, 175, 195, 203, 204
Thomas (Tregos), 153*n.*
Thomas (Wenvoe), Edmund, 154, 158, 166, 170
Thomas, John, 111
Thomas, Michael, 142
Thurloe, John, 102
Tintern, 25, 79
Tories, 198, 219 (*see also* Court Party)
Torrington, Earl of, *see* Herbert
Torbay, 227–8
Tor y coed, *see* Vaughan
Trafford, Francis (Col.), 89–90, 103
Traeth Mawr, 174
Trawscoed (Card.), *see* Vaughan
Trawscoed (Mer.), 132*n.*
Trawscoed (Montgom.), *see* Lloyd, Thos.
Trawsfynydd, 31
Tredegar, 26 (*see also* Morgan)
Tredomen, *see* Gunter
Trefriw, 7
Tregibby, *see* Phillips
Tregos, *see* Thomas
Tre'rddol, *see* Bold
Trevalun, *see* Trevor
Trevor (Brynkynallt), 83

Trevor (Brynkynallt), Sir Edw., 80, 83–4, 87, 88
Trevor (Brynkynallt), Marcus Col.), 12, 87, 100, 102, 103 (*see also* Dungannon)
Trevor (Brynkynallt), Arthur, 70, 88, 95, 102
Trevor (Brynkynallt), Sir John, 205–6, 209, 212, 217–18 and *n.*, 232
Trevor (Trevalun), 83, 87, 189
Trevor (Trevalun), Sir Richard, 56, 80–1, 84
Trevor (Trevalun), Sir Sackville, 35, 80–1
Trevor (Trevalun), Sir John (2), 126–8, 143, 162, 172, 178
Trevor (Trevalun), Sir John (3), 46, 126, 172, 178, 194, 218*n.*
Trevor (Trevalun), Sir Thos., 143, 172
Tudors, 16, 47, 76, 131 (*see also* Theodore)
Tudor, Siôn, 183
Tunman, Thos., 166, 168
Turks, 101
Twisleton, Geo. (Col.), 139, 147, 154, 161, 163, 173
Tyrconnel, Earl of, 230, 231

U

Ucheldre, *see* Meyrick
Ulster, 84, 107
Usk, 204
"Usquibagh", 201
Ussher, Jas, 84
Ussher, Robt., 87

V

Valle Crucis, 27, 120
Van, *see* Lewis
Vaughan (Caer Gai), Rowland, 7, 23. John, 11*n.*, 132 and *n.*, 161
Vaughan (Caer Gai), John, 11*n.*, 132 and *n.*, 161
Vaughan (Clyro), 187
Vaughan (Clyro), Roger, 184
Vaughan (Cors y gedol), 7, 212
Vaughan (Hengwrt), 8, 84, 105, 113

Vaughan (Glan y llyn), Howel, 131, 191

Vaughan (Golden Grove, Derwydd, Derllys, etc.), 16, 81, 83, 141, 165, 169, 175, 180, 184, 186, 188, 211–13 (see alo Carbery)

Vaughan (Golden Grove, Derwydd, Derllys, etc.) (Sir), Henry (1), 150, 188

Vaughan (Golden Grove, Derwydd, Derllys, etc.), Henry (2), 150

Vaughan (Golden Grove, Derwydd, Derllys, etc.), Richard, 176

Vaughan (Golden Grove, Derwydd, Derllys, etc.), John, Lord, 200

Vaughan (Llangyndeyrn), Wm., 16, 33–5, 76, 213

Vaughan (Llwydiarth), 116, 127, 129, 131, 212–13, 229, 231

Vaughan (Llwydiarth), Edw. (1), 113, 116, 122, 128, 139, 151, 156, 162, 163, 167, 174n., 191

Vaughan (Llwydiarth), Edw. (2), 131, 201, 229, 232

Vaughan (Llwydiarth), Owen, 231

Vaughan (Pantglas), 3n.

Vaughan (Tor y coed), Sir Edw., 132, 142

Vaughan (Trawscoed), 20, 211

Vaughan (Trawscoed), Sir John (Judge), 150, 151, 211

Vaughan (Trawscoed), Henry, 150

Vaughan (Trawscoed), John, 211

Vaughan, Rice, 112, 129, 156, 163

Vaughan, Sir Wm. (Shropshire), 98

Vaynol, see Williams

Virginia, 48, 89

Voelas, see Wynne

Vychan, Sir Griffith, 36, 116

W

Wake, Capt., 90

Walbeof, Chas., 134, 150

Walker, Sir Edw., 97

Waller, Sir Wm., 114

Walpole, Sir R., 213

Walter, 138 and n.

Warwick, Earl of, 135, 160

Watkin Clywedog, 17n.

Watkins (Llanigon), Wm., 120, 121, 150, 166, 171

Welshpool, 218, 224, 227, 228, 230

Welsh Language, 6–8, 13–14, 29, 36, 40–3, 46, 51, 52, 53, 62–3, 67, 122 (see also Bards)

Welsh Trust, 47, 63

Wentwood, 19, 204

Wentworth, Sir T., 60 (see also Strafford)

Wenvoe, see Thomas

Whigs, 156, 201, 202, 208, 224, 228 (see also Country Party)

Whippergundy, 13

Whitchurch, 226

Whitelock, Sir Bulstrode, 132

Whitley, Roger, 199, 200, 217

Whyte (Friars), Rowland, 159, 174

Wiliems, Thomas, 7, 29, 38, 52, 55

William of Orange, William III, 73, 108, 202, 207, VI passim

Williams (Caebalfa), Henry, 122, 133, 145, 155, 166

Williams (Caebalfa), Richard, 150, 196, 202

Williams (Cefnheyley), Roger, 124, 144, 154

Williams (Edwinsford), 175

Williams (Glascoed and Llanvorda) (Sir), Wm., 75, 210, 211, 213, 218, 220, 221, 222 and n., 223, 227, 232

Williams (Llanfihangel Ysceifiog), Thos., 142, 146, 147, 158

Williams (Llangibby), Sir Trevor, 97–9, 124, 144, 169, 195, 198, 202, 204, 208, 210, 232

Williams (Meillionydd), John, 159, 167

Williams (Penrhyn), John (Abp.), 23, 33, 77, 87–90, 96–100, 130, 175, 192

Williams (Penrhyn), Sir Griffith, 175

Williams (Penrhyn), Sir Robt., 175

Williams (Penrhyn), Edmund, 175

Williams (Vaynol), Sir Wm. (2), 130, 160, 161, 212

Williams (Vaynol), Sir Wm. (3), 212

Williams, Griffith (Bp.), 85

Williams, John (Capt.), 134, 150, 155, 166, 168

Williams, John (goldsmith), 47

Williams, Rice, 125
Williams, Sir Roger, 183
Williamson, Sir Jos., 198, 201, 202, 203
Willington, *see* Dymock
Wiston, 215
Windham (Dunraven), 124, 133, 171
Wittewronge, Sir J., 135
Wogan (Wiston, Boulston, etc.), 151, 185, 187, 215
Wogan, Thos., 132, 141, 165, 167
Wogan, Sir Wm., 203, 207, 209, 232
Wood, Anthony, 226
Wood (Rhosmor), 131, 147, 159, 179*n*.
Woollen industry, 24–5, 29, 31, 46, 85
Worcester, 71, 226
Worcester, Earls and Marquises of, 2, 3, 9, 10, 25 (*see also* Raglan)
Worcester, Earl of (3), 14, 55
Worcester, Earl of (4), 58, 64–5
Worcester Mquis. of (1), 64–5, 91, 124
Worcester, Mquis. of (2), *see* Glamorgan
Worcester, Mquis. of (3), 72, 196, 202, 204, 205, 207, 208 (*see also* Beaufort)
Worcester, Mquis. of (4), 204, 209, 210, 219–20, 229, 232
Worcestershire, 60, 88
Word for God, 155, 156, 159, 164
Wrexham, 14, 18, 27, 31, 49, 71, 104, 112, 113, 130, 144, 152, 154, 157, 162, 167, 172, 193, 205, 221

Wyn, Elis, 18
Wynne (Berthddu), Robert, 231
Wynn (Dolarddyn), Gabriel, 120, 128, 139
Wynne (Gwaenfynydd), Owen, 225
Wynn (Gwydir), 27, 38, 130, 160, 175, 189
Wynn (Gwydir), Sir John, 9, 10, 59, 179, 185, 199
Wynn (Gwydir), Sir Richard (1), 160, 180
Wynn (Gwydir), Sir Owen, 160, 167
Wynn (Gwydir), Sir Richard (2), 167
Wynn (Gwydir), Maurice (1), 46, 143, 164, 175
Wynn (Gwydir), Maurice (2), 199
Wynn (Glyn), Wm., 7, 146
Wynn (Llangoed), 159
Wynn (Penhesgin), 159
Wynn, Ruabon (Wm.), 144, 157, 167
Wynne (Melai), 157, 174
Wynne (Melai), John, 199
Wynne (Voelas), 157, 164
Wynn (Wynnstay), 131, 191, 213
Wynn (Wynnstay), Sir Watkin Williams, 213
Wynnstay, *see* Wynn

Y

Yardley, John, 156, 168
York, 67
York, Duke of, 70, 207*n*., 216, 217 (*see also* James II)
Yorkshire, 96, 126, 131
Ysgafell, 133*n*., 155*n*.